Labor Markets and Wage Determination

ERRATA

LABOR MARKETS AND WAGE DETERMINATION
The Balkanization of Labor Markets and Other Essays
By CLARK KERR

Page 17, paragraph 4, should read as follows:

Meanwhile, labor economics has gone in two different directions from the earlier body of literature. One direction is toward statistical and theoretical analyses of a neoclassical type (the "Chicago School" came to replace the "Wisconsin School"). Some of this work—most of it at an advanced level of methodological sophistication—has confirmed old insights as new discoveries, since the earlier literature had been largely forgotten or ignored. This development made great advances to bring labor economics into contact with main-stream economics.

Labor Markets and Wage Determination

THE BALKANIZATION OF LABOR MARKETS AND OTHER ESSAYS

Clark Kerr

PUBLISHED FOR THE
Institute of Industrial Relations,
University of California, Berkeley

University of California Press

BERKELEY · LOS ANGELES · LONDON

University of California Press
Berkeley and Los Angeles, California
University of California Press, Ltd.
London, England
Copyright© 1977 by
The Regents of the University of California
ISBN 0-520-03070-2
Library of Congress Catalog Card Number: 75-17291
Printed in the United States of America

Contents

PART III. The Impact of Bureaucratic Controls

PART IV. "The California School"

Foreword

Labor market analysis owes much to the writings of Clark Kerr. Perhaps it is appropriate for one who has had the privilege of a long and close association with him to comment on the scope and impact of these essays, which have never previously been gathered into a book. The compilation is a most fortunate event not only for those who have read many of the essays at different times and in various sources, but for younger scholars who will be impressed by their freshness and vigor and their timeliness and relevance for many current problems.

There is a long-standing, fundamental dispute among the proponents of labor market analysis. The problem is to determine the relative importance of "market forces" (notably maximization of gain by individual buyers and sellers exposed to competitive conditions and confronted by costs of information and mobility) and "institutional influences" (usually either behavior not consistent with optimal exploitation of opportunities for gain or group behavior designed to provide the members with some insulation from the forces of competition). The positions of the various parties to the debate might be described by paraphrasing James Tobin's famous statement about a similar debate over the importance of money supply: Market forces do not count; market forces do too count; market forces count for everything. The first position has been attributed to John R. Commons and most of the older institutionalists before and after the First World War; the third, to Milton Friedman and many newer neoclassicists after the Second World War.

The second position was originally espoused (at least in part) by the older neoclassicists like Henry C. Simons and later by newer institutionalists like Slichter, Kerr, and Dunlop. Nowhere was the eclecticism of this approach more lucidly displayed than in the celebrated essay on "The Balkanization of Labor Markets." In it, Kerr discusses the contributions made by "institutional rules to the creation of more boundaries between labor markets"; and he associates different forms of job control ("manorial" and "guild") with different forms of unionism (industrial and craft, respectively). He notes that tendencies toward the different types of job control have existed in the absence of formal union rules and policies; and he cites the influence of "the specificity of skills and the money costs of transfer." In the "Effect of Environment and Administration on Job Evaluation" he stresses the impact of external market forces (as well as union politics and rivalry) on this important characteristic of the "internal labor market." Indeed the same caution and balance which characterize Kerr's assessment of the effect of unionism on relative wages is evident in his treatment (in other papers) of the effect of unionism on the general level of money wages and on the distribution of income.

Subsequent work in the human capital area has concentrated on competitive, allocationally efficient market forces. But in the fifties, the idea developed that markets might be segregated into areas of all-around good jobs (with high pay, good promotional prospects, and job security through seniority or attachment to a structured market) and all-around bad jobs (low pay, dead-end, short-lived) with special attention to services and trade as a "sponge sector." The idea was revived in the late sixties by young economists, led by Doeringer and Piore. Although they were critical of the Pollyanna implications of neoclassical analysis and analyzed the properties and characteristics of "internal" as well as of "secondary" markets, they at first explained the differences almost exclusively in terms of technological peculiarities and human capital analysis. More recently, however, the role assigned to unions by some analysts of market segmentation has again been upgraded. Such upgrading received unintended support in the sixties from work on the quantitative impact of unionism on interindustrial wage structures. Although the quality and the results of these studies vary widely, they generally suggest greater union influence than the market-forces-count-for-everything school had expected. In a recent attempt to distinguish quantitatively among Kerr's three market classifications ("manorial," "guild," and "open"), Arthur Alexander finds that "manorial" industries (with good jobs) show lower mobility and higher wage incomes than could be predicted solely on the basis of human capital characteristics (as summarized by age and experience) of their employees, and that such "structural" characteristics as capital intensity, product market concentration, size of firm, and unionism play an important role. Thus the broader interpretations of market segmentation and their renewed emphasis suggest that the pendulum of intellectual fashion has swung once more in the direction of the balanced approach followed by Kerr, Dunlop, Reynolds, and their contemporaries.

Whether events and increased analytic sophistication will prompt the revival of more subtle and controversial aspects of this institutionalism remains to be seen. In denying much of a role to unions and other private market organizations as a means of accounting for persistent wage dispersion within labor markets, conventional analysis asserts the explanatory sufficiency of costs of acquiring various kinds of information; in denying much of a role to inflationary agents, it stresses limitations on their power to buck countervailing competitive forces (to which they themselves contribute). In both cases it is assumed that individuals and their organizations fully exploit whatever opportunities the market holds for them. In these essays, however, the latter assumption is not made and is indeed implicitly denied. Kerr attributes wage disperson in part to "inertia" — to the fact that "the hard core of the employed" are "sufficiently satisfied with their current jobs." He attributes the "selective impact of union power" on different types of wage differential to the differential "intensity of motivation" arising from the interdependence of worker preference functions as well as to "the amount of power requisite to effect such changes." He attributes the limited inflationary and distributional impact of American unions to their "reasonableness" — the absence of a particular programmatic thrust and bite which in other countries may proceed from radical ideological heritage. This reasonableness, he goes on to say (in "Economic Analysis and the Study of Industrial Relations") can cause restraint if the institution is granted a certain degree of union security; but he warns that there are limits to the tradeoff between wage restraint and institutional security. The existence, the raison d'etre, and the limitations of the tradeoff all constitute a lesson which should commend itself to the contemporary policymaker.

Kerr's accomplishments and contributions, of course, range far beyond the context of these essays, just as the essays greatly exceed in scope the issues and problems which prompted this Foreword. Among his extracurricular activities was the founding of the Institute of Industrial Relations at Berkeley, which he directed for seven years. The institute is now in its thirtieth year, combining a program of academic research with teaching in the labor, management, and minority communities. This emphasis was, characteristically, imparted to it by Clark Kerr, whose personal career has also been stamped by a unique combination of scholarly, policy-oriented, and administrative achievements.

Lloyd Ulman
Director
Institute of Industrial Relations
University of California, Berkeley

September 1975

Introduction:
The Study of Labor Markets
and Wages After World War II

THE PERIOD after World War II (roughly from 1945 to 1960) saw a great thrust forward in the study of industrial relations in the United States:

There was intense public interest in industrial relations after the organizing disputes of the late 1930s, the wartime troubles in defense related industries, and the great strikes at the end of the war. New basic public policies were being debated and adopted, like the Taft-Hartley (1947) and Landrum-Griffin (1959) acts.

Academic interest increased with the prominence of the field in public debate, the new popularity of interdisciplinary studies, and the entry of many young social scientists into higher education (to match the "GI rush") who looked for "hot" fields and new approaches. A field of study that had once belonged to a small number of labor economists now attracted political scientists, sociologists and psychologists.

Among the many social scientists was a relatively small number that constituted a new generation of scholar-participants. They had gained practical experience with industrial relations during World War II in addition to earlier theoretical training in their disciplines. They had found that the theory they had learned in the classroom did not help but hindered them, at least temporarily, in understanding situations. Consequently, they sought to bring together theory and practice. Most new work that attracted substantial attention came from this group of scholar-participants. Only a few others, without comparable wartime experience, made major contributions in the immediate postwar period.

New institutes and centers were established to advance the study of industrial relations at Princeton, MIT, Cornell, Minnesota, Illinois, and California — both in Berkeley and Los Angeles, by the end of 1945.

New and enlarged professional opportunities in industry, government, unions and teaching attracted many more students to the study of industrial relations and contiguous fields like personnel administration; there were jobs waiting for them after graduation.

It was an exciting time. New approaches were developed, new ideas brought forth and disputed. The study of industrial relations, as other fields of study before, experienced its greatest expansion — with both quantitative and qualitative consequences. In the previous years the field was without a core. It had consisted then of:

Neoclassicists, like Hicks, who applied established theory to an attempted understanding of labor markets, wages and strikes.

Institutionalists, like Commons, Perlman, and Hoxie, who were interested in historical processes and in organizational practices. Some, like Commons and Perlman, the early leaders of the "Wisconsin School," and Witte and Taft, who succeeded them, supported trade unions.

Marxists, like Foster, who attacked the "misleaders of labor" in the unions and argued the need for a working class revolution instead of "bread and butter unionism."

Anti-monopolists, like Simon and Hayek, who viewed unions as monopolies that should be broken.

The "Human Relations School," led by Mayo, that saw the factory and the office as the modern version of the tribe, with the manager as the tribal chief of the community.

These separate schools went their respective ways. The first school knew much theory but little practice; the second was steeped in practice but rejected existing economic theory; the third and fourth had ideological positions to uphold regardless of the factual situation; the fifth neglected to acknowledge that the modern worker may belong to several tribes, not just one, and may not willingly follow the chief in any of them.

There were great exceptions, particularly Douglas at Chicago and Slichter at Harvard, who provided the models for the postwar developments in which they both participated. They were the principal forerunners, and their work still stands above that of their followers.

The postwar explosion produced:

A combination of theory and practice that led to middle-level generalizations that stood between overall principles or ideologies and case by case or historical period by period studies. The earlier neoclassicists (except Marshall) knew little practice, and the prewar historians were prejudiced against theory.

An interdisciplinary view combining insights from each of the social sciences, although economics remained the center.

A rejection of ideology. Marxists and anti-monopolists alike were rejected; and, though to a lesser extent, so were the Wisconsin and Human Relations schools — the one pro-labor and the other pro-management. The field became more unified in outlook and more neutrally professional in approach. Many labor economists served as arbitrators in industrial disputes and this encouraged an attitude of neutrality.

An effort to see reality in its several dimensions. This approach stood against both the excessive hostility and the excessive expectations raised by the sudden growth of the mass labor movement. The labor movement meant neither the destruction of all that was once thought good nor the introduction of a new utopian period. It changed industrial society in a moderate degree, rather than in kind. Countervailing forces were a central theme. So were the many mixtures of good and bad effects.

A concern for policy. This included policies for public institutions, for management, and for unions. Workable policies were of central interest: What would work among the "bumps and grinds" of the real world; not what might work in the "best of all possible worlds."

An effort was made to relate existing theory more realistically to practice and to draw new generalizations from the complexity of actions; to see industrial relations from several disciplinary vantage points, not just one; to reject the blinders of ideologies; to reflect upon what was happening rather than to build Procrustean beds for facts from theories and ideologies — to let the bed fit the man rather than the man fit the bed; and to suggest policies that would be more rational and effective. All this led to problems, including a tendency sometimes to generalize too much from too few observations, and to be too little concerned with finding and contemplating the exceptions to the new generalizations. There was more by way of new insights than by way of precise proof. But the study of industrial relations was greatly advanced — beyond Hicks, Commons, Foster, Hayek, and Mayo; although Douglas and Slichter still stood as the great American pioneers with Marshall and the Webbs standing behind them in historical line. The field now had a core.

The essays that follow were written during the postwar period.[1] My interest in industrial relations began as a graduate student when I worked with Paul S. Taylor at Berkeley in the course of the cotton picker strike in California in 1934.[2] During World War II, I was Wage Stabilization Director of the War Labor Board for the West Coast, then Vice Chairman of the Regional War Labor Board for the Pacific Northwest and Alaska and, later, Chairman of the National Meat Packing Commission. In 1945, I became the founding director of the Institute of Industrial Relations at Berkeley. During the post-war period, I was active as an arbitrator in many industrial disputes and served, for a time, as Impartial Chairman of the Pacific Coast longshore industry. These experiences, and academic training at Swarthmore, Stanford, and Berkeley, are the bases for the essays.

All essays here appeared in the reprint series of the Institute of Industrial Relations. The institute was then and still is one of the leading centers for the study of industrial relations. The essays reflect the work and discussion going on in the institute and also constitute a partial review of the nationwide literature as it developed during the period (1945-1960). I have made no effort to bring the essays up-to-date. They stand as a reflection of the state of the discussion at the time they were written. However, I would not now change my views on any of the important matters of which they treat. Many observations, it seems to me, apply as much, and sometimes even more, today than when they were first set forth. I shall note some of the applications later.

Since 1960, the field of industrial relations in the United States has developed substantially, particularly in three directions. The first is the introduction of more careful statistical and theoretical analysis of wage determination and labor market behavior that clarified the facts and illuminated the conclusions of the earlier period. The second is the great expansion of studies of manpower utilization and human capital development. The third is the bringing to bear of Marxist thought in the field. The study of industrial relations in the United States, until recently, has been imbalanced by lack of contact with the thought of Marx (a few teachers, like Gulick, aside). Marx as an analyst of social processes (though not as a political activist) had much to contribute to an understanding of the evolution of industrial society, particularly in the identification of the broad issues that so interested him (much less in his specific analyses and predictions). He was concerned with the general ad-

---

1. For a second set of essays on industrial relations between labor and management, on industrial peace, and on the industrial system, see *Labor and Management in Industrial Society,* (New York: Anchor/Doubleday, 1964).

2. See Paul S. Taylor and Clark Kerr, *Documentary History of the Strike of Cotton Pickers in California, 1933,* U.S. Government Printing Office, 1940.

vance of history rather than with a single moment and with connections among social phenomena (as between economics and politics) rather than with any one aspect in isolation. Now the gap created by the absence of Marxist thought in the study of industrial relations is being filled in a preliminary way. The essays included here do not benefit from these three and other post-1960 developments.

The essays are concerned with efforts (1) to disaggregate what was once called "*the* labor market," (2) to see the likely limits to union power in setting wages, (3) to observe how bureaucracy handles policy and changes it in the process, and (4) to define what came to be known as the "California School."

I. Disaggregation of the Labor Market

The pure model of the labor market assumed that there was a single labor market; all workers were actively in it seeking to maximize their net advantages; all jobs, by implication, were open to the person with the best bid; and this resulted in a "going rate" for each occupation which adjusted supply and demand. Exceptions were recognized, such as certain noncompeting labor groups as set forth a century ago by Cairnes — members of each group were held within the confines of their class. But competition still led to a going rate within the groups.

However, in fact there often was no going rate but rather a wide dispersion of rates within the same labor market area. War Labor Board policy in World War II initially called for finding *the* going rate and then applying it. Finding it was the job of the Bureau of Labor Statistics. The bureau found instead a wide variation of rates. The anticipated simple application of the going rate became a complex task of judgment as to which of the many actual rates should be made into *the* going rate. When a going rate was found, it was almost always "a sure sign of collusion, not of the working of market forces." Things were quite otherwise from what they were expected to be. The cold wind of reality blew over the once sheltered theories.

Most workers in the labor market at any time were not actively trying to improve their net advantage — they constituted instead what I called the "hard core of the employed." They were attached to their jobs or their areas as in a "marriage contract," as Boulding put it. There was no single labor market but many labor markets, each with its own characteristics and rules for entry and movement within.

The "Balkanization of Labor Markets" (1955) sets forth what was then a new view about labor markets. There were the "ins" and the "outs." The outs are in what is now called the secondary market of the unprotected (what I call, drawing on Lloyd Fisher, the "structureless" market), and the ins are in the primary market of the protected (which I call the structured market). I divided structured markets into two types: the "guild" for craft workers and the "manorial" for noncraft workers.[3] Both represent a new "enclosure movement," where jobs rather than land are captured by and for the ins. Competition takes place mostly at "ports of entry" where the outs seek in competition with each other to get in. Inside the "internal markets"[4] are "families of jobs"[5] where rates of pay are interrelated in an hierarchical fashion. Outside, in the "external markets," are "the non-citizens without rights."[6] Thus, "managed markets" under the influence of public policy were seen as becoming more of a necessity, as we now experience — for example, in federal affirmative action programs, since primary markets often do not meet, in their conduct, the test of "welfare."

"Labor Markets: Their Character and Consequences" (1950) sets forth the theme of the separation of the "wage market" and the "job market." They had been viewed as the same market and, as Hicks said, "potential mobility is the ultimate sanction for the interrelation of wage rates."[7] The job market and the wage market were seen as operating together. But if some job markets are protected and not governed by potential mobility into them, then wage rates are less interrelated. The wage market is separated, in part at least, from the job market; and "wages tend to be unequal," not equal. "The wage market and the job market are substantially disjointed." This leads toward "producer" and away from "consumer sovereignty." And the "system of wages" may have to be "regarded by economists as an independent variable." Wages can and do, to a substantial degree, go their own not so merry way outside the

3. Corina summarized these views: "The institutional market is distinguished by the substitution of institutional rules for frictions as the principal delineator of job market limits." (John Corina, *Labour Market Economics*, [London: Heinemann, 1972], p. 14.) Structureless markets are defined by frictions; structured markets by rules. A recent attempt has been made to divide actual markets into "manorial," "guild" and "unstructured." See Arthur J. Alexander, "Income, Experience and Internal Labor Markets," *Quarterly Journal of Economics* (February 1974).

4. The concept of "internal markets" has been further developed particularly by Peter B. Doeringer and Michael J. Piore in *Internal Labor Markets and Manpower Analysis* (Lexington, Mass.: Heath, 1971).

5. John T. Dunlop has elaborated the concept of the "job family" and "seniority districts" in "Job Vacancy and Economic Analysis," in *The Measurement and Interpretation of Job Vacancies: A Conference Report*, National Bureau of Economic Research (New York: Columbia University Press, 1966).

6. Myrdal later wrote of the "underclass" and Harrington of the "culture of poverty." (See Gunnar Myrdal, *Challenge to Affluence* [New York: Random House, 1963]; and Michael Harrington, *The Other America* [New York: Macmillan, 1964].)

7. J. R. Hicks, *Theory of Wages* (London: Macmillan, 1932, 2nd ed.).

control of the job market; and in this phenomenon lie many of the economic distresses of the day.

Hicks[8] later wrote in a most influential article of the "labor standard" replacing the gold standard as a determinant of the price level since wages followed a course largely of their own and prices had to follow along — the general level of wages had become largely independent of the job market. The Phillips curve[9] shows the trade-off between unemployment and inflation, but the trade-off is a much more costly one if many job markets are protected from wage competition — it takes more unemployment to hold down the rate of inflation.

"Stagflation," a relatively new phenomenon, is one result of the separation of the wage market and the job market — wages can go up even as jobs go down; and unemployment is less of a solution to inflation — it does not reach most of the ins for whom an independent wage policy is made; and it puts a heavy burden on the outs and on those who are barely in — they are severely hurt with only modest gains in holding down inflation. The general rule is: the less wages are set by the job market and the more they are set in wage markets sheltered from job competition, the less impact unemployment will have on inflation and there is less trade-off of more unemployment for less inflation. Therefore, the solution in terms of the gains to be realized is costlier. This is the current and future problem, but it began much earlier.[10] Many more internal markets are now more protected from external forces; and external forces vent their wrath more on the unprotected — the outs and the consumers. Yet public policy still tries to reach the wage market through the job market, thus reducing output, and putting heavy pressure on structureless markets but having little influence on structured markets.

The "Effect of Environment and Administration on Job Evaluation" (1950) considers the working of protected internal markets, where job evaluation finds its home, but as affected by external forces. Internal markets are not entirely immune from external forces, although some are more immune than others — for example, internal markets in the high wage plant. The internal

8. J. R. Hicks, "Economic Foundations of Wage Policy," *Economic Journal* (September 1955).

9. A. W. Phillips, "The Relation Between Unemployment and the Rate of Change of Money Wages in the United Kingdom, 1861-1957," *Economica* (November 1958).

10. For a discussion of how unemployment has had less impact on wage levels in the United States (a less responsive Phillips curve), see R. A. Gordon, "Wages, Prices and Unemployment, 1900-1975," *Industrial Relations* (October 1975). See also the conclusion of George L. Perry that "Phillips curves exist but are quite flat in most countries" ("Determinants of Wage Inflation Around the World," *Brookings Papers on Economic Activity — 2* [Washington, D.C.: 1975]). An absolutely flat line would, of course, have no explanatory value.

market reacts to what is considered to be "right"; the external market to what is "necessary." The engineer tends to reflect the first as he administers the plan with its principles; and the employment manager the second as he operates in the market. Not only is management divided in the points of view between the engineer and the employment manager; but so are the workers over what is right and what is necessary. There is a continuous conflict between "internal logic" and the "external environment"; and this leads to continuous compromise. Another conflict, magnified increasingly as industrial societies mature, is the comparative reward for skill and for job desirability. We observed that the comparative disagreeableness of a job, rather than the skill it entails, will require a higher and higher relative weighting in setting wages. Truer today than yesterday, the observation will be even more valid tomorrow as higher and higher premiums will be paid for disagreeable work.

If there were only one labor market setting wages everywhere all the time, then there would be no conflict between internal and external systems of evaluation — the market, responding to supply and demand, would rule supreme; but there are internal as well as external markets, each responding to different considerations and so causing universal problems.

"Migration to the Seattle Labor Market, 1940-1942" is not included here but I mention it, for historical reasons.[11] It was the first modern labor market study made in the field under the auspices of the Social Science Research Council. (It was followed shortly by a study by Myers and Maclaurin.[12]) Early in the war, Seattle greatly expanded its employment and so offered an opportunity to learn who moved and why. Some now commonplace findings were: the large reserves of workers potentially available; the comparatively higher mobility of younger persons; the greater likelihood of a worker making small jumps in skill and geographical location than a large jump; the small importance of cost of physical movement (which in neoclassical theory was the main impediment to movement and thus a main cause of wage differentials); the importance of the "push" of an unfavorable situation versus the "pull" of a better situation; and the importance of sources of information and, in particular, of the great reliance on friends.

The standard view had been that *the* labor market was a unified and unifying phenomenon. The new view was that labor markets were plural in their structures, their characteristics and their effects — fractionated labor markets

11. Clark Kerr, *Migration to the Seattle Labor Market Area, 1940-42* (University of Washington Press, 1942). (Reprinted, Westport: Greenwood Press, 1970.)

12. Charles A. Myers and W. Rupert Maclaurin, *The Movement of Factory Workers* (New York: Wiley, 1943).

and disjointed wage structures were the rule, not the exception. The economic world was not so nearly the best of all possible worlds as the neoclassicists had thought and there was room for social policy to bring improvements.

II. THE LIMITS OF UNION POWER OVER WAGES

Unions have often been viewed as monopolies led by and consisting of "economic men" intent on maximizing their material advantages. This has contributed to fears of exploitation of the economy by some and to hopes of capturing the illicit gains of the capitalists by others. Great harm, on the one hand, and great good, on the other, have quite inconsistently been anticipated by different observers as the result of the mass organization of workers for the first time in American history. The essays included in Part II explore what organized power by workers does accomplish. The general conclusion of the essays is that neither Hell nor Heaven is the most likely result, but some of each and often not much of either.

"Labor's Income Share and the Labor Movement" (1957) treats of the impact of unionization on labor's share of national income. The general answer is: not a great deal, mainly because the employer has escape routes through higher prices and substitution of other resources and methods. The employer can be pushed but in turn there are those whom he can push. There are exceptions, particularly when product markets have "hard" prices as in a depression or when there are effective price controls; or when the labor movement politically can obtain redistribution of income for the workers through taxation and government expenditures. Labor's share, *as a share,* can also be reduced by labor-induced policies to achieve full employment — for profits usually benefit more than wages. Either way, it seems that the labor movement is not likely to affect labor's share much in either direction in the long run (although with more workers and fewer self-employed, labor's share tends to rise in the long run for other reasons). While labor's overall share may not be much affected by organized labor power, efforts to increase it can result in redistribution *within* labor's share as some segments improve their position vis-à-vis other segments. The battle, thus, is labor versus labor rather than labor versus capital. The ins with power can gain at the expense of the outs without power.[13]

"The Impact of Unions on the Level of Wages" (1959) comes to an

---

13. H. Gregg Lewis found that "unionism . . . has raised the average relative wage of union labor by about 7 to 11 percent and reduced the average relative wage of nonunion labor by approximately 3 or 4 percent." (*Unionism and Relative Wages in the United States* [University of Chicago Press, 1963], p. 194.)

opposite conclusion about union power. Unions can have a major impact on the general level of money wages. They can hold it down, as when they are an "agent of the state" in a controlled economy or when the slow adjustment of contracts lags behind in an economic upswing. They can raise it, as when they act as an "enemy of the system" or when they take advantage of a government supported policy of full employment. There are many situations and many possible results.

Why this potentially great impact on the level of wages and not on the share? The basic answer is that the employer can protect his profits better from worker efforts to seize them than consumers can protect themselves from price increases under the joint assault of unions and employers. Employers can better escape from the upward pressure than can consumers. Also, labor's share relates to real terms — to real shares of the pie — which set harsher limits on actions than do the money terms of the general level of wages.

The essay concludes that union action in the United States in the long run has been only "moderately inflationary." Current circumstances (1975) reinforce the judgment for the same reason as set forth earlier — "the general reasonableness of the unions and their leaders in the context of the type of society in which they evolve."

"Wage Relationships — The Comparative Impact of Market and Power Forces" (1957) looks at wage structures which are divided into five categories — interpersonal, interfirm, interarea, interoccupational and interindustry. It concludes that union power has potentially great impact on the first two, much less on the last two, with the third in an intermediate position. The general rule is that unions have the greatest impact where they have the greatest motivation to equalize rates (in interpersonal and interfirm wage structures) and where the least power is needed to accomplish the task; and the least impact where there is the least motivation (in interoccupational and interindustry wage structures) and where the most total power must be applied.

The essay relates interoccupational and interindustry wage structures mostly to the skill level of the occupation and, in turn, of the industry, and to the comparative supply of and demand for skill at different stages of economic growth. The basic rule is: "The lesser the degree and the greater the rate of industrialization, the wider will be the occupational differentials and the greater the premium for skill; and the greater the degree and the lesser the rate of industrialization, the narrower will be the occupational differentials and the greater the premium for distasteful work." Interindustry differentials are largely set by interoccupational differentials and thus follow the same general rule of narrowing as the economy advances. This rule applies to both managed and market economies, which means that managed economies also reflect market forces in this area of wage structures. A recent study of experience in China confirms the observation.[14]

"The Short-Run Behavior of Physical Productivity and Average Hourly Earnings" (1949) is included because the favored norm of economists and policy makers is that money wages should rise with productivity and thus the price level would remain stable. The essay considers this norm and seeks to set forth "a realistic appraisal of the likelihood of its being followed." It concludes that "the short-run gearing of wages to productivity in the future is unlikely to be achieved with any great precision." Intervening history has emphasized the validity of this conclusion. Dangers were seen ahead even though the overall performance of the years 1840 to 1914 and 1919 to 1945 seemed to meet this norm. The main problems in meeting the norm were considered to be: (1) wages and productivity respond quite differently to the different phases of the business cycle and not at all in harmony with each other; (2) the experience of different industries is quite various and, in practice, hardly likely to add up to what the norm requires; and (3) many considerations, in addition to productivity, affect employers and unions as they set wages. The push and pull of power and of markets are greater than the attraction of the norm.

Overall, the impact of union power compared to market forces is mixed — in some places and some times the impact is great, in other places and at other times little or even none at all. The answer to the question of whether union power or the labor market is the more influential is: yes and no. Reality is more complex than theory or ideology once supposed.

III. THE IMPACT OF BUREAUCRATIC CONTROLS

I had the opportunity to observe wage controls at work both with the War Labor Board in World War II and later as Vice Chairman of the National Wage Stabilization Board during the Korean War. How well do they work and under what circumstances? Are they a potential solution to persistent inflation?

"Governmental Wage Restraints: Their Limits and Uses in a Mobilized Economy" (1952) examines the experience in World War II and the Korean War. The general answer is that wage restraints work well overall only in a national crisis and then only for a short time. The recent experience of the

---

14. See Christopher Howe, *Wage Patterns and Wage Policy in Modern China* (Cambridge University Press, 1973).

early 1970s confirms this conclusion. In the long run and in less than a crisis, however, wage restraints can help reduce "individual runaways." Thus they can hold wage increases more to their normal pattern than if runaways set new patterns to be emulated. The essay is concerned with what may reasonably be expected of wage restraint efforts; and the use of wage restraints will be a recurring issue in the indefinite future.

Reasons why wage restraints are not very effective, except under limited circumstances, are that (1) unions will not accept them, (2) employers can administer wage schedules in ways to increase earnings substantially despite stabilization of schedules, (3) the public representatives and officials involved in application of wage restraints are more mediators between the parties than they are representatives of the public interest, and (4) the public is interested in industrial peace and in production as well as in stabilization.

One contribution that wage restraint can make, however, is bureaucratic delay. A good bureaucracy can delay actions at least six months without building up unacceptable levels of frustration. There are circumstances, however, where wage restraint may *raise* wages by setting a minimum level of increases — in the course of taking care of maximum situations — which is higher than would otherwise prevail.

The essay is concerned with wage restraint in response to external national crises. Wage restraints are even harder to effect when the crisis is internal to the nation, in the absence of an external threat from another nation or nations.

A related essay, not included here, entitled, "The Distribution of Authority and Its Relation to Policy,"[15] examines how administrative structures can affect policy. Administration is by people and policy application reflects the surrounding administrative structure. The general rule for persons being restrained and wishing to minimize the restraint is (1) to get their own agency, (2) to arrange to meet no opposition within this agency, and (3) to minimize review and control from above. These tactics have affected the history of regulatory agencies in recent peacetime years and not just in the area of wage controls. The general rule to avoid regulatory manipulation by special interests is (1) to have an agency cover several or many institutions and groupings of institutions at once, (2) to arrange for opposition interests to be represented within the agency, and (3) to make the agency subject to review of its actions rather than independent.

The experience with these two periods of wage restraint (World War II and the Korean War) leads to these conclusions: (1) it works best in the short run

15. In *Problems and Policies of Dispute Settlement and Wage Stabilization During World War II*, U.S. Bureau of Labor Statistics (Washington, D.C.: 1950).

and in a time of national crisis; and (2) how well it works depends, substantially, on how it is administered, on whose organizational strategy wins out — actual results depend as much on the specific forms of administrative application as on formal policy.

The conclusion that governmental wage restraints have only moderate long-run effectiveness adds to the weight of the earlier conclusion that unemployment in the labor market is also only moderately useful in holding down the rise in the general level of money wages. The two conclusions indicate that the control of inflation within narrow limits is at least very difficult and perhaps even unlikely — now that the labor standard has replaced the gold standard. Neither string to the bow — wage restraint or unemployment — is adequate for the purpose; yet governmental policy has been shifting back and forth from the use of one to the use of the other. This means either that other methods than these two (whatever they may be) must be relied on to halt inflation or that efforts must be made to assure that the inevitable inflation that will take place is reasonably fair in its impact on individuals.

The essays taken together lead to a disappointing conclusion. They agree with the recent views of Galbraith that privately administered inflation will occur in the absence of restraints, but disagree with Galbraith that restraints are likely to be effective. Inflation, substantial in amount, appears to be endemic in our industrial society.

IV. "THE CALIFORNIA SCHOOL"

"The California School," as it came to be called,[16] sought to combine economics and politics in analyzing industrial relation situations, not to rely on economics alone. In a way, it returned to the older tradition of "political economy." Lloyd Fisher was the political scientist. He was particularly interested in the separation of interests between leaders and members; he was a follower of Robert Michels and a believer in the inevitability of "the iron law of oligarchy."[17] Arthur Ross and I were economists by training. All three of us had served with the War Labor Board. The central contribution of Ross was the concept of the "orbits of coercive comparisons."[18] My particular

16. See, for example, B. C. Roberts, "Trade Union Behaviour and Wage Determination in Great Britain," in *The Theory of Wage Determination,* edited by John T. Dunlop (London: Macmillan, 1957).

17. Robert Michels, *Political Parties* (Glencoe, Ill.: Free Press,1949; first published in 1915), particularly Chapter 2 of Part VI.

18. Arthur M. Ross, *Trade Union Wage Policy* (Berkeley: University of California Press, 1948), Chapter 3.

contribution was the concept of the union, not as a monopoly selling labor, but as a "wage-fixing institution."

I once explained the California School at a meeting (1954) under the auspices of the International Economic Association:[19]

Professor Kerr said that, though there was no "California School" or line, he wished to explain what this "line" was! It held that trade unions were primarily political institutions which responded both to external economic stimuli and to the internal political environment. Externally the union might be concerned with economics and/or politics, but internally it was politically activated. Professor Dunlop's models were ingenious, interesting — and nonsense! If one looked at the United States wage structure, the dispersion of wage rates was much less than would be permitted by the very different characteristics of demand, etc. Unions did not respond as much as one might expect to such elasticities. Perhaps the California school had overemphasized internal political factors in the union; for example, the importance of new and rival unionism. The two papers [then under discussion] represented efforts to reconcile the Harvard and California "lines." He himself would reconcile them by saying that which one was correct depended on the question one was asking. The political model was the better model for explaining internal decision-making, but economic forces were easily the most important factor in the long run in fixing wages. In the long run, political factors had little impact on wages. The union was, so to speak, operating in a "narrow corridor" of action.

"Economic Analysis and the Study of Industrial Relations" (1947) was an earlier effort to explain the California School. It was given at a conference in May 1947. The essence of the "school" was said to be the "combination of economics and politics" in consideration of a number of topics, as several essays here indicate. The central dispute came to be over the model of the trade union. The only model at the time was the pioneering "economic model" as set forth by Dunlop.[20] The "political model" was subsequently set forth best by Arthur Ross in a famous article late in 1947.[21] It drew on some of the ideas noted above; as Ross indicated in the prefatory note to his subsequent book:[22] "I have worked in close cooperation with Professor Clark

19. Dunlop, *The Theory of Wage Determination* (Macmillan, 1957), p. 387.

20. John T. Dunlop, *Wage Determination Under Trade Unions* (New York: Macmillan, 1944).

21. Arthur M. Ross, "The Trade Union as a Wage-Fixing Institution," *American Economic Review* (December 1947).

22. *Trade Union Wage Policy, op. cit.* R. A. Gordon also influenced this conception with his at least partially "political model" of business leadership. (See R. A. Gordon, *Business Leadership in the Large Corporation*[Washington, D.C.: The Brookings Institution, 1945], pp. 3-10.) See also the essay of Lloyd H. Fisher on "The Price of Union Responsibility" where he describes "the trade union as a continuing political body" (*Proceedings*, National Conference of Social Work [1947]. Also included in E. Wight Bakke and Clark Kerr, *Unions, Management and the Public* [New York: Harcourt, Brace, 1948], pp. 144-148. In this same volume, see the section on "Union Leaders and Members," pp. 178-180, which I wrote.)

Kerr and Mr. Lloyd Fisher, and the ideas expressed in the monograph are theirs as well as mine."

Despite the joint development of the central ideas, I have always felt that Ross rather overdid the political side. He was too concerned with conditions of new and rival unionism immediately after World War II when politics in unions were often at a white heat, and too little concerned with economic constraints. My view of the "wage-fixing institution" was that it was not selling labor, as Dunlop said, but fixing a wage at which labor was then individually sold. The comparison intended was more with a government bureau setting wages in a bureaucratic fashion to meet certain standard conditions (like the cost of living) and to avoid undue trouble (such as failing to match a "pattern"). I once contrasted (see "The Impact of Unions on the Level of Wages") union bargaining in a "state of excitement" as against a "state of normality." Ross was heavily influenced by the "state of excitement" which prevailed at the time he wrote. Dunlop, on the other hand, I thought, was too interested in applying standard economic theory, relying on the model of "economic man," to wage determination.

I now would contrast (a) the "competitive political model" of unionism, where there is a state of internal leadership or external organizational rivalry, with (b) the "bureaucratic political model" of unionism. Both are political models. However, they behave differently. The more standard case is the "bureaucratic political model." I once wrote (in "Labor Markets — Their Character and Consequences") of the "further bureaucratization of unions." But right after World War II, with organizing strikes by unions, AFL versus CIO rivalry, and the creation of new unions, the "competitive political model" was in the ascendancy. However, as Lloyd Fisher would always point out, unions are mostly "one-party governments." This is the long-run reality.

Some craft unions act as monopolies "selling labor," as Dunlop set forth. Thus, three models are necessary: (1) the competitive political model, (2) the bureaucratic political model, and (3) the economic monopoly model. Each explains some situations. However, more situations more often follow the bureaucratic political model than either of the others. Unions are mostly one-party governments with an entrenched leadership setting wages, along with employers, at levels that satisfy many pressures and respond to many goals (including doing as much as necessary to keep up with the cost of living and any "coercive" wage patterns and thus satisfying the membership, but not much more) and not even substantially maximizing monopoly power. Their leaders behave more like reasonable bureaucratic managers than like competitive political candidates or grasping exploiters. This is fortunate, since wage rates would be much higher and there would be more inflation than there already is if either of the other two models, or the two together, were predominantly followed in practice. Long live the bureaucratic political model!

The rise to dominance of the bureaucratic model has depended on these developments: the end of rival unionism (AFL versus CIO), the steady application of the "iron law of oligarchy" as new unions become older unions, the acceptance of union security through some version of the union or closed shop by employers, and the expansion of industrial unionism (craft unions are more likely to follow the monopoly approach).

Generally, unions are run more like quasi-governmental bureaucracies than like either economic monopolies or competitive political parties. They take less advantage of their potential economic power and act less driven by political competition than the Dunlop and Ross models, respectively, might suggest, and behave themselves more like well-meaning bureaucracies responding effectively to standard conventions and staying out of excessive trouble both internally and externally. It is fortunate for the economy that they usually do act this way. More and more the bureaucratic political model is the standard; society can live better with it than with the other two models; either of the other two would cause more trouble with employers, with government, and among unions than the bureaucratic model. It minimizes trouble, which is what good governmental managers do, while accomplishing what is minimally necessary.

In any event, much literature has been written on the controversy over union models and it continues to appear.[23]

The California School made contributions to more realistic models: (1) of the labor market, (2) of the wage setting process, (3) of governmental administration of labor policies, and (4) of trade union behavior. It elucidated the reasons beyond such important phenomena as (1) continuing inflation in the presence of substantial unemployment, (2) the ever greater comparative exploitation of the outs in the labor market coincident with greater protection of the ins; (3) the comparatively moderate impact of the union movement on the workings of the economy, and (4) the development of diverse wage structures that seem to be without much rhyme or reason.

In 1945, on the urging of Governor Earl Warren, the Institute of Industrial Relations at Berkeley was established to take a fresh look at the expanding world of industrial relations in the American economy, to provide better

23. See Wallace W. Atherton, *Theory of Union Bargaining Goals* (Princeton University Press, 1973).

understanding of current developments, and to contribute to more effective private and public policy. These essays were part of that effort.[24]

I should like to conclude with a brief note on what the whole related literature (1945-1960) in labor economics, not just the essays here, have meant to the more recent development of industrial relations and to economics generally.

The literature examined aspects of the economy in a period of historic change. More "visible" hands were at work than just the "invisible hand" of Adam Smith. More organizations controlled more of the economy with greater power. We were moving, as Hicks has put it, from "flexprice" to "fixprice."[25] This literature, early, looked at some selected developments in the course of the movement: at labor markets responding to rules as well as to frictions; at wages depending on power as well as market forces; at the inherent behavior of power groups and the "power elite." What was going on? Why? What were the impacts? What was good social policy in the new context?

Unfortunately, there was little contact between this body of literature and main-line economic theory which then concentrated on macro phenomena using mathematical techniques, as against a micro and institutional approach. Recently, however, the economic theorists have shown more interest in micro problems and institutional behavior because much could not be explained satisfactorily without such reference.[26]

Meanwhile, labor economics has gone in two different directions from the earlier body of literature. One direction is toward statistical and theoretical analyses of a neoclassical type (the "Chicago School" came to replace the "Wisconsin School"). Some of this work — most of it at an advanced level of methodological sophistication — has confirmed old insights on new discoveries since the earlier literature. The development made great advances to bring labor economics into contact with main-stream economics.

Another direction has been Marxist-type analysis. Here, too, while the issues of interest have often been similar, the older literature has been rejected on ideological not methodological grounds. It was "liberal" in tone, not "radical." The new Marxists have helped to define the issues that are

24. I should like to thank August Frugé, Director, and Grant Barnes, Sponsoring Editor, of the University of California Press for their encouragement and assistance in bringing these essays together for publication; and Lloyd Ulman, Director of the Institute of Industrial Relations, University of California, Berkeley, for his interest in this project at the time of the 30th anniversary of the founding of the Institute and for his contribution of the Foreword.

25. J. R. Hicks, *The Crisis in Keynesian Economics* (Oxford: Blackwell, 1974).

26. See the comment in Perry, *op. cit.,* "institutions are important and can lead to wage behavior that would be unpredictable from equations that one could normally fit."

"relevant" to public policy and public discussion. They have served to keep labor economics in contact with institutional behavior, the broad sweep of history, the current range of problems, and the emerging policy issues.

Thus labor economics has split again, this time into neoclassical and Marxist camps with little relation to each other or to the tradition of the 1945-1960 period. The new neoclassicists have studied what could be studied while using the best modern methodology; the new Marxists have studied what needed to be studied, sometimes regardless of the best modern methodology, in terms of their social concerns. Unfortunately, the methodology is more limited than the range of problems, and the ideology more confining than the range of good possible solutions.

It remains to be seen how the problems of today, such as managed labor markets, managed wage rates, stagflation, exploitation, may once again produce approaches to labor economics to make it a single discipline that combines theory and institutional practice; that uses but goes beyond statistical and mathematical analysis; that relates to ideology but is not confined by it.

PART I. Disaggregation of the Labor Market

The Balkanization
of Labor Markets

L ABOR MARKETS are more talked about than seen, for their dimensions most frequently are set by the unknown and, perhaps, mystic ideas in people's minds. A worker wishes to be employed in a certain area and at a certain type of job, and an employer wants employees drawn from certain groups and possessing certain characteristics. Unless it is said that each worker always has his own market area and each employer his,[1] there must be some adding of worker and employer preferences to get designated "markets."

These preferences vary from person to person and from time to time for the same person, and when they are totaled the "market" that they constitute has vague and varying contours but no ultimate limits short of those for American society itself. For example, there is said to be a market for waitresses in Oakland with certain women normally attached to it and certain employers hiring from it. Since, however, a woman need not always be a waitress once having bccn one and a woman never having been one can become one and

Reprinted by permission from *Labor Mobility and Economic Opportunity*, The Technology Press of M.I.T., and Wiley. Copyright: 1954 Massachusetts Institute of Technology.

1. If this is said, then the term "market," with all it implies, might better be dropped. Instead, we should pay attention to the scales of preference of individual workers and individual employers. The approach might well constitute a gain for realism and for precision but a loss for comprehension. It probably is true that no two people are alike, and for some purposes this is the relevant generalization; but it is also probably true that all people need to eat, and for other purposes this is the relevant generalization. The use of the term "labor market" implies that there is enough uniformity of behavior among certain workers and among certain employers to warrant generalizations about the actions of each group. Thus it might be said that the labor market for waitresses in Oakland is characterized (among other things) by sellers who want part-time employment and buyers who prefer married women, or by high turnover, or by a lack of formal structure.

since a restaurant employer can hire a girl from San Francisco as well as from Oakland, the market is by no means a self-contained one with precise limits. Preferences of workers and employers are also relative to time. In a depression, a "waitress" may consider herself also available for work in a laundry, and a restaurant employer in wartime may be willing to hire former laundry workers to serve as waitresses.

Most labor markets are similarly indefinite in their specification of the sellers and the buyers. Such a labor market is merely an area, with indistinct geographical and occupational limits within which certain workers customarily seek to offer their services and certain employers to purchase them. But any single worker or any single employer may decide to go elsewhere. This might be identified as the "free choice" market or the "natural market,"[2] for which the individual and changing preferences of workers and employers set the hazy limits.

THE INSTITUTIONAL MARKET

An increasing number of labor markets are more specifically defined at any moment and have their dimensions less constantly changed over time. These are the "institutional markets." Their dimensions are set not by the whims of workers and employers but by rules, both formal and informal. These rules state which workers are preferred in the market or even which ones may operate in it at all, and which employers may or must buy in this market if they are to buy at all. Institutional rules take the place of individual preferences in setting the boundaries. Such institutional rules are established by employers' associations, by the informal understandings of employers among each other (the "gentlemen's agreement"), by companies when they set up their personnel policies, by trade unions, by collective agreements, and by actions of government. They contrast with the independent preferences of the individuals who are directly involved.

Economists once spoke of *the* labor market. Each worker competed with all other workers for jobs, and each employer with all other employers for workers. Cairnes, however, early saw there were noncompeting groups:[3]

No doubt the various ranks and classes fade into each other by imperceptible gradations, and individuals from all classes are constantly passing up or down; but while this is so, it is nevertheless true that the average workman, from whatever rank he be taken, finds his power of competition limited for practical purposes to a certain range of

2. See Clark Kerr, "Labor Markets: Their Character and Consequences," *American Economic Review* (May 1950).

3. J. E. Cairnes, *Political Economy* (New York: Harper, 1874), pp. 67-68.

occupations, so that, however high the rates of remuneration in those which lie beyond may rise, he is excluded from sharing them. We are thus compelled to recognize the existence of non-competing industrial groups as a feature of our social economy.

Cairnes used the word "compelled" advisedly. For the existence of "non-competing" groups adds both complications to economic analysis and impediments to the maximization of welfare. Economic society would be both simpler to understand and closer to the economist's prescription if there were only one labor market.

In the long run, perhaps over several generations, it may be correct to talk about *the* labor market. Unless society has a hereditary class system, social mobility over time will permit, if not all, at least many individuals or their descendants to prepare themselves for any specific line of work. But a medical practitioner of today can hardly be said to be competing in the market with the unborn son of a pipe fitter. Yet in the long run, defined as the time it takes for the greatest occupational shift to work itself out, *the* labor market may be said to exist.

In the long run, all families may compete with all other families, but in the short run, most individuals are not in competition with each other. In fact, at any time the standard case is one man faced by one job — this one job is available to only this one man, and this man has only this one job available to him. We are more concerned, however, with labor markets in the short run when several men and several jobs, rather than all men and all jobs or one man and one job, may face each other. In the short run, a worker can make himself available for several jobs, according to his preferences, and an employer can make a job available to several workers, according to his preferences.

The noncompeting groups of Cairnes were the several socio-economic classes (manual, white-collar, professional workers, and so forth). We have found, however, that each of these classes is composed in turn of many largely noncompeting groups. Painters do not compete with bricklayers, or typists with accountants, or doctors with lawyers; nor individuals in Portland, Maine, with those in Portland, Oregon (except perhaps in certain professions). Barriers to movement are set up by the skill gaps between occupations and the distance gaps between locations. Beyond the specificity of skills and the money costs of physical transfer, lie such various but no less important impediments to competition as lack of knowledge, the job tastes of workers, their inertia and their desire for security, and the personal predilections of employers. The competitive market areas within which somewhat similar men look for somewhat similar jobs, and within which somewhat similar employers try to fill somewhat similar jobs, are normally quite restricted. It has even been suggested that the only meaningful definition of a labor market is one which calls each place of employment a separate market[4] and, perhaps, beyond that, each separate class of work at each such place. More commonly, it is said that a labor market covers the several employers in the same industry in the same area. Thus there are markets and submarkets, all more or less interrelated with each other. The introduction of institutional rules, as we shall see presently, generally creates a larger number of such markets and universally makes them less interrelated.

Institutional rules put added structure into labor markets. Lloyd Fisher has lucidly described the "structureless market" for harvest labor in California.[5] The characteristics of this market serve as a point of contrast for the market types to be described later. The structureless market, according to Fisher, has five conditions: (1) there are no unions with seniority and other rules, (2) the relation between the employee and the employer is a transitory, impersonal one, (3) the workers are unskilled, (4) payment is by unit of product, and (5) little capital or machinery is employed. The employer prefers one worker to another only if he accepts a lower piece rate and the worker one employer over another only if he will pay a higher piece rate. Rates vary greatly over time, but at any moment of time are uniform over space. There are no structural barriers to the mobility of workers and to the fluidity of rates. The only nexus is cash.

Structure is introduced into labor markets even without institutional rules. Many workers have skills which restrict the occupational area in which they seek work, and the number of these skills limits the supply to the employer. Moreover, workers and employers form attachments for each other which neither like to break lightly — "You must realize that the labor market is like the marriage market"[6] and separation is for cause only. Thus most jobs, even without institutional rules, belong to single workers or to small groups of workers. The craft exists without the craft union, and informal job ties exist

4. "There are thus as many labor markets as there are employers of labor," Gordon F. Bloom and Herbert R. Northrup, *Economics of Labor and Industrial Relations* (Philadelphia: Blakiston, 1950), p. 265. Lloyd G. Reynolds states: "the firm is the hiring unit and . . . each company employment office is really a distinct market for labor." *The Structure of Labor Markets* (New York: Harper, 1951), p. 42.

5. Lloyd H. Fisher, "The Harvest Labor Market in California," *Quarterly Journal of Economics* (November 1951).

6. Kenneth Boulding's comment in "Selections from the Discussion of Friedman's Paper," in David McCord Wright, editor, *The Impact of the Union* (New York: Harcourt, Brace, 1951), p. 254.

without formal seniority rules. Institutional rules, however, add new rights and new preferences and strengthen the old ties.

Institutional labor markets create truly noncompeting groups. Markets are more specifically delimited, and entrance into them, movement within them, and exit from them more precisely defined. Such labor' markets find their definition not in the composite of individual preferences but in precise rules. "Natural" frictions are replaced by institutional ones; the free and ignorant man by the exclusive and knowledgeable group. Market forces, seemingly impersonal in the aggregate but exceedingly personal in individual situations, give way to personnel rules which may seem exceedingly impersonal when applied to specific workers. Fraternity triumphs over liberty as "no trespassing" signs are posted in more and more job markets.

The sources of this enclosure movement are not far to seek. Employing units are larger, and bureaucratic rules take the place of individual judgments. These rules accept or reject classes of people, instead of the single individuals who met or failed to meet the tests of judgment or the prejudices of the small employer or the foreman. Workers have organized into unions which seek to establish sovereignty over a "job territory." Within this job territory work the citizens who belong to this private government; outside are the noncitizens without rights. The demands of all citizens will be met before the petitions of the aliens are considered. The institutionalization of labor markets is one aspect of the general trend from the atomistic to the pluralistic, and from the largely open to the partially closed society.

TYPES OF INSTITUTIONAL MARKETS

Many barriers divide the totality of employment relationships into more or less distinct compartments. These barriers have five sources: (1) the preferences of individual workers, (2) the preferences of individual employers, (3) the actions of the community of workers, (4) the actions of the community of employers, and (5) the actions of government. The controls on movement flowing from the last three are defined as institutional rules, whether they are written or merely understood, as compared with the "free choices" flowing from the first two.

The institutional rules of employers, workers, and government are enormously varied, reflecting as they do a diversity of environments and desires, and consequently it is difficult to generalize about them. There are, however, two general systems of rules, each with important subtypes. We shall discuss here only the two broad systems and not all the variations of each, significant as they are. The two systems are the communal-ownership approach of craft groups and the private-property method of industrial workers.

Communal Ownership — The craft union asserts proprietorship on behalf of its members over the jobs falling within a carefully defined occupational and geographical area. Employers needing the specified occupational skill in that area must hire union members or take the consequences. The building, printing, maritime, and teamster trades illustrate this type of arrangement.

Workers enter the market through the unions; and the unions have preferences just as do employers. They may be in favor of or against Negroes, or women, or students, or Communist party members, and these preferences will show up in the labor supply made available.[7] Entrance is sometimes through closely supervised apprenticeship systems[8] which require the worker to choose his specific occupation early in life and make initial sacrifices in order to gain admittance. These apprenticeship programs are usually pursued with government aid. Admission may also be by transfer card from another local. Occasionally, as in the case of the typographical workers, the man with a transfer card has equal rights with some local members. More frequently, however, he must go to the end of the list and wait until all local members are employed. The transfer card gives him preference only over new applicants for membership. When work is abnormally plentiful, some unions issue work permits, analogous to visas, which entitle outsiders to temporary employment. When employment returns to normal, they lose their privileges. They are renters, not owners.

Once fully in the market, the craft worker can move anywhere within it. Sometimes, when there is a hiring hall with rotation of work, as for longshoremen on the Pacific Coast, he may move throughout the market. Inside the market, wages, working conditions, and job requirements are equalized, and the worker has an unusual knowledge of conditions and job opportunities. Sometimes worker performance is standardized also,[9] so that no employer need prefer any worker any more than any worker need prefer any employer. Though the men within the market are equal with each other, they are unequal with others outside the market. A little equalitarian island has been created in the midst of a sea of inequality.

7. Thus, the "membership function" of the union, because of its restrictive preferences, may lie to the left of the "market-supply function." See John T. Dunlop, *Wage Determination under Trade Unions* (New York: Macmillan, 1944), p. 33. The employer may also, because of his preferences, draw from less than the total supply of efficient workers potentially available to him.

8. The classic discussion of apprenticeship, as of other union rules, is by Sumner H. Slichter, *Union Policies and Industrial Management,* (Washington: The Brookings Institution, 1941).

9. When it is not standardized, competition among workers is by degree of skill. The more skilled workers are in greater demand.

Movement of workers is vitally affected. Occupational identification is unchanging and, largely because of this, other types of movement are encouraged — from one plant to another and even one industry or one locality to another. Since some fluidity is necessary in a progressive society, a tight tie to occupation forces a looser tie to employer, industry, and locality. Movement is primarily horizontal in the craft market. The worker gets his security not from the individual employer but from his skill, the competitive supply of which is controlled by his union; and he is known as a carpenter and not as an employee of a certain company. Just as the worker is free to move from employer, so also are employers free to encourage such movement. "Gentlemen's agreements" against "pirating" are not the mark of the craft trades.

Ejection from the market is controlled by the union. An employer can discharge a man from a specific job but not from the market. Few discharge grievances are filed in craft markets because the man gets his security from union control of the market and not from the employer. The union, however, may eject a man, but its reasons are not normally the same as those actuating employers. Political sins are given a higher order of value as compared with the economic sins which an employer is more apt to punish. Union ejections, which are infrequent, are not so subject to appeal to third parties as are employer discharges.

The communal-ownership system is by no means an oddity. A check of contracts covering 350,000 workers in the San Francisco Bay area in all the major industries (construction, food and drink, retail, transportation equipment, wholesale, service, local transportation, metal and machinery, oil, chemicals, lumber and furniture, hotels and restaurants, public utilities, and others) showed 190,000 workers covered by some variant of the closed shop, i.e., membership in the union must precede employment. The San Francisco Bay area is, of course, strongly unionized and does not include a significant amount of heavy industry.

Private Property — In the industrial enterprise, the central rule is to each man one job and to each job one man. The typical market consists of one job for which one man is available. This is an exaggerated description of the average situation, for ability usually counts as well as seniority, but since the trend is toward strict seniority provisions it may stand as a statement of the central tendency. The man on the job (given good behavior) is the only man eligible for it, and when he leaves the next man on the seniority list (given minimum ability to perform the task) is the only eligible candidate. The market has been reduced to the irreducible minimum.

The production contract does not define the occupation. It sets forth the plant or company or industry. The plant or company or industry is the market. New workers are hired by the company,[10] not the union, but the union may impose its scale of preferences on the employer. It may, for example, refuse to accept Negroes or it may, alternatively, prohibit the employer from discriminating against Negroes. Bargained rules, however, usually first become operative once the employee is hired. The union then seeks to set a rising scale of jobs and a rising hierarchy of workers. As jobs open up, the workers move up in order; and as they close they move down in order. The worker temporarily laid off still holds his place on the seniority roster. For each job there is a worker and thus a whole series of submarkets where one job and one man are paired.

Two important qualifications must be entered here. First, many contracts do not provide for straight seniority but for some combination of seniority and ability. Jobs are posted and all men who claim the necessary qualifications may compete. But this is still an internal submarket to which persons outside the plant have little or no access. Second, usually there are several families of jobs — production, maintenance, sales, white-collar — each with a contact point with the outside world and with an internal hierarchy of men and jobs related to each other. These families of jobs constitute noncompeting classes within the plant.

The employer, and occasionally the union (for nonpayment of dues or some other offense against the union), can separate the man from the market, usually subject to appeal to a third party. Institutional rules, set forth in a contract, often specify the proper causes for discharge — inefficiency, insubordination, and so forth.

The worker is held within this marketing apparatus not alone by prospects of advancement within the plant. He may be tied to it by a pension plan as well. More important, perhaps, is what would happen to him if he wished to leave. First of all, he would need to quit his job before finding another one since other employers, under the customary gentlemen's agreement against pirating, would be reluctant to hire him away from his firm;[11] and, second, in most cases, he would need to start again at the bottom of the seniority ladder in some other plant with lower status and income.

Movement, as in the craft case, is affected, but in a reverse fashion.

10. For a study of employer hiring preferences, see E. William Noland and E. Wight Bakke, *Workers Wanted* (New York: Harper, 1949).

11. For a discussion of the importance of "gentlemen's agreements" see Charles A. Myers and W. Rupert Maclaurin, *The Movement of Factory Workers* (New York: The Technology Press and Wiley, 1943), p. 39.

Movement to another employer is greatly discouraged but change of occupation is almost automatic.[12] The important market for the worker is the internal plant market with its many submarkets spelled out in great detail. Movement is vertical in the plant instead of horizontal as in the craft market; and workers fight over seniority rights instead of unions over craft jurisdictions. The "haves" are separated from the "have-nots" not by a union card, but by a place on the seniority roster. When the "haves" compete among themselves, it is more in relation to the accumulation of seniority than in relation to the possession of skill.

Governmental policy supports both the communal-ownership and the private-property systems. Apprenticeship programs bolster the former; unemployment compensation rules, since they do not require an employee to leave his accustomed occupation or place of residence to accept work as a condition for the receipt of benefits, help hold workers available for openings in the same craft[13] or the same plant. These rules accept worker attachment to craft and to employer,[14] and support a pool of workers in slack times into which the union or employer can dip.

Neither the craft nor the industrial institutional rules are completely new departures. Even without formal contracts, the craft worker holds to his craft, and the industrial worker to his plant. Employers hired craft workers for craft jobs and promoted from within before closed shops and seniority clauses tightened the rules. The institutional rules, however, do match men and jobs more precisely in the craft case, and the man and the job in the industrial case, than was done informally before their introduction.[15]

INSTITUTIONAL LABOR MARKETS IN OPERATION

Ports of Entry — Not all jobs are open at all times to all bidders except in the structureless market. Even in the absence of institutional rules, most employers consider a job not open for bid so long as the incumbent fills it

12. Most labor market studies find the worker's chief attachment is to his occupation, yet the essence of the seniority approach is to create an employee largely devoid of narrow occupational attachment.

13. In some states, unemployed workers report to the union hiring hall to demonstrate their availability for work rather than to the employment service.

14. A study in Nashua, New Hampshire, found, however, that many workers took lower-paid jobs in preference to staying on unemployment compensation. But this was a situation where a large plant had ceased operation and would not reopen. Charles A. Myers and George P. Schultz, *Dynamics of a Labor Market* (New York: Prentice-Hall, 1951), p. 100.

15. The case of the operating crafts in the railroad system is interesting, for it has elements of both the craft and industrial patterns. Normally, craft workers can obtain transfer cards, but production workers cannot transfer seniority from one plant to another. On the railroads, seniority rights are rigidly defined but employees do have the right to take their seniority to another location and "bump" less senior men there.

satisfactorily; and employers generally prefer to promote from within to canvassing the outside market. Institutional rules, however, set sharper boundaries between the "internal" and "external" markets and define more precisely the points of entrance.[16] In the craft case, the internal market is the area covered by the jurisdiction of the local union, and in the industrial case it is the individual plant. The port of entry in the former instance is the union office, and union membership (achieved through apprenticeship, transfer, or application) provides access to all the jobs on the inside. In the latter case, there are usually several ports of entry (each reached through the company personnel office) — common labor for production workers, lower clerical occupations for the white-collar workers, and junior posts for sales and executive personnel, among others — although if qualified candidates are not available almost any job on an *ad hoc* basis may be opened to outsiders.[17] The external market is the totality of the labor force outside this one market or submarket, or at least that part of it which potentially might like to gain entry.

Thus the internal market has points of contact with the external market rather than interconnections all along the line-up of jobs. Workers inside the market, though they may compete with each other in a limited way, are not in direct competition with persons outside. Outside workers compete directly with each other, not with the inside workers, to gain admittance.

At these ports of entry, the individuals are selected who may enter. Employers have their hiring preferences which are usually dominant when it comes to hiring into the plant, although unions can and do affect these prefer-

16. Labor markets are of two broad types: (1) the structureless and (2) the structured. In the structureless market, there is no attachment except the wage between the worker and the employer. No worker has any claim on any job and no employer has any hold on any man. Structure enters the market when different treatment is accorded to the "ins" and to the "outs." In the structured market there always exist (1) the internal market and (2) the external market. The internal market may be the plant or the craft group, and preferment within it may be based on prejudice or merit or equality of opportunity or seniority or some combination of these. The external market consists of clusters of workers actively or passively available for new jobs lying within some meaningful geographical and occupational boundaries, and of the port or ports of entry which are open or are potentially open to them. It may happen that some markets have only one port of entry, but this can hardly be the standard case as Bloom and Northrup, and Reynolds, state (Bloom and Northrup, *op. cit.*, p. 265, and Reynolds, *op. cit.*, p. 42). They may be right where certain large manufacturing plants are involved, but more commonly such a cluster of workers will face several ports of entry. The extreme cases would be (a) one worker facing one port of entry and (b) large numbers of workers facing a large number of ports of entry. The more structured the market, the more precise will be the rules on allocation of opportunity within the internal market and the fewer will be the ports of entry and the more rigid will be the requirements for admission. Institutional rules do not usually introduce structure into a market — it often arises from the individual preferences of workers and employers — but they uniformly add to it.

17. Thus there are more ports of entry in a period of prosperity than in a period of depression.

ences; and the unions have theirs[18] which determine who gains access to the craft, although employers can and do affect them also.

The process of selection is also the process of rejection. Decisions are made in favor of certain individuals but at the same time against others. The individuals and groups which control these ports of entry greatly affect the distribution of opportunities in economic society. The rules that they follow determine how equitably opportunity is spread and the characteristics for which men are rewarded and for which they are penalized. The controlling individuals and groups may and do choose between prospective efficiency and prospective social acceptability. Since labor resources are being distributed, as well as individual opportunities, the comparative emphasis on efficiency and on acceptability affects the productivity of the economic system. When men fail to find jobs, it may be because there are not enough jobs to go around, or because they do not know about the jobs which do exist or do not think such jobs fit their expectations, or because they do not meet the specifications set by employers and unions. In the last case, as the specifications become more formal and cover more jobs, determination of the specifications becomes of increasing concern to persons in the external market who are universally unrepresented in the councils which set the specifications. For society to remain free and open, many ports of entry should exist and the immigration barriers should not hold outside the able and the willing.

Impact on Movement—One can only surmise how institutional rules affect latent mobility (the willingness and ability to move with given incentives),[19] but actual movement is, in totality, probably reduced.[20]

18. For a discussion of union preferences, see Clyde Summers, "Admission Policies of Labor Unions," *Quarterly Journal of Economics* (November 1946).

19. For the distinction between "mobility" and "movement" see Clark Kerr, *Migration to the Seattle Labor Market Area, 1940-1942* (Seattle: University of Washington Press, 1941), p. 151: "Relatively immobile groups may move in large volume, and potentially mobile groups may remain stationary depending on the circumstances they face."

20. See Lloyd G. Reynolds and Joseph Shister, *Job Horizons* (New York: Harper, 1949), p. 48; and Reynolds, *The Structure of Labor Markets, op. cit.,* pp. 55, 148, and 255. See also statement in Joseph Shister, "Labor Mobility: Some Institutional Aspects," *Proceedings of the Third Annual Meeting, Industrial Relations Research Association, 1950* (Madison, Wis.: 1951), pp. 42-59: "Union policies reduce the amount of voluntary mobility, on net balance." Other evidence, however, is exactly to the contrary. Lipset and Gordon conclude: "Union members appear to be more mobile both area- and job-wise than do non-unionists. . ." Seymour M. Lipset and Joan Gordon, "Mobility and Trade Union Membership," in Reinhard Bendix and Seymour M. Lipset, editors, *Class, Status and Power* (Glencoe: The Free Press, 1953), p. 498. The two statements are, I think, reconcilable. Reynolds and Shister drew their conclusions from the New Haven labor market survey and Lipset and Gordon from the Oakland study. New Haven is a manufacturing town and most unionists there are probably covered by seniority rules which tie them to the individual plant. Oakland is a community of small shops and a distributive center, and

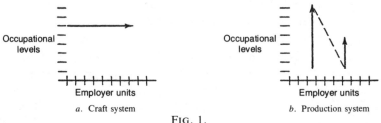

a. Craft system   b. Production system

FIG. 1.

Whether the average union member moves less often than the nonunion member, he certainly moves in a somewhat different direction following the formal channels set by the institutional rules. The craft worker moves horizontally in the craft area (Fig. 1a), and the industrial worker vertically in the seniority area (Fig. 1b). Interoccupational movement is reduced for the former and employer-to-employer movement for the latter. Thus they are both captives, albeit ones who surrendered voluntarily or even enthusiastically, of the rules which guide their working careers. Job rights protect but they also confine. Reduction of insecurity also brings reduction of independence.

Both craft and industrial workers probably have their geographical movements restricted, although some craft systems (such as specialized construction or typographical) force or permit great change of physical location, and some employers require reassignment from one location to another as the price of continued employment. Movement from industry to industry in the craft case may be greatly increased (maintenance workers) or greatly reduced (longshore workers); but in the industrial case it is always restricted. Change of employment status from employed to unemployed and back again is reduced in both cases, since both systems are designed to yield greater employment security; and changes from participation in the labor force to nonparticipation and back again are also minimized since both types of arrangements usually require a high degree of attachment to the work force if rights are to be preserved.[21]

---

most unionists are probably subject to craft rules which permit or even encourage them to move from employer to employer. The two studies come to opposite conclusions because they are based on observations of two contrasting situations. To be fully useful in determining the effect of unionism on mobility, two questions should have been asked in both studies: (1) Did the worker belong to a craft or an industrial union? and (2) How does each type of movement (see the following footnote) relate to union status? For certainly union membership affects both the number and the nature of the moves differently for the industrial unionist and for the craft unionist.

21. Movement of workers is of six types: (1) one occupation to another, (2) one employer to

Institutional rules affect the movement of unprotected workers also. Some jobs are never open to them, and others only under certain conditions. Also the fewer people who leave their jobs because they do not wish to forfeit their security, the fewer other people can leave theirs for there are fewer places to which they may go. The production worker is particularly affected. If he loses employment in one seniority area (he is discharged or the plant closes, for example), he must drop to the bottom of the list in the next area to which he gains admission (see Fig. 1*b*); or he may, of course, never get back into a seniority area (the case of the production worker who becomes a janitor). The more secure are the "ins," the greater the penalty for being an "out."

Competition among workers is reduced. The internal and external markets are joined only at restricted points; and within the internal market, craft jobs are likely to be fairly standardized and industrial jobs filled in accordance with seniority, so that workers are not actively contesting with each other for preference. Beyond this, the distribution of work opportunities by the craft union and the rehiring rights of the industrial contract tend to hold unemployed workers in a pool attached to the craft or plant and thus keep them from competing for jobs so actively elsewhere.[22]

All societies are stratified to a degree, although the degrees vary enormously, and a key element in any society is the character and the intensity of stratification. For our purposes here we shall designate three systems of organization: the "open," the "guild," and the "manorial." The pre-Cairnes classical version of the labor market was of the truly open type — all workers competed for all jobs all of the time. The guild system stratifies the labor force horizontally. Walter Galenson has described such a "closed labor market" under the control of craft unions as it operates in Denmark.[23] The manorial system places its emphasis not on skill but on attachment to the place of work and thus on vertical stratification. The industrial worker may demonstrate (albeit for somewhat different reasons) the same perpetual adherence to

---

another, (3) one industry to another, (4) one area to another, (5) between employment and unemployment, and (6) into and out of the labor force. (A single move may, of course, combine several of these changes.) Craft rules generally reduce (1) (5), and (6) and usually also (3) and (4), but greatly increase (2); industrial rules generally reduce (2), (3), (5), and (6), and usually also (4), but increase (1).

22. The craft and industrial systems react quite differently to the impact of large-scale unemployment. The former is more likely to resort to some form of work-sharing and the latter to layoffs in order of seniority; the former responds to the claims of equal opportunity, the latter to a diminishing scale of property rights in the job.

23. Walter Galenson, *The Danish System of Labor Relations* (Cambridge: Harvard University Press, 1952), pp. 195-200. See also remarks by Gladys Palmer on European labor markets in a paper presented to the Industrial Relations Research Association, May 1952.

the plant as the serf did to the soil of the estate, although he does have opportunities for upward movement unknown to the serf.

The institutional rules we have been discussing move the labor force farther away from the open system of the classical economists which never, however, was as open as they thought it was or hoped it might be. But as it moves toward the guild and manorial systems, which will predominate? For they follow quite different principles of societal organization. The conflict in the United States evidences itself in the conflict between craft and industrial unions over the representation of skilled workers in industrial plants, in the effort of skilled workers in such plants to have their own job families and seniority lists, in the insistence of craft workers that their wages follow the market rather than the dictates of a job evaluation plan dedicated to internal consistency. In Denmark, the guild system is dominant; in Germany, with all the paternalistic devices of large employers and the life-long attachment of the worker to his plant, the manorial system, and this is one source of the union insistence on codirection at the plant level.

The stratification of the labor force affects the worker as citizen. Is he a free-roving mobile person ranging widely horizontally and vertically and probably having a middle-class outlook,[24] is he a carpenter, or is he a UAW-GM man? How he is located economically will affect his view of society and his personal identification with society and its constituent groups, and thus his political behavior.

Institutional Rules and Wage Setting — "Potential mobility," Hicks noted, "is the ultimate sanction for the interrelation of wage rates."[25] Other sanctions do exist and many times are the more important, but the less the potential mobility of workers the less the economic pressures that relate wage rates to each other. Institutional rules, to the extent that they reduce mobility, also lessen the economic pressures. As we have seen, some internal markets are quite isolated from their external markets by the working of these rules, and the interrelatedness of wage rates may be traced more to political, ethical, or operational than to labor market considerations. How do the rules we have been discussing impinge on the wage-setting process?

Extensive discussions with craft union leaders and the employers dealing with them in the San Francisco Bay area indicate that these unions do not generally use their control over the supply of labor to force up wage rates. They employ it rather to adjust supply to demand once the wage has been

24. Lipset and Gordon, *op. cit.*
25. J. R. Hicks, *The Theory of Wages* (London: Macmillan, 1935), p. 79.

fixed.[26] If the supply falls too far short of demand, the employers are encouraged to introduce machinery or look to another craft for workers or even to non-union men. If the supply is too great, some union members are unemployed. This is politically uncomfortable for the union leaders and may require the members to undertake some work-sharing device. Further, employers may point to this unemployed group at the next wage negotiations and the members may be less willing to support wage demands with an effective strike threat. All in all, it is better to adjust supply to demand as closely as possible. This is done by controlling the flow of new members and by issuing work permits.

In neo-classical wage theory, supply (which is assumed to be relatively fixed in the short run) and demand are the independent variables which simultaneously determine the wage and the volume of employment. The standard craft market process runs instead along these lines: (1) the wage is set by collective bargaining in response to many considerations (including economic ones) and usually for a one-year duration; (2) demand which changes constantly determines the amount of employment at the fixed rate; and (3) supply is constantly adjusted by the union to keep close contact with the changing volume of jobs offered by the employers.[27] Control over supply is used more to preserve the integrity of the wage rate rather than to create it.[28] The wage rate determines supply more than supply the wage rate. Demand itself is subject to some control (foremen are limited in the work they may perform; one man may handle only so many machines; certain work must be reserved for a certain craft, and so forth). Demand, the wage rate, and supply all respond to more or less control by the bargaining institutions.

The production case is a different one. Industrial unions cannot control the supply of workers. Their attention is turned rather to stabilizing the demand for labor so that all workers with seniority rights may have assured employment, for example, by introducing the guaranteed wage or heavy dismissal

26. "The jobs must be rationed among the seekers for jobs. And this is the important economic function the so-called restrictive practices play." Milton Friedman, "Some Comments on the Significance of Labor Unions for Economic Policy," in *The Impacts of the Union, op. cit.*, p. 213.

27. The supply curve may be shown as a straight line which stops at or shortly before the volume of jobs normally expected at the fixed wage rate. If demand moves to the right temporarily, the supply line can be temporarily extended by the issuance of work permits, which can be cancelled if it moves again back toward the left.

28. This sets the craft groups apart from certain professional groups. These professional groups do not control the wage (the fee) and so they influence it by control of supply.

bonuses.[29] These devices have no appeal to the craft unions. But, for the industrial union, the supply of workers with seniority rights is fixed, and this makes it more conscious of the impact of fluctuating demand. Institutional rules have two further wage results. Since seniority ties workers to the plant, the industrial union must be more concerned with the effect of a negotiated wage rate on employment. Were it not for seniority rules, wage rates probably could not have deteriorated comparatively so greatly for telegraph and railroad employees during the past quarter of a century. The seniority tie to the industry has reduced the minimum price which would hold the workers in the industry. Industrial unions, also, are more willing than are craft unions to make exceptions to the common rate to meet the necessities of the individual company and its employees. Further, institutional rules by reducing the contact points with the external markets encourage formal or informal job evaluation plans as a means of setting rates acceptable in the internal market.

Under both systems of rules, wage rates are less effective in allocating labor (just as the movement of labor is less potent in setting wage rates) than they are in less structured labor markets.

The Locus of Control — This reconstitution of labor markets reflects the shift in locus of control from the individual entrepreneur to the bureaucratic manager and to the work group. And with this shift goes a change in values. The entrepreneur felt personally the pressure for efficiency and expressed personally his prejudices, sometimes quite violent, about men. The hired manager and the work group both respond more to considerations of security, of order, and of certainty — and, in the case of the craft group, of preservation of the all-around skilled worker. By making men alike and jobs alike and placing each in a certain order, decisions are more or less automatically made by the rules rather than by individual men;[30] but these rules can reflect prejudice just as men in their actions can evidence it. These prejudices may be the same (racial) or different (seniority, instead of merit), but prejudices, or perhaps better, value judgments, they remain. The rule of law is still the rule of men — once removed.

A further shift in locus of control may lie in the future. If the laws of the private governments of industry and labor fail by too great a margin to meet the definition of welfare as conceived by the public at large, then government

29. Once the wage has been set, the craft union tries to adjust supply to demand; the industrial union, demand to supply.

30. The rules are a method of settling the intense disputes between men over job preferment. While the rules settle the individual disputes, they are themselves subject to dispute. See, for example, Leonard R. Sayles, "Seniority: An Internal Union Problem," *Harvard Business Review* (January-February 1952).

may enter the labor market and try to impose its set of values. For example, in Denmark there is agitation against the closed labor market; and in the United States against discriminatory practices. The "managed labor market" may succeed the institutional market.[31]

CONCLUSION

Institutional rules in the labor market, as we have seen, establish more boundaries between labor markets and make them more specific and harder to cross. They define the points of competition, the groups which may compete, and the grounds on which they compete. The study of the import of these rules,[32] though less exciting than the examination of wage policies, is more needed. It is debatable whether wage policies of unions and employers have much impact on wage determination. It is not debatable that institutional rules in the labor market do have substantial effects on the performance of our economic system. These rules increasingly affect both the opportunities held open to workers and the contributions which they can make to the national product.

When private functional governments establish rules which so affect the unrepresented worker and the unrepresented consumer, the cry for public intervention is not long in being sounded even though it may not be very loud. Sir William Beveridge has called for "organized mobility" in the labor market,[33] as have others. This cannot be accomplished mainly as a consequence of guaranteeing full employment, as he claims, although full employment does reduce some barriers; for craft unions will want to control entrance to the craft, and industrial unions to provide for seniority rights, regardless of how full employment may be. Nor may the market be made much more fluid by other governmental actions. Seniority rules probably restrict the freedom of the worker and retard his efficiency more than the craft rules which are the customary target of criticism, yet government is not going to do much about them. At most, governmental policy can make more equitable the rules affecting entrance at those points of entry left open by the private agencies. Security will not be taken away from those who own the jobs, but nonowners can be placed on a more equal footing one against another in contesting for the vacancies.

31. See Kerr, "Labor Markets: Their Character and Consequences," *op. cit.*
32. For a list of research suggestions see Gladys L. Palmer, *Research Planning Memorandum on Labor Mobility,* (New York: Social Science Research Council, 1947).
33. William H. Beveridge, *Full Employment in a Free Society* (New York: Norton, 1944), p. 172.

Labor Markets:
Their Character and Consequences

A DOUBLE LIFE has developed for the term "labor market" and this has been the source of much confusion. Some economists employ the term in one sense; some in the other; and some in both at the same time without realizing or acknowledging the actual or potentially different meanings.[1]

THE WAGE MARKET AND THE JOB MARKET

Two processes, among others, are going on all the time in our economy: wage rates are changing and individuals are moving among jobs. The two processes may or may not be closely connected. It is out of their changing degree of association that the confusion develops.

Conventionally, in wage analysis, the labor market is the totality of jobs for which, given the achievement of equilibrium and an allowance for "other advantages,"[2] the same wage is paid. It is the area within which the single price pertains. Local labor markets are separated by costs of movement, which result in price variations. Granting that some imperfections exist, the labor market is the area within which the single price would exist if the imperfections did not interfere. The labor market sets the price. This is the economists' traditional view.

There is another sense in which the term is used, more particularly by employer, union, and government administrators but also by economists. The labor market is the area, defined occupationally, industrially, and geographi-

Reprinted from *American Economic Review* (May 1950).

1. Carl Campbell and Lloyd H. Fisher were particularly helpful in the development of this paper.

2. J. R. Hicks, *The Theory of Wages* (London: Macmillan, 1935), p. 7.

cally, within which workers are willing to move and do move comparatively freely from one job to another. Movement within the area is fairly easy and customary; and migration into it or out of it is less frequent and more difficult. The market is defined by resistance points on the scale of mobility. There are a multitude of markets and more than a single price may be paid in each; and a single price may cover more than one market, although each of such markets may be otherwise quite different. The market is the mechanism which distributes jobs.

In this discussion, whenever a distinction is made, the first will be designated as the "wage market" and the second as the "job market"; and the two need not encompass in each instance the identical composite of jobs. In fact, it is out of their potential and frequently actual separateness that some of the more interesting and important problems evolve.

MODELS OF THE MARKET

The markets with which we are concerned may and do vary almost infinitely in structure and dynamics. Five general models or ideal types represent, but do not fully describe, the differences which are in kind as well as in degree.

1. *The Perfect Market* — This model is the accepted measuring device of economists. A "market place," in the historical sense, exists as a result of free entry and exit, complete knowledge, a sufficiency of relatively small and undifferentiated buyers and sellers, and the absence of collusion. Perfection is achieved if the product market also displays these characteristics; and the consumer reigns supreme in the allocation of resources and the determination of the rewards to individuals.

Under these circumstances, the dichotomy of the wage market and the job market does not exist. Physical movement of workers and the wage setting process are inextricably interwoven. The single price prevails and the market is cleared.[3]

Wages . . . tend to that level where demand and supply are equal. If supply exceeds demand, some men will be unemployed, and in their efforts to regain employment they will reduce the wages they ask to that level which makes it just worth while for employers to take them on. If demand exceeds supply, employers will be unable to obtain all the labour they require, and will therefore offer higher wages in order to attract labour from elsewhere.

2. *The Neoclassical Market* — Hicks considered the above "a good simplified model of the labor market. . . . [Wages] do turn out on the whole very

3. *Ibid.*, pp. 4-5.

much as if they were determined in this manner."[4] It is, however, a "simplified model" and some minor amendments to it have often been deemed necessary in order to approach reality more closely. The "neoclassical market" emerges. It departs from perfection but still performs its economic tasks adequately.

This was the market as seen by Alfred Marshall.[5] The supply of skilled workers is inelastic because of the extended period of time involved in acquiring skill. Unskilled workers are at a disadvantage because of the perishability of the service they have to sell. Unions exist but they are only sufficiently strong to offset market imperfections introduced by combinations, formal or informal, of employers. Workers do differ from one another.

Yet, all in all, the market is the main determinant of wages. Workers have sufficient knowledge of alternative opportunities and do, despite some inertia, move quite readily in the direction of net economic advantage. Wages may for a time be above or below the "competitive level" but over time they tend toward equality for workers of equal qualifications. Resource allocation approaches the optimum in the long run. While neither the product nor the labor market is perfect, the consumer retains his sovereignty. Adjustments, while not delicately made, are amply pleasing: all is for the best in the best of all possible worlds.

This model has frequently been held to be a fairly accurate description of reality:[6]

. . . for the general tendency for the wages of laborers of equal efficiency to become equalized in different occupations (allowance being made for other advantages or disadvantages of employment) has been a commonplace of economics since the days of Adam Smith. . . . The movement of labor from one occupation to another, which brings it about, is certainly a slow one; but there is no need to question its reality.

3. *The Natural Market* — Abundant evidence now testifies that it would, in the absence of collusion, be almost more correct to say that wages tend to be unequal rather than the other way around. The avalanche of wage data by occupations and by localities during World War II at first bewildered and later convinced War Labor Board economists. Occupational wage rates, locality by locality, in the absence of collective bargaining displayed no single "going rate" but a wide dispersion.[7] Absence of a single price was found to be the

4. *Ibid.*, p. 5.
5. Alfred Marshall, *Principles of Economics*, 8th edition (London: Macmillan, 1938). See particularly pages 525-579.
6. Hicks, *op. cit.*, p. 3.
7. Richard A. Lester, "Wage Diversity and Its Theoretical Implications," *Review of Economic Statistics* (August 1946).

general rule.[8] A sure sign of collusion, not of the working of market forces, came to be the existence of a uniform rate. The market, it seemed, set rather wide limits and within these limits employers could develop policies as high-, medium-, or low-paid firms, and workers could accept high, medium, or low rates. Nonwage conditions of unemployment, such as welfare provisions, sick leave with pay, and so forth, were found to reinforce rather than offset the rate inequalities.

The explanation of the prevalence of this type of market behavior is, in part, the two contrasting views of the market of the economist and the worker. To the economist, the job market is an objective fact. It consists of those jobs among which the workers could pick and choose and move without substantial cost for retraining or physical transference. To the worker, the market is much more ill-defined and subjectively described. It may consist only of other jobs within his own plant, or, more likely, those jobs about which he has information, largely from friends, and which fit his own conception of himself as to trade and income level. The worker operates within the market as he sees it, and his view is limited by lack of knowledge and a restricted conception of himself (particularly as to occupation).

Although the majority of the workers are vaguely conscious of the job market, they cannot be said to be actively in it.[9] They are sufficiently satisfied with their current jobs or fearful of the uncertainties to be encountered in movement so that they are not weighing the advantages of other jobs as against their own. Unless ejected from their current jobs they are only passive participants in the market. Not only by choice but also by necessity is this the case, for many employers, as demonstrated by a current study of employer hiring practices in the San Francisco Bay Area, prefer not to hire persons employed elsewhere. From the point of view of the smooth functioning of the job market, they are the hard core of the employed. Some persons, however, are aggressively in the market — largely the unemployed and the otherwise unsettled workers (mostly the young). Their numbers are not normally sufficiently great or their conception of the market adequate enough to provide such volume of movement as would equalize net economic advantage.[10]

8. Allowance, of course, had to be made for the lack of identity of job specifications and worker performance, but rate discrepancies were too great to be explained away by these considerations.

9. In a study by the Institute of Industrial Relations, University of California (Berkeley), of 935 heads of families in the Oakland labor market area, it has been found that among the employed only 13.5 percent were actively interested in finding another job.

10. The business cycle affects both the number of people actively in the market and the workers' views of themselves. In a depression, more people are industriously seeking jobs and they define the range of acceptable jobs less strictly, but the market, objectively viewed, has

The natural market may thus be defined as one in which the average worker has a narrowly confined view of the market and, in addition, is not an alert participant in it. Unions do not exist. Employers, while not formally organized, either because of smallness of number or informal co-operation (the "tacit, but constant and uniform combination, not to raise the wages of labor above their actual rate" of which Adam Smith spoke[11]), can exercise some monopsonistic influence in the labor market. Sovereignty is jointly held by the consumer and the employer. Wages are not set uniformly at the competitive level, and resources are not utilized to the best advantage. The operation of the job market does not determine wages but, rather, sets the limits within which they are fixed and influences the specific levels within these limits.

4. *The Institutional Market* — The institutional market is distinguished by the substitution of institutional rules for frictions as the principal delineator of job market limits; of institutional and leadership comparisons for physical movement as the main basis for the interrelatedness of wage markets; and of policies of unions, employers, and government for the traditional action of market forces as the more significant source of wage movements. Strong unions interested in policy and capable of having policies range alongside of large employers and employers' associations likewise interested in policy and capable of having policies. The purpose of these policies is, in fact, to curtail the free operation of supply and demand. The pertinent policies relate to the definition of job markets, the determination of rules affecting entry into, movement within, and exit from these markets, and the setting of wage rates. Formal rules, consciously selected, supplant informal practices determined by market conditions. Nor are policies solely developed by the private governments of industry and organized labor, but also by public government which may intervene to assure that monopoly encroachments do not entirely eliminate competition from the market, that wages do not fall below a given level, and that employment be maintained at acceptable levels.

This is, in its full-blown development, a relatively new kind of market in the United States and has assumed large-scale importance only within the past two decades. The wage market and the job market are substantially disjointed

---

greatly contracted. During a period of full employment, while workers contract their notions of suitable jobs, more jobs are open and uncertainty of re-employment is much less of a barrier to movement, so that, on balance, the market works more adequately; and it is during such periods, and particularly during periods of overly full employment, as one would expect, that rate spreads are narrowed.

11. Adam Smith, *An Inquiry Into the Nature and Causes of the Wealth of Nations* (New York: Modern Library Edition, Random House, 1937), p. 66.

and can and sometimes do go their quite separate ways. For many kinds of labor there are no spatial boundaries within which it can be said that supply and demand considerations determine wages. Men find and lose employment within a restricted job market but the wage market is an orbit — an "orbit of coercive comparison."[12] This orbit frequently is spatially quite unlimited. It is the sphere of influence of organizations, policies, and concepts of equity. The job market area and the orbit of wage influencing considerations become quite distinct entities.

The job market no longer alone sets the upper and lower bargaining limits for wage determination. Its operation generally widens these limits, for institutional policies often make it harder for labor, and sometimes capital, to migrate and and thus lower the minimum workers will accept and raise the maximum employers will offer since withdrawal is less possible. Customarily the more significant limits are set by the danger points at which the survival of leaders and associations and coalitions is threatened. Bargaining limits are fixed as much by political as by economic inducements.

Within these limits, it is not economic bargaining power by itself which concludes the settlement but also such largely noneconomic considerations as "patterns" and commonly accepted principles of equity. It is not so much what can be done economically which is important but what must be done politically — on both sides. Employers' associations and large corporations, as well as trade unions, have a political life which claims attention just as do the economic goals.

The wage rate under conditions of bilateral monopoly and bilateral oligopoly is economically indeterminate. "The theory of the determination of wages" is no longer, as Hicks said, "simply a special case of the general theory of value," for the "free market" no longer exists.[13] If wages should be set at the competitive level, it would be by chance and not by virtue of any economic law.

The single price does usually exist but as a consequence of policy and not the operation of market forces. Its existence proves that market forces have been supplanted by institutional controls. This single rate may not clear the market, and, if it does, this may result from control over entry rather than the achievement of a competitive equilibrium position. Supply and demand do adjust and can be adjusted to the wage rate rather than wages adjusting to supply and demand. This is not to say that supply and demand have no effect

12. Arthur M. Ross, *Trade Union Wage Policy* (Berkeley: University of California Press, 1948), p. 53.
13. Hicks, *op. cit.*, p. 1.

on price, but only that their influence is often both indirect and muted. If the market is cleared, it is more likely to be the result of other factors, such as the policies of government and of private investors, than of wage adjustments.

Consumer sovereignty has now been supplanted by producer-consumer sovereignty. The policies of unions and employer groups as well as the choices of consumers affect the distribution of resources and the assignment of rewards.

5. *The Managed Market* — Economists, in the past, most commonly viewed the labor market as sufficiently perfect; but a number of them, more recently, have deemed it unsupportably imperfect. A major shift has taken place from defense to attack. Some form of managed market is offered as the solution for the shortcomings. One group favors a return to competition — to "compulsory individualism"; another group favors a step farther toward positive participation by the state. In either event state control should replace, in part or in whole, private control.

a) Compulsory Individualism. Henry Simons favored the abolition of trade unions since they seek to destroy free labor markets: "I simply cannot conceive of any tolerable or enduring order in which there exists widespread organization of workers along occupational, industrial, functional lines . . ."[14] since "unionism . . . enables an aristocracy of labor to build fences around its occupations, restricting entry, raising arbitrarily the costs and prices of its products, and lowering the wages and incomes of those outside, and of the poor particularly."[15] Along with limitations on trade unions, he favored antitrust prosecutions to increase competition in the product market. Hayek, apparently, favors the same approach.[16]

b) Collective Determination. Meade sees the same problem — "trade unions are monopolistic bodies with the power and the incentive to rig the market"[17] — but basically a different solution. In addition to enforced competition in the product market, or, lacking that, socialization, he proposes consideration of two solutions: limitation of single bargains to employees of a single employer; and government fixation of individual wage rates so as to equalize supply and demand.[18] Beveridge sees a somewhat different problem and supports a more specific program which includes government control of

14. Henry C. Simons, *Economic Policy for a Free Society* (Chicago: University of Chicago Press, 1948), pp. 121-122.

15. *Ibid.*, p. 138.

16. Friedrich A. Hayek, *The Road to Serfdom* (Chicago: University of Chicago Press, 1944). See particularly p. 36.

17. James Edward Meade, *Planning and the Price Mechanism* (London: Allen and Unwin, 1948), p. 68.

18. *Ibid.*, p. 76.

prices; limitation of wage increases through employer resistance, the action of arbitration tribunals, and the self-discipline of the trade unions; the planned location of factories; and "organized mobility" through the greater willingness of workers to change place and occupation, the dropping by the unions of restrictive rules, and the greater and perhaps compulsory use of the government employment service to guide movement.[19]

Lindblom, who seems unsettled as between compulsory individualism and collective determination, believes that "unionism and the private enterprise economy are incompatible."[20] Despite doubts as to feasibility, he considers certain measures necessary: (1) the breaking of the monopoly power of unions by prohibiting strikes over wage issues, (2) the reviewing of wage changes or the direct fixation of wages by public authority, and (3) the prohibition of all joint collusive activities of unions and employers.[21]

The managed market, particularly as suggested by Simons, Meade, and Lindblom, would, through government intervention, seek to tie wage setting and worker movement more closely together. Wages, so far as possible, would, through enforcement of competition or government fixation, be set at the competitive rate and labor resources would be properly utilized. Producer control would be limited and consumer supremacy restored.[22]

REALISTIC ALTERNATIVES

Among these five models, the first, the perfect market, is truly a "labor market," since worker movement and wage movement interact precisely. The second (the neoclassical market) and the last (the managed market) are, by customary standards, sufficiently satisfactory wage setting and labor distributing mechanisms. In the former case this is due to natural forces and in the latter to government intervention. The two remaining models (the natural market and the institutional market) are usually counted the least satisfactory, since they operate so imprecisely in allocating resources to their most efficient uses and in setting wages — yet they are and have been by all odds the most common types.

Regardless of the alternatives with which one might choose to be faced, the

19. William H. Beveridge, *Full Employment in a Free Society* (New York: Norton, 1945), pp. 166-175 and 198-203.
20. Charles E. Lindblom, *Unions and Capitalism* (New Haven: Yale University Press, 1949), p. v.
21. *Ibid.*, pp. 243-245.
22. The "socialist market" — an advanced form of collective determination — if of the type suggested by Oskar Lange would also emphasize consumer's sovereignty. See his essay in Benjamin E. Lippincott, editor, *On the Economic Theory of Socialism* (Minneapolis: University of Minnesota Press, 1938).

perfect market and the neoclassical market are not currently obtainable in the United States. The natural market, while still the most ordinary occurrence, is on the wane. The growth of unions, of large enterprises, and of employers' associations is reducing its prevalence. The trend is against it. The managed market, though adumbrated by federal and state bans on the closed shop, cannot conceivably be fully introduced at the present time: (1) unions will not be destroyed or strikes over wages prohibited, as suggested by Simons and Lindblom; nor (2) will wages be fixed or reviewed by the government, plants be located by government decree, or hiring of any or all workers be forced through the employment service, as suggested by Meade and Beveridge. The economist's usual version of a satisfactory market, if it ever existed, is not going to be put together soon again in the United States, either by enforced atomistic competition or government wage fixing. The first is impossible of achievement and the second, while possible, would not, because of private pressures, lack of knowledge, lags in obtaining information and making adjustments, and difficulties of enforcement, be reasonably effective in obtaining the desired result. The institutional market will, instead, gain in importance. In the United States, the near future, at least, is on the side of stronger private governments. The consequences of institutional markets, consequently, warrant particular attention.

TESTS OF PERFORMANCE

No single test of the ability of wage and job markets to execute appropriate functions is sufficient. Wage and job markets serve more than one purpose and their effective working capacity needs to be evaluated against more than a single criterion. Nor should a perfect record on any test be expected. Human relations seldom lend themselves to the divine attribute of complete excellence. The degree of satisfaction of the minimum requirements of society is a more realistic if less consummate test than of the maximum desires of economists. The operational impacts of institutional wage and job markets will be matched against certain of these societal requisites.

1. *The Wage Structure* — Ideally, the occupational and industrial wage structure should reflect alike the disutility flowing from the work and the utility of the service rendered. For closely similar work and workers, closely similar rates should be paid; and rates should be dissimilar in proportion to the dissimilarity of work and workers. There is no evidence that such a Utopian wage structure has ever fully existed. It is a useful norm for theoretical speculations but an unusable departure point for empirical studies. Such studies must compare, unsatisfactory as this comparison may be, develop-

ments where institutional controls (more specifically collective bargaining) are applied with developments in areas not responding directly to such controls, although these areas need not display "the competitive level" of wages.

One consequence of contemporary institutional controls in the labor market is evident. They conduce to the single rate within the craft or industrial field which they cover. The best, although not thoroughly convincing, evidence now indicates they have surprisingly little effect, however, on interindustry differentials, confirming the conclusions of Paul Douglas of a quarter of a century ago.[23] Whether this is because other forces such as productivity, comparative changes in employment, governmental policy, and product market configurations far outweigh unionism, or because collective bargaining while strengthening the power of the workers also leads to an offsetting augmentation of the strength of employers, or because union rates pull non-union rates after them, or for some other reason, it seems to be a fact that collective bargaining has much less of an ensuing result on interindustry differentials than commonly supposed.[24]

Sir Henry Clay has noted that in England before World War I, "wages, it may fairly be said, constituted a system, since there were well-understood rates for most occupations; the relations between these were stable and generally accepted, and a change in any one rate would prompt demands for a change in other rates."[25] This "system" resulted, in part, from commonly

23. Paul H. Douglas, *Real Wages in the United States, 1890-1926* (Boston and New York: Houghton Mifflin, 1930), p. 562.

24. See particularly John T. Dunlop, "Productivity and the Wage Structure," in Lloyd A. Metzler and others, *Income, Employment, and Public Policy: Essays in Honor of Alvin H. Hansen* (New York: Norton, 1948), pp. 341-362; Arthur M. Ross and William Goldner, "Forces Affecting the Interindustry Wage Structure," *Quarterly Journal of Economics* (May 1950); and Joseph W. Garbarino, "A Theory of Interindustry Wave Structure Variation," *Quarterly Journal of Economics* (May 1950). Dunlop explains interindustry variations in wages primarily by four factors, not including unionism: "changes in productivity and output, the proportion of labor costs to total costs, the competitive conditions in the product market for the output of an industry, and the changing skill and occupational content of the work force of an industry" (p. 362). Ross and Goldner find that "Among the industries which were substantially unorganized in 1933, subsequent increases in earnings were associated with changes in the degree of organization. However, those which were already substantially organized in 1933 have lagged behind all other groups." They add: "From an analytical standpoint, the difficulty is that these three influences (unionization, employment change and oligopolistic market structure) have been operative in substantially the same groups of industries. Statistical means are not at hand to disentangle their separate effect or to establish which, if any, is the primary cause." (This article is the sequel to an earlier one by Ross, "Influence of Unionism Upon Earnings," *Quarterly Journal of Economics* [February 1948].) Garbarino concludes: "The foregoing discussion has attempted to illustrate the relationship between each of the variables in the wage model and changes in earnings. Such a relationship seems to exist for both productivity and concentration while for unionization the results are inconclusive."

25. Henry Clay, *The Problem of Industrial Relations* (London: Macmillan, 1929), p. 74.

accepted rules of equity and from institutional controls. Both militate against economic forces which tend to pull the "system" apart. As institutional controls spread and deepen, the "system" may become increasingly formalized with "historical relations" and "patterns" taking the place more and more of supply and demand. Widely pervasive political interrelationships instead of physical movement of workers will tie the wage structure together. It may eventually appear that the "system of wages" will have to be regarded by economists as an independent variable, rather than a dependent variable at the mercy of a myriad of economic causes.

By and large, the wage structure has not been distorted from its pre-existing mold as one would expect if unions were exploiting to the full their economic monopoly power. But then unions are not primarily economic monopolies but political organizations. The political test of meeting workers' notions of equity has more of an impact on wage policy than the economic test of income maximization.

If collective bargaining has had no revolutionary effect on the wage structure except to bring the single rate within the industry and within the craft, then, by means of wage influences, it seems likely its impact on the allocation of resources has often been exaggerated.[26] This does not mean that the wage structure under collective bargaining is ideally designed to allocate resources, but only that it has not been changed so greatly from its "natural" state, bad as that may have been.

There is some real question how effective a wage structure can be in distributing labor in any event. Wages are only one of several important considerations which repel workers from some jobs and attract them to others.[27] The push of unemployment, for example, is often more effective than the pull of higher wages.

26. Collective bargaining can have three principal impacts on wage rates: (1) on intraindustry and intracraft relationships, (2) on interindustry and intercraft differentials, and (3) on the general level of money wages as distinct from the structure (to which the next chapter refers); and in these three principal ways, through wage influences, can change the allocation of resources. Most attention is normally paid to the second (impact on interindustry differentials); but the first (impact on intraindustry and intracraft relationships) and the third (impact on the general level of wages) may be the more significant. Equalizing rates within the industry and craft and raising the general level of wages can substantially affect resource allocation, even if interindustry differentials are not much changed. Equalizing rates can affect, for example, which firms survive and the relative profitability of those which do; and raising the general level, for example, can affect the relative proportions of labor and capital utilized and relative amounts of final products and services demanded since the demand for some is affected more than for others when prices rise in response to higher costs. In general, however, it seems that resource allocation may be less affected and in somewhat different ways than is often stated.

27. See, for example, Lloyd G. Reynolds and Joseph Shister, *Job Horizons* (New York: Harper and Brothers, 1949), Chapter 2; and W. Rupert Maclaurin and Charles A. Myers,

If institutional controls change the wage structure surprisingly little from its former conformations, it remains to be asked whether governmental wage fixing would bring it any closer to the competitive norm. No definitive answer is, of course, possible. It may be suggested, however, that much the same equitable considerations, albeit more uniformly applied, and equivalent pressures, though emanating even more from political incentives and less from the market, would leave their mark and we should be as far as ever from the flexible, equilibrating wage structure.

The institutional market does bring the single rate within the industry and craft, although by a different process. In adjusting interindustry and intercraft rates it may represent an economy of means. The market can be tested and the wage structure adjusted more quickly and with less physical movement than would be the case in the natural market.

2. *The General Level of Wages* — The institutional market undoubtedly causes the general level of money wages to behave differently than it otherwise would, and a large literature has developed around this point. Here again, however, there may be a tendency to view with too much alarm. Wages always rise under conditions of full employment. The upward movement appears more spectacular under conditions of collective bargaining but possibly may not be as great as in its absence. At least the case for the opposite view is by no means clear. During World War II, nonunion wages on the average must have risen as fast or faster than union wages, although many other factors were at work aside from unionization. Wage levels in unorganized areas generally went up more than in such highly organized areas as Seattle and San Francisco, although here again other forces serve as explanations, too. Experience in other democratic capitalistic nations also indicates that a high level of institutional controls has not been associated with abnormal wage advances but rather the opposite.

Unionism is not normally introduced into a society under conditions of *ceteris paribus*. Employers coalesce, also, and formally or informally have policies, too; and the government, through settlement of labor disputes, if in no other fashion, becomes involved. The new force of unionism is met by increased countervailing force. The problem of undue wage increases under full employment is more the result of full employment than of unionism.

"Wages and the Movement of Factory Labor," *Quarterly Journal of Economics* (February 1943). For a contrary view, based on apparently less valid evidence, see J. L. Nicholson, "Earnings, Hours, and Mobility of Labour," *Bulletin of the Oxford University Institute of Statistics* (May 1946).

Institutional controls while conceivably dampening the upward surge of wages during full employment certainly retard their downward tendency during depression; and thus the overall effect may well be to raise the general level of wages. Given reasonable resort to other methods than wage control of achieving price stability, a continued growth of employers' associations, a further bureaucratization of trade unions, a continued rise in man-hour output, and a volume of employment not overly full, the impact of unionism on the overall level of labor costs and purchasing power may be quite tolerable.

3. *The Distribution of Job Opportunities* — Under our system we depend on the choice of individuals to allocate human resources. But it is not alone resources which are being allocated but also job opportunities. The economic goal of efficient utilization of manpower is at least matched in importance by the political goal of equality and opportunity.

Institutional rules, in a sense, create markets — markets with specific occupational, industrial, and geographical boundaries and with rules affecting entry, movement within, and exit. Both unions and employers have policies affecting these dimensions and processes, but those of the former at their fullest development tend to be the more precise and restrictive. Selig Perlman's term, "job territory,"[28] well conveys the emphasis on citizenship and noncitizenship, immigration restrictions and quotas, and passports.

Instead of ill-defined markets existing most significantly as subjective impressions of workers and employment managers, markets become a finite entity. This is especially true of the hiring hall which is a market place, a bourse. Balkanization of job markets results, and these Balkanized markets operate differently internally and in their external relations than "natural markets." Internally, wages and conditions are more uniform, knowledge more complete, and movement is according to more formalized guides for conduct, such as seniority. Among markets, movement is both reduced in totality and redirected.

Union policies variously control, guide, and influence market processes. Control is illustrated by closed shop arrangements where access to the market is solely through union channels; guidance by the practices in the garment trades, for example, where the unions actively distribute work and workers but lack full control; and influence by the mass-production industries where union rights, such as seniority, and union membership by itself, identify the individual worker more closely with the company and the industry. Both the recently completed New Haven labor market study[29] and the current Oakland

28. Selig Perlman, *A Theory of the Labor Movement* (New York: Macmillan, 1928), p. 273.
29. See Reynolds and Shister, *op. cit.*, p. 48.

study[30] demonstrate that, for whatever reason, union members are less mobile. Formal policies of employers and employers' associations also effectively influence hiring and movement from job to job within the company.[31]

These institutional policies affect less importantly the number of jobs available and the adequacy of supply to match them than they do the selection of those workers to whom individual opportunities are open. In addition to qualifications related to job performance, other attributes precedent to employment are frequently required. Perhaps the most socially questionable impact of institutional controls is on the availability of free access to jobs. This prompts the suggestion that the admission policies of unions and employers are of key importance in the operation of institutional markets.

4. *Freedom of Competition and Freedom of Association* — All forms of freedom are not fully compatible. Freedom of competition, a most laudable objective, and freedom of association often run counter to each other. Economic groups most frequently associate for the purpose of reducing or eliminating competition. Yet freedom of association is as basic a political right as freedom of competition is an economic blessing. Freedom of competition can only be assured in job markets by destruction of freedom of association, since freedom of association leads directly to institutional controls. The first can only be completely obtained by the complete elimination of the latter; and complete fulfillment of the latter can lead to the destruction of the former. Since it is not likely, nor proper, that either freedom should thoroughly supplant the other, a compromise of their claims is in order. Since associations are the aggressor, it is proper public policy to see that none becomes too strong as against any other, against the state, or against the individual, and that they be required to act responsibly. There will be some cost to freedom of competition, but then the policy of Simons is not without its different and greater costs. Both the causes of political freedom and economic efficiency must be served. The achievement of J. M. Clark's goal of "responsible individuals in responsible groups" is, however, no simple task.[32]

5. *Consumer and Producer Sovereignty* — Economists historically have favored consumer sovereignty, and there is no adequate substitute for it in a free society. Institutional controls cause this sovereignty to be shared with producer groups. While this most frequently reduces economic well-being, decisions of producer groups can display some wisdom as well; and producers

---

30. Reported in Reinhard Bendix and Seymour M. Lipset, *Social Mobility in Industrial Society* (Berkeley: University of California Press, 1959).

31. See F. Theodore Malm, "Hiring Procedures and Selection Standards in the San Francisco Bay Area," *Industrial and Labor Relations Review*, January 1955.

32. John Maurice Clark, *Alternative to Serfdom* (New York: Knopf, 1948), Chapter 5.

can have some minimum demands for security and recompense which they can properly assert against the wishes of consumers.

6. *Preservation of Law and Order* — Some job markets make more of a contribution to industrial stability than others. Institutional controls are generally accepted or tolerated. With all their faults, they lend a certain order and discipline to industrial life. Destruction of unions and presumably of employers' associations, as suggested by Simons, or prohibitions of strikes over wages, as suggested by Lindblom, or government wage fixing, as suggested by Lindblom and Meade, would be lacking in that minimum voluntary approval which is indispensable to enforcement in a democracy.

CONCLUSION

Among the five models of the labor market which we have set forth, the trend is unmistakably toward the institutional market. It will always miss high excellence but it can be an adequate economic mechanism. It probably has rather less of an impact on the wage structure and the general level of wages than is frequently assumed, while reflecting freedom of association, allowing expression of a measure of producer concern, and contributing to overall public tranquility. Such a market requires, however, particularly careful scrutiny of the efficiency and equality with which it distributes jobs. It is more likely to lack as a job distributing market than as a wage setting market, although it is the latter aspect which more often generates the greater concern.

Compulsory atomization and compulsory wage fixation should both be rejected and institutional markets accepted as the best alternative (although far from the best theoretical market form), and such modifications in them should be attempted as are deemed necessary to the protection of the legitimate welfare of individuals, groups, and the economy at large.

Most economists in the past have been too little critical of labor markets; some now are too much so. In an effort to achieve what is perfect, they would lose what is acceptable.

Effect of Environment
and Administration
on Job Evaluation

M OST MODERN business managements have given plenty of attention to the question of how to evaluate the employee's job — the amount of skill and responsibility that are involved, the conditions of work, and so on. A large and growing literature takes up the process of describing, weighing, and applying all the internal factors that enter into a determination of what is a just wage. A plant or industry wage structure, however, may often be controlled by other considerations stemming from the environment in which the structure operates. Yet these external considerations are being comparatively neglected in current discussions of the problem.

The fact that the wage structures of plants and industries are subject to these two, in a very real sense contradictory, forces has long been recognized. Adam Smith pointed out the situation in his famous *Wealth of Nations* when he distinguished between differences arising "from certain circumstances in the employments themselves" and "from the policy of Europe, which nowhere leaves things at perfect liberty."[1] The five famous circumstances which he listed under the former heading — agreeableness of the work, difficulty of learning the trade, constancy of employment, the trust reposed in

Written with Lloyd H. Fisher. Reprinted from *Harvard Business Review* (May 1950).

Authors' note: The authors gratefully acknowledge assistance from a large number of persons, particularly Benjamin Aaron, former Chairman of the National Airframe Panel of the National War Labor Board; Arthur Allen, former Chairman of the West Coast Aircraft Committee (Region Ten); Theodore Grant, Executive Secretary of the Southern California Aircraft Industry Committee; Wendell Cooke and William Brodie of the United Automobile Workers; Tom McNett, Dale Reed, Richard Powell, C. E. Bently, and Harold J. Gibson of the International Association of Machinists; A. F. Logan, Ralph Newell, and Byron Hartley of the Boeing Aircraft Company; and D. H. Cameron and S. R. Mercer of the Lockheed Aircraft Company. May Jamieson assisted in the preparation of much of the historical material.

1. Book I, Chapter X.

the workmen, and the probability of success — have their modern counterparts in the factors which enter into job evaluation plans.

Important as these matters of internal logic and mechanics may be, however, the crucial test of the plan is its suitability to the external environment —
to the community, industrial, and market situations and to the local status of
labor unions. Consequently, while a plan may suit the neat and orderly mind
of the engineer, the ultimate question remains whether or not it is appropriate
in the current scene as a whole. This is especially true today, when the
different parts of the economy are so interdependent, when conditions in one
plant or industry are so sensitive to conditions in another.

Of course, sound wage structures are subject to the forces of internal logic
and of external environment *both at the same time;* neither can be completely
dominant. If a job evaluation plan were compromised to meet every prevailing wage rate in the community, for instance, it would be a sorry relic indeed.
And, on the other hand, as William H. Davis, the former chairman of the
National War Labor Board, has observed:

> There is no single factor in the whole field of labor relations that does more to break
> down morale, create individual dissatisfaction, encourage absenteeism, increase labor
> turnover, and hamper production than obviously unjust inequalities in the wage rates
> paid to different individuals in the same labor group within the same plant.[2]

The fact remains that the failure of a plan to account for recognized wage
levels in the business community is an open invitation for employee dissatisfaction and labor union strife to arise. And so, as we shall discuss in detail
later on, job description and evaluation plans which purport only to set
relative rates within the plant or industry do not go far enough. Note, too, that
the more powerful the forces in the external environment, the greater the
compromise of the plan's internal consistency that may be necessary.

This article is a case study of an industry-wide experience which, to a
unique degree, because of the scale of application and other circumstances
involved, illustrates the effect of environment on a job description and evaluation plan. Needless to say, there are administrative problems involved — and
the ultimate record of any plan inevitably depends on the quality of its administration, which is almost as neglected in current discussion as are the
environmental factors.

Our examination of this experience will not be concerned with a description
of the plan itself, nor will it treat in detail such questions as whether the plan
did or did not include all the elements that should affect the compensation for

2. *6 War Labor Reports* 594.

labor services performed and whether the factors chosen received their appropriate weight and emphasis. The particulars are well set forth elsewhere,[3] and the essential nature of the plan will be evident as the discussion proceeds. It is enough for present purposes to note that the plan was modeled particularly after the General Electric system, did not differ greatly from many other job description and evaluation systems, and was inherently a sound one. Nor is it the purpose of this presentation to pass judgment on the merits of job description and evaluation as a technique. That is the business of each employer and each union in the light of the circumstances faced.

Rather, this is (1) a report on a venture in systematic wage determination in an environment of labor scarcity, union organization, and industry-wide bargaining; (2) a record of the problems encountered; and (3) an analysis of the administration of a job description and evaluation plan under such conditions. Certain of the problems which arose in the execution of this job description and evaluation plan in the West Coast airframe industry are eternal problems which have been and will be faced at many other times and in many other places. Accordingly, a further section of the article presents some generalizations drawn from this experience, which businessmen in other industries may be able to use as "precepts" and "caveats" for their own efforts with job description and evaluation plans.

SIGNIFICANCE OF THE EXPERIENCE

Just as the character of a person is often best revealed under conditions of critical pressure, so the character of a job description and evaluation plan shows up under similar circumstances. The plan ordered into effect in 1943 by the National War Labor Board in the West Coast airframe industry provides an outstanding case because, subjected as it was to a number of strong pressures, many of its weaknesses and strengths, its traits and proclivities, inevitably came to light. It is almost certainly true that a plan encounters fewer difficulties in a single plant than in an entire industry; in a slack market than in a tight one; and in unorganized establishments than in ones recently organized by aggressive and rival unions. The case at hand was spared none of these stresses and strains.

3. Robert D. Gray, *Systematic Wage Administration in the Southern California Aircraft Industry* (New York: Industrial Relations Counsellors, 1943); F. H. Johnson, R. W. Boise, Jr., and D. Pratt, *Job Evaluation* (New York: Wiley, 1946); and U. S. Bureau of Labor Statistics, *Wage Stabilization in California Airframe Industry*, Bulletin No. 746, 1943. For a history of the plan in California, see Southern California Aircraft Industry Committee, *Wage Stabilization in Southern California Aircraft Industry* (mimeographed), 1946.

(1) The plan, in Southern California, was applied to the entire industry rather than a single plant or company. It therefore represented, at one and the same time, an effort to distribute the wage bill equitably within the several industrial establishments and also to standardize wages among them.

(2) The plan was ultimately subject to collective bargaining in all but one company (Northrop), and the presence of active and aggressive unions had a great effect. Both the United Auto Workers (UAW) and the International Association of Machinists (IAM) represented substantial segments of the industry, and intense rivalry existed between them.

(3) The plan operated during the war period with its generally heavy demand for labor and the postwar period when scarcities were related to specific skills. The insistent pressures that manpower shortages exerted upon the wage structure were an important part of the experience.

The plan was tested in a further fashion. Boeing Airplane Company in Seattle and the six companies in Southern California (Consolidated Vultee Aircraft Corporation, Douglas Aircraft Company, Lockheed Aircraft Corporation, North American Aviation, Inc., Northrop Aircraft, Inc., and Ryan Aeronautical Company) were all covered by the same general plan, with the same factors and about the same weighting of them; but several significant features were not identical, and the environments were quite distinguishable. The results of the plan, as well, were markedly different both during and after the war. An opportunity was thus created to relate different results to differing characteristics and environments.

The Environment — The plan operated in an environment established by five sets of circumstances:

(1) Fluctuations of Employment. At the start of the war in Europe, the West Coast airframe industry employed about 30,000 workers. At peak employment this number reached 300,000. From the position of a minor industry, in a few short years the aircraft industry became one of the industrial giants on the Pacific Coast, exerting a dominant influence on the industrial and employment patterns of the three major communities in which the industry was located — Los Angeles, San Diego, and Seattle. After the war employment dropped to about 75,000.

(2) Changes in Job Structure. The prewar aircraft industry, small and experimental, had used custom methods in the production of its planes and required considerable versatility of labor. The enormously expanded war production made necessary a complete reorganization of production methods. It became of the first importance to break down complex jobs into simple ones and to substitute semiskilled for the skilled workers whose supply was quickly

exhausted as employment in the industry expanded tenfold. Although custom methods had to be discarded, the product did not become sufficiently standardized to permit true assembly-line methods with a full complement of purely repetitive tasks. The multiplication of separately described jobs, as the simplification process spread, set the stage for a formal job description and evaluation system as the method of determining compensation for employees.

With the exception of the motion picture industry, the aircraft industry emerged with a greater variety of jobs and a wider range of skills than any other industry in the nation. The extraordinary range of separate skills required for the production of planes —those of cabinet workers, sewing machine operators, sign painters, upholsterers, nurses, machinists, patternmakers, drop-hammer operators, radio mechanics, and so forth — contributed greatly both to the need for systematization of the wage structure and the difficulty of bringing it about.

(3) The Labor Market. There was during the war intense competition in the labor markets in which the West Coast airframe companies operated. Not only was competition for labor strong among the airframe companies themselves, but with the development of allied and subsidiary enterprises to supply the prime contractors (enterprises which manufactured products ranging from the smallest parts to entire subassemblies) keen competition for labor developed between the aircraft companies and their suppliers.

Beyond this there was the most severe competition from the shipbuilding industry, which was undergoing the same kind of rapid growth as was the aircraft industry and had an equally insatiable demand for labor of all types. Boeing additionally competed with the expanding lumber industry as well. Competition, particularly for skilled employees, occurred not only in local labor markets but in some degree throughout the West and the nation. The labor market eased considerably after the war but remained tight for two or three years for some skills, particularly those also involved in the construction and furniture industries.

(4) Federal Controls. The Federal Government could not and did not remain impassive. Even before the application of nation-wide wage stabilization in the fall of 1942, the government was quite concerned. The airframe companies were competing for manpower with any means at hand. New and untrained employees were hired at rates above those paid to experienced personnel. Lack of uniformity of job titles persistently resulted in the same work's being performed under different titles at varying rates. The resulting internal wage structure was chaotic and productive of numerous grievances. Rapid turnover, mounting unrest, and rising costs were among the results.

Following earlier encouragement of joint efforts at standardization, the National War Labor Board in March 1943 ordered into effect at all Southern California Plants the Southern California Aircraft Industry (SCAI) plan,[4] a "point system" of job description and evaluation with a heavy weight (about two thirds) for skill factors, encompassing ten grades, each with a rate range. This plan was unilaterally developed by the companies. The NWLB at the same time rejected a plan jointly negotiated by the IAM and Lockheed; and this, among other factors, led to dissenting votes by the labor members of the NWLB and Public Member Wayne Morse. In September 1943 the Board approved unanimously a plan agreed upon by Boeing and the IAM[5] which differed from the SCAI plan, aside from its bilateral origin, mainly in having single rates instead of rate ranges and, on grounds of "effective prosecution of the war," a higher level of rates attendant upon each grade.

The Board established the West Coast Aircraft Committee (WCAC), with divisions for California (Region X) and the Pacific Northwest (Region XII) to supervise administration of the orders and adjudicate disputes arising under them. This intervention ended, of course, with the conclusion of the war. Had it never occurred, it is less likely that the plan in Southern California would have been industry-wide, for at least Lockheed and the IAM would probably have gone their own way.

(5) Union Organization. The economic and governmental environments alone will not suffice, however, as explanations of the vicissitudes encountered in the introduction and administration of the plan. There was a complicated political environment as well. With the exception of Northrop which remained unorganized by any union, all the plants had either been organized just recently or were currently in the throes of organizing campaigns. Aside from the two major unions, the IAM and the UAW, the National Union of United Welders of America represented in several plants a group of employees for which there was the greatest large-scale demand and most serious shortage.

The IAM was a craft union built around journeyman machinists with high levels of skills. While it had adapted its structure to industrial organization, its background predisposed it more to a system of job grades differentiated largely by skill and even to rate ranges expressing "premiums" for skilled mechanics. The UAW carried over to aircraft organization experiences and points of view from the automobile industry. This strongly conditioned it in favor of flat rates narrowly spread from bottom to top of the structure and set

4. *6 War Labor Reports* 581-715.
5. *11 War Labor Reports* 268.

by *ad hoc* bargaining, and against a heavy weighting for skill. Its wage structure philosophy was much less compatible with the SCAI plan than was that of the IAM.

The UAW and the IAM, and to a lesser extent the Welders, were each aggressively seeking expanded jurisdiction in unorganized sectors of the industry, as well as at each other's expense. All three viewed the SCAI plan, in part, as it affected their competitive positions *vis-à-vis* each other. They searched for the strategic advantages and disadvantages in the plan as it related to their organizational programs and as it related to the several groups and factions among their organized constituents.

At Boeing, the IAM, with a union shop, was protected during the war from rival unionism, and the plan there was less subject to the stresses of interunion rivalry and divergent union philosophies.

Problems Encountered

A system of wage compensation is never so broad as the influences which affect it. What is true of wage systems in general is true of job evaluation particularly. The logic of evaluation plans is primarily an internal logic, its equities internal equities, and its objectives a set of rates mutually consistent with one another. But a factory or even an industry is a limited environment. The influences which bear upon it and its employees are seldom self-contained. It may work out its interior relationships with great skill, ingenuity, and perceptiveness and still have its plans founder because their scope is narrower than the influences which must be accommodated.

Thus the SCAI plan, throughout its course, struggled with the effects of influences it could not control, with issues which, though they arose from outside the system, nevertheless established powerful claims that could not be ignored and usually had to be compromised.

The Market and the Plan — The most difficult and pervasive problem in the administration of job description and evaluation in the Pacific Coast aircraft industry arose from the frequent conflicts between measures of external and measures of internal equity. The price of a job in the market is one well-established measure of its worth. The SCAI plan established a different measure of its worth. The conflicts between these different standards made for continuous obstacles to the consistent administration of the plan.

Whether an evaluation plan can be administered consistently with the principles which it is supposed to embody depends, in large measure, on whether the labor market is tight or loose and whether wage rates in the market are rising, stable, or falling. The history of the SCAI plan has been, for the most part, a history of operation during a period of war, with its extraordinary demands for manpower and with the severe pressures upon wage structures and wage levels which were the consequences of those demands; and during a postwar period of relatively full employment.

The marked difference between the Boeing experience and that of the Southern California plants emphasizes the importance of this relationship between internal and external standards of reference:

(a) By virtue of a higher wage level at the outset and general wage increases on two occasions, rates of pay at Boeing were somewhat higher than community rates in the Seattle area, which on the whole held unusually stable. In consequence the structure of evaluated rates was under much less pressure than was the rate structure of the Southern California aircraft industry. The chairman of the Pacific Northwest division of the WCAC was able to announce that all modifications in the evaluation plan at Boeing had been made at a cost that would not exceed 2½ cents per hour added to the average rate of pay.[6]

(b) The Southern California aircraft plants, on the other hand, because of their relatively lower wage level were confronted with a larger number of unfavorable rate relationships. (Rates of pay in Southern California generally rose comparatively rapidly during the war.[7]) The cost of all adjustments made in these plants, where the plan was peculiarly subject to other pressures also, added 15 – 20 cents per hour to the average rate of pay.

It should be noted that both the figures of 2½ cents and of 15–20 cents relate to costs encountered during the administration of the plans. The initial introduction of the plans in 1943 also added to average hourly earnings; the March 2 and September 4 orders at Boeing added about 16½ cents an hour to average hourly earnings, and the March 5 order in Southern California about 6 or 7 cents. Moreover, the comparison between Boeing and the Southern California industry is not exact since the Boeing data summarize the cost of re-evaluation only and the Southern California costs reflect upgrading and merit increases as well. Yet the comparison is more valid than would appear from the differing definitions. At Boeing there were no rate ranges and therefore no merit increases; and, by the testimony of those responsible for the

6. *Statement on Aircraft Order 62* (WCAC — Region XII). The cost ultimately turned out to be about two cents.

7. See Nedra Bartlett Belloc, *Wages in California: War and Postwar Changes* (Berkeley: University of California Press, 1948).

administration of the plan, the effect of individual upgrading was more than offset by work simplification and the consequent increase in the proportion of persons working at lower paid jobs.

Labor market pressures were not confined to the war period. Highly skilled mechanics were in great demand in the airframe plants for a substantial time after the war. This was due in part to the industry's loss of an advantage over the general market which it had built up during the war. Airframe wage increases, in the first three wage rounds after the war, failed to meet the patterns for manufacturing industry. At the same time — although the labor market was much looser, particularly for unskilled and semiskilled workers (no difficulty was experienced in retaining or recruiting workers at those levels) — craft workers were in great demand by other industries, and the general increases in their rates almost universally exceeded the standard manufacturing pattern.

The airframe companies, disadvantaged in their competition for skilled workers by their craft rates already at the top of their structures, took many steps to offset the shortages — in-plant training, breaking down jobs into less skilled tasks, stepping up recruiting. Two moves were particularly interesting for their bearing on the job evaluation plan. One was the farming out of work to outside commercial enterprises which could and did pay rates outside the limits of the plan; the integrity of the evaluation plan was thus formally preserved. Another, as in the case of at least one company when upholsterers were desperately needed by the airframe companies as they shifted from war to passenger planes, was to pay rates substantially above the top of the highest grade; thus production and labor market necessities completely overrode the limits set by the plan.

It was, however, in the Southern California plants during the war that market pressures on the plan were felt most severely, that the conflicts between internal and external measures of equity were the most marked, and that the manipulations of the plan were prevalent. Where there was a need to manipulate, the techniques were many. Among these were three devices of major importance:

(1) Re-evaluation and Redescription. When a job is re-evaluated, the presumption is that the plan remains unimpaired. The factors employed have not been changed, the degrees of the factors remain as before, the weight assigned to each degree is unaltered. The process of re-evaluation is simply the agreement or decision that a higher degree of some factor better measures the worth of the job than the degree previously assigned.

As labor became scarcer during the war, the shortage which earlier was particularly acute for skilled classifications became equally or more acute in the unskilled and semiskilled categories. The SCAI plan was particularly vulnerable to shortages of unskilled and semiskilled labor, since it rewarded skill much more substantially than factors such as job hazards and job conditions. The plan was not long in effect when it became increasingly difficult to find workers to fill the disagreeable jobs. Such a job was the occupation of sandblaster. The factors of job conditions and job hazards had already received the full weight possible under the plan, and so, by agreement of the parties, all other factors were increased in evaluation so that the wage rate resulting would prove more attractive.[8]

Related to re-evaluation of jobs was redescription. By changing a job description, it was possible to embrace lower paid workers in a higher paid rate, or to add a task to a job which would make possible re-evaluation at a higher level.

(2) Upgrading. The SCAI plan did not determine the distribution of employees through the classification system. Wage increases took place without any apparent modification of the plan itself. The task of the plan was to develop the structure of job classification and the standards and criteria according to which the jobs would be distinguished and the distinctions according to which they would be compensated. The balance belonged to administration. Among the tasks left to administration, accordingly, was the determination of how many employees were to be classified in the A, B, and C grades of the various jobs, whether the pyramid would have a broad base or a relatively narrow one.

The largest single classification of workers in the Southern California plants had the title of general assemblers. The average rate at which all general assemblers (grades A, B, and C) were employed in July of 1943 was 88.6 cents per hour. By June 1945 the average rate of compensation for all general assemblers was $1.074. Thus an increase of 18.8 cents per hour was achieved without either a general wage increase or a re-evaluation of the job. Over the entire 15 classifications for which a report was made to the War Labor Board, the weighted average increase was 16.0 cents per hour.[9]

It is perhaps to be expected that under normal circumstances the average rate of compensation will rise as the labor force grows more experienced. But the wartime experience of the aircraft industry was one of rapid turnover and dilution of skill. New recruits to the industry were less experienced than those

8. *Order 63* (WCAC — Region X).
9. Data from Southern Aircraft Industry Committee.

already in the industry so that the effect of expansion and turnover was undoubtedly to lower the level of skill and experience for which the higher average rate was paid.

Boeing minimized a creeping rise in average hourly earnings through generalized upgrading by careful observance of pre-existing shop agreements with the IAM setting the ratio of workers in the A, B, and C grades.

(3) Rate Ranges. One of the differences between the Boeing and the Southern California versions of the evaluation plan concerned the matter of rate ranges. In the Boeing plants, the compensation for a graded job was at a fixed single rate, and all persons employed at that classification received the same rate of pay. In Southern California, the rate of pay received by an individual might vary by as much as 20 cents per hour from that received by another individual performing the identical job.

Depending upon the labor grade in which the job was classified, the permissible range of payment in Southern California varied from 5 cents to 20 cents per hour, with the most common ranges being to 10 cents and 15 cents. Whether an individual received the low, the medium, or the high rate in his range was supposed to depend upon the efficiency with which the particular individual performed his duties. But in fact the rate range functioned as an expansion joint built into the wage system, allowing the wage structure to respond to pressure without serious structural damage. Unfortunately no precise measure of the magnitude of this type of increase is available; but the several companies made increasing use, as the war went on, of the top one third of each rate range.

The plan also permitted downward movement of average hourly earnings through (1) redefinition and re-evaluation of jobs at lower levels (2) downgrading, and (3) tighter administration of rate ranges. Simply reversing the developments which began after the installation of the plan would presumably have led to a reduction of 15–20 cents in average hourly earnings, even without any revision of rate steps. The evidence on any reversal of the wartime inching-up trend is not clear. In the postwar period average hourly earnings rose roughly proportionately with the general wage increases negotiated, and a prima facie case can be made against company utilization of downward flexibility. On further examination the case is not so clear. A reduction in employment can and has raised average hourly earnings in airframe plants by 10 cents per hour, since it raises the skill mix and the average seniority of the employees; and employment was much reduced below wartime levels. Further, the real test of a depression had not been met by the end of 1949.

Management — A House Divided — Despite the attempts at system and objectivity which a point evaluation plan represents, the success of a job evaluation plan depends heavily upon a common desire of many groups to make the plan work. And these groups do not begin with common problems or common interests.

There are bound to be differences in objectives between management and union. In addition, where more than one union holds bargaining rights, there is likely to be union rivalry. Where a single union represents less than the entire workforce, there may be conflict between the organized and the unorganized employees. Within the union itself there are distinctions between the needs and ends of officials and the rank and file. Furthermore, there may also be differences among the several levels and functions of management, and in the case of an association of several firms there may be a conflict of interest among the constituent employers.

In the West Coast airframe industry most, if not all, of these conflicts and differences existed in greater or lesser degree. In such a situation the job description and evaluation plan may become a major instrument of partisan gain. A job description and evaluation plan, depending so greatly upon cooperation and harmony for success, may become the battleground upon which conflicting interests contend for advantage.

Differences among the various levels and functions of management deserve particular scrutiny. The job description and evaluation program in the West Coast airframe industry was not equally compatible with each of the several levels and functions of management. On occasion, this incompatibility led to open conflict. The technical personnel of management closely associated with the formulation of the plan — engineers and wage analysts — were likely to look upon the plan as a finely tooled machine with each of its parts interdependent and therefore not to be tampered with. On the other hand, those of management charged with industrial relations had to deal in more flexible concepts. They needed to meet the give and take of collective bargaining. To function at all, some room for maneuver was essential.

Another kind of problem in the administration of a plan is raised by the special position of the foreman as an agent of management. He is likely to prove unreliable for evaluation purposes, since he is only marginally a representative of management. Although he exercises supervisory functions in the name of the company, his relationships to the workforce are likely to be close and his sympathies and even his loyalties divided. His vantage point is not high enough to see the wage structure as a whole, and his sense of status is served by an overevaluation of the importance of the work he supervises. For the SCAI plan the problem was complicated by the fact that in some plants the foreman's rate of pay was tied to the pay scale of those under him.

In one Southern California plant, the classification assignments made by the foremen were audited and revealed extensive overassignment. In one department of the plant, the audit revealed that of 70 assemblers classified at the B level, some 36 were performing work that fell clearly within the duties of C assemblers. In part, the cause lay with the general laxity of management working under war contracts, since the necessity for close calculation of labor costs was not great. In part, however, the equivocal position of the foreman in modern industry must be held responsible. In part, also, departmental superintendents were responsible, for they had a recruiting job to do within the plant just as the plant had within the labor market.

Largely back stage, but no less acute for that reason, a conflict within the individual management groups existed in almost every plant under the plan. The industrial engineers wanted to preserve the integrity of their scientific method; the industrial relations men, to adjust to the pressures and to engage in the tactics of collective bargaining; the production supervisors, to ease their administrative tasks; the personnel representatives, to recruit readily, reduce turnover and grievances, and raise morale; the accountants, to contain costs within set limits. Reconciliation of diverse points of view was not limited to the union-management arena.

The Industry as the Area of Single Decisions — An industry is even less likely to act as a unified decision-making unit than is the management group in an individual company. The authoritative structure conducive to conformity is absent. Divergent institutional policies, in addition to divergent personal points of view, impede uniformity of outlook. In order for a single decision to emerge, the differing policies of independent companies must be harmonized instead of the differing approaches of dependent individuals within the managerial hierarchy. If, as in the West Coast airframe industry, the companies are large and competitive and distinguished by a wide range of policies toward the labor force, conciliation is a task of the first order.

Only under the pressure of unusual circumstances did the airframe industry act at all jointly. The tight labor market, government control flowing from a monopoly of purchases and supervision of wages and industrial disputes, and fear of whipsaw tactics by the rival unions were the coalescing forces. Even then, although the plan was identical at all plants, the separate companies in Southern California administered it differently. By way of illustration, Lockheed and Northrop, for quite separate reasons, evidenced more laxity or generosity (depending on the point of view) than the other companies. The only real discipline was through the Federal Government, and that was not entirely effective.

The greatest single difficulty in industry-wide job description and evaluation, aside from delay, conflict in decision making, and variegated administrative policies, arose when the Southern California industry attempted "composite job descriptions" covering all plants. Each company had its own combination of tasks to fit its type of production. In an effort to include under one title and description jobs in different companies, each with its own make-up of tasks, the job descriptions became very broad and their limits hazy. The effort of reaching agreement was exceeded only by the effort of administering the "composite jobs." The mass filing of "reclassification" grievances was, if not invited, at least made possible as thousands of workers claimed to fall within the ill-defined boundaries of higher paid jobs.

Boeing avoided these difficulties. It did not become a member of the SCAI committee until after the war when its rate structure came closer into line with those in Southern California and was thus less suspect by the other companies, and then chiefly for the sake of the sharing of information on practices. It had at all times its own job titles and job descriptions keyed to its own needs. This eased both the introduction and administration of the system.

Once the war was over, three of the six companies — Ryan, Consolidated, and Lockheed — withdrew from membership in the SCAI committee, although the latter two subsequently rejoined. Each company developed its own variation of the original SCAI plan. Enforcement of a minimum consistency of approach was limited to the influence of joint factual analysis and exploration of proposals.

The Union as Manipulative Agent — Union leadership is a form of political leadership, and those elected to office in a trade union play a role not dissimilar to elected representatives of the public. Upon their ability to perform successfully in that role, given a degree of democracy, depends their survival as the chosen representatives of the members.

Obviously no job evaluation plan can meet the demands made upon it by all of those whose wages are governed by it. However just it may be, an evaluation plan can only mete out a kind of abstract equity. This, to be sure, is true of any type of systematization and is not exclusive to evaluation plans. Yet it cannot be doubted that job evaluation, particularly under a point system, offers less scope for negotiation and therefore less room for political compromise than the ordinary wage structure.

During the war and the period of wage controls, this seeming inflexibility was of some political advantage to union leadership in the West Coast Aircraft industry. As responsibility for the failure to secure satisfactory general wage increases could be laid to the War Labor Board, inability to meet the demands of individual members for reclassification could be laid to the job evaluation program.

But in peacetime the same protections did not exist. The union official frequently could not serve his membership and the plan alike. He found it difficult to support a mysterious technical formula which in the employees' view claimed to dispense equity as a nickelodeon dispenses music. The relative positions of jobs, as determined by the point system, often conflicted with the opinions of the workers themselves. Workers, like most mortals, were prone to exaggerate the importance of their jobs and therefore their worth under an evaluation system. Further, there developed a concern for position in the hierarchy of labor grades which was in large measure independent of the compensation proper. The worker was thus prepared to believe that the evaluation plan which failed to meet his standards of value was a poor plan — whatever the objective facts.

The union official, as a prudent political leader depending upon the support of his membership for continuance in office, commonly found it unwise to defend the plan on the slim grounds that the facts were on its side. At the same time he found it possible, particularly in Southern California, to make fairly constant, if small, gains for his constituents as proof of his representative value. Efforts to "squeeze the gold" out of the plan tended, in part, to increase and subside in response to the timing of elections. Pre-election flurries of interest were particularly noticeable in several of the Southern California plants.

While this sort of pressure was not unknown at Boeing, more secure union leadership minimized its effect. Even at Boeing, however, union officials were not insulated from membership pressures. The largest group of employees, the B mechanics, received an increase of only 3½ cents per hour as an immediate result of the September 1943 order of the War Labor Board, while the average increase at that time was 12 cents. The union officials, while the technical case was rather unsubstantial, pressed insistently, but ultimately fruitlessly, for re-evaluation of the jobs.

Among the most serious threats to the consistent administration of a job description and evaluation plan are those that arise either out of the struggles of rival unions for jurisdiction or out of the threat of craft unions to an industrial jurisdiction.

The Boeing plants were less affected by rival unionism than were the California companies. The jurisdiction of the IAM was secure and had been established well before the outbreak of war. Furthermore, the Boeing plants constituted the entire aircraft industry of the area and were therefore not susceptible for use as proving grounds or demonstrations of union strength for the benefit of workers in other plants that the union hoped to organize. Notwithstanding this fact, there is some reason for believing that craft rates within the Boeing structure, as well as in Southern California, were set higher than could be readily justified under the plan. With relatively high rates paid to craft workers, the task of organization for the competitive craft unions was more difficult, and the threat of craft incursions upon the industrial jurisdiction much diminished.

The major battleground for rival unionism was the aircraft industry of Southern California. There the IAM and the UAW were aggressively seeking expanded jurisdiction. Also, as noted, a craft union held bargaining rights for an important group of welders. The effect of this rivalry upon the operation of the SCAI plan was pronounced.

The SCAI plan and the achievements of each of the unions under it became one of the primary tools of organization. Credit for devising various strategies to squeeze more from the SCAI plan than was intended was a solid argument for choosing this union rather than the other union. An "angle" or a particularly sizable volume of grievances vigorously prosecuted became the "currency" of organizing efforts. Success in the manipulation of the plan was the strongest evidence of where the workers' self-interest lay. The UAW instructed its shop stewards to look for the "many thousands of dollars in hidden pay increases" available through the plan.

Union rivalry was among the important reasons why no sense of union loyalty to the SCAI plan developed in Southern California. In the presence of strong competitive unionism, the objectives of territorial gain took precedence over orderly administration. (It is only in times of peace that the domestic arts can flourish.) A further reason was the lack of institutional security for the unions. The unions were fighting for members all the time. One method of attracting them was evidence of ability to make individual gains for them under the plan, as against nonmembers. Over 4,000 wage-rate grievances were filed at Lockheed in a single year. That is indicated by the fact that at Boeing, where the union shop guaranteed members, the plan was not subject to the same assault.

The Contract and the Plan — A job description and evaluation plan, where collective bargaining prevails, must coexist with the labor agreement. The two are related, not only (1) through the union security provisions of the contract as they influence the political situation of the union and (2) through the grievance machinery and its adequacy for handling the volume of cases normally incident to the introduction of a plan, but particularly (3) through the seniority clauses. A job evaluation plan sets up a wage structure, while seniority clauses affect the flow of employees through this structure. The two must be compatible.

The Boeing experience is instructive. In the postwar period there was a clash between the job description and evaluation system and the contractual provisions on seniority, and out of this clash developed two years of negotiations ending in a five-month strike and at least temporary loss of contractual relations by the IAM. This came between the parties after a decade of satisfactory relations.

The fault lay both with the job system and with the seniority clause. Boeing had far more separately described jobs, about 750 of them, than had the Southern California plants. The more distinct jobs there are in the structure, with the narrower employee training associated with them, the more flexibility a company needs in promotions, transfers, and demotions if it is to operate efficiently. This is particularly true in an airframe plant where changing models, methods, and production schedules require the constant shifting of employees.

Boeing had virtually no flexibility at all. The contract provided for plant-wide seniority. Under the seniority provisions of the contract, each employee was entitled to a preferment for any position in the plant for which he was qualified in direct relationship to his position on the seniority list. In the event of a layoff, the individual dropped could lay claim to any job held by a person of lesser seniority provided the job requirements could be met. The employee was given two days at company expense to select the job on which he would like to show capacity and a 30-day trial period in which to demonstrate his capacity; at the end of the period, the burden of proof was placed on the company if it claimed the employee was not competent.

Wholly apart from the merits and demerits of plant-wide seniority in any industrial context, it is clear that the greater the specialization in assignment and training, the less operable is plant-wide seniority. The equitable considerations which led to the adoption of the principle of seniority were nullified, in part at least, by the inability of Boeing workers to qualify over any significant occupational range, despite the trial periods. Pulverization of skill into small elements greatly complicated and magnified the normal difficulties in administering plant-wide seniority.

As employment and type of work fluctuated up and down after the war, chaos resulted. (In contrast, the steady upward movement during the war, while it required considerable training, did not pose insuperable difficulties.) Factory workers about to be laid off "bumped" workers of less seniority holding other factory positions (and "factory indirect" clerical positions as well), of course demanding 30-day trials. Much resentment among the "bumped" employees resulted. Everyone was insecure. Some employees were bumped on an average of five times a month. The paper work for the company was immense. Ten men had to be moved to lay off one. The company often had to rehire ten men to get one it wanted. Senior employees could demand a whole series of trials before they found a job on which they were acceptable permanently. Inefficiency was the order of the day.

It is easier to bestow seniority rights than to take them away. At one time in the negotiations certain union leaders, realizing the difficulties, talked with the company about establishing a limited number of occupational groups, within which the workers would receive broader training and within which seniority would apply. The opposition of other union leaders and of the senior and more influential members of the union prevented the proposal from being seriously considered. The senior employees would have lost their virtually completely protected positions, and junior members also felt threatened for fear they could not broaden their narrow skills to fill the requirements of the new occupational groups.

To the narrowly trained and highly specialized worker, a tight little job cubicle offered protection from the anxieties of the learning process. This was a far cry from the IAM's original philosophy of all-around journeyman machinist and from the prewar job structure at Boeing, reflecting the IAM approach, which called chiefly for "mechanics" classified as premium men, journeymen, specialists, production workers, helpers, and beginners.

The established union leaders viewed the occupational group suggestion as an attack on the entire seniority principle. Negotiations broke down and relations between the parties were severed.

The Southern California plants largely avoided this difficulty with their seniority clauses, although there was no dearth of other complex problems. All their contracts called not for plant-wide but rather for occupation-wide or department-wide seniority. Merit was generally given much greater emphasis as against straight seniority; and the Southern California plants had something less than half as many separately titled jobs.

Summary of Environmental Considerations — An internal wage structure exists within an external environment. This environment consists primarily of (1) the job structure, (2) the labor market, (3) the management hierarchy, (4) intraindustry relationships, (5) the political situation of the union or unions, and (6) the collective agreement, all intertwined. The importance of these environmental forces elevates over-all strategy in the introduction and administration of a plan above its internal design.

ADMINISTRATION

A job evaluation plan within a plant or industry must be administered as well as devised. Once evolved it cannot be left to its own devices. However neat the scheme of factors, weights, points, and grades, a job evaluation plan is still inanimate. A plan cannot of itself automatically enfold a set of tasks and issue forth a series of jobs neatly slotted and tagged as to price. Nor can it keep a wage structure up to date. Yet administrative considerations are largely neglected in the literature[10] in favor of elaborate discussions of the details of the plans themselves. Actually the technical core of a plan, on which so much attention is lavished, has generally less bearing on the ultimate results than either the environment into which it is injected or the policies by which it is administered.

Precision and Imprecision — The technical apparatus of a point job description and evaluation plan, such as the SCAI plan, consists of two related parts. One is relatively objective in character — the job description, which is simply an account of the job as it is. The other is a value judgment — the factors and the points associated with each factor, which constitute the pricing scale according to which the jobs are compensated once the general wage level is known.

It is apparent from even the briefest experience with a job description and evaluation plan that even in its relatively objective phases it is compounded of many nonobjective elements. Reasonable men might agree on the factors which ought to be compensated and what relative compensation was proper for each of them, but disagree on the duties of the job. Or if agreement was reached on job duties, there would remain the conflicts over the degrees of skill, hazard, or physical exertion associated with them.

Job descriptions at Boeing and in Southern California were of a very different character from each other. At Boeing each individual job was described precisely. In Southern California, where the plan was industry-wide, the job descriptions were composite — an attempt to include within a single job description the variations in duties which might characterize the job at the

10. Major exceptions are two perceptive studies: Helen Baker and John M. True, *The Operation of Job Evaluation Plans* (Princeton: Princeton University, 1947); and Edward Robert Livernash, *An Analysis of Job Evaluation Procedure*, unpublished doctoral dissertation, Harvard University, 1941.

several plants — and therefore necessarily somewhat unprecise. Both precision and imprecision had their special problems.

At Boeing, the union took the position that the employee was responsible only for the duties recorded in the job description. Any assignment of work for which the description made no provision was likely to be attended by a demand for more money to compensate for increased duties or met by a flat refusal to perform duties which were not specified in the description.

In Southern California, the broad terms of the job description often provided for duties which were in fact broader than the job itself required, resulting from time to time in the denial of the full job rate to workers because the actual duties assigned were not so broad as provided for in the description. Conversely, employees claimed that performance of any duties within a broad job description entitled them to the full rate.

In many instances, the descriptions were found inconclusive. The most frequent fault lay in the common failure of job descriptions to distinguish between levels of skill. In some instances A and B jobs were indistinguishable. To be sure, the inability to distinguish between A and B jobs was not always a fault of the description. Sometimes the jobs themselves were not distinct enough to warrant separate classifications.

The Worth of a Job — Utility versus Disutility — In addition to the indeterminateness of job descriptions as a technical tool, it was discovered both in Southern California and in Seattle that the plan overvalued skill in relation to the factors of job disutility, such as job conditions and physical application.

The reasons for this are reasonably clear. As the aircraft industry moved from a small enterprise to a giant industry, its earliest and most urgent demands were for skilled labor. Processes were not yet standardized; assembly-line techniques were still to be introduced. The industry was not yet equipped to absorb the large numbers of semiskilled and unskilled workers necessary for mass production. Thus in the early stages of the SCAI plan the all-important need was for skill, and the plan reflected this need. As the industry moved toward mass production, the demand for semiskilled and unskilled workers grew enormously. The plan, however, having been developed under the influence of shortages of skilled workers, was poorly adapted to the recruitment of semiskilled and unskilled workers, particularly where job duties were unpleasant. Under the original plan, too little skill offset too much job disagreeableness as a determinant of compensation.

The WCAC of Region XII moved to correct the distortion at Boeing by providing that a sixth degree of the factor "Job Conditions" be added for jobs in which there was "more than one exceptionally disagreeable element or factor which is continuous or a combination of such exceptional elements or factors."[11] A similar step was taken in Southern California, in the course of restudy, by the addition of five points to the fifth degree of "Job Conditions" and the addition of a sixth degree as well.

Job Evaluation as a Caste System — Many difficulties arise from the tendency of job description and evaluation plans to become divorced from the total environment in which they operate. The objectives and therefore the techniques of job evaluation tend to become inbred. Precision rather than adaptability becomes the governing criterion and with it a strong propensity to greater elaboration and specificity than the industrial situation can support.

One of the graver dangers which were inherent in the job evaluation system of the West Coast airframe industry arose from the narrow classifications of workers. The classification not only governs the rate of pay; it governs also the assignment of work and therefore the occupational skill which the worker will acquire from his job. Where work assignments are confined within narrow boundaries, each employee becomes a specialist on a particular job and dependent therefore upon the continued existence of just such a job for his industrial efficiency and perhaps his employment. The occupational structure of the plant becomes a series of small cubicles without lateral communication and with greatly restricted mobility. The path of movement, if it exists at all, tends to be vertical through levels of the same job rather than horizontal through related jobs.

Psychologically and socially, the specialization which is fostered by detailed description systems leads to the development of a caste outlook. Within the specialized job the worker is secure and well-equipped. In any other job he would be insecure, poorly trained, and frequently inadequate to its requirements unless a period of training was provided. He comes to prefer the safety of his limited duties where he has already met the standards to a new situation in which he must prove himself able to meet new and unfamiliar standards.

On the management side there is a loss in flexibility of assignment which is sometimes a serious impediment to the efficient conduct of the enterprise. Since the range of competence of the worker is sharply limited, the labor force upon which management draws must be sufficient not only in the aggregate but also in each narrow occupational classification.

One of the real wartime emergencies at Boeing developed from the caste outlook encouraged by extreme job specialization. Workers refused to perform even minor tasks which lay outside their job descriptions and insisted

11. *Aircraft Order 51* (WCAC — Region XII).

instead that other workers whose job descriptions included those tasks be brought in to perform them, sometimes while the original group stood idle. The company claimed "sabotage" of the war effort; the union, "exploitation," since employees were asked to perform work which had not been taken into account when their jobs were evaluated. By action of the WCAC, the dispute was resolved by providing that employees should perform work outside their specifically described job duties when it was "incidental" to their other tasks and at the same time involved general or a lower level of skill.[12]

The Product or the Process — The job evaluation plan of the West Coast aircraft industry placed a high value on skill and thus a relatively low value on responsibility. Whether the fact was recognized or not, the relative weights of skill and responsibility constituted a decision as to the sources of job value — the high value for skill indicating a choice of job process as the principal source of job value, whereas a high value for responsibility would have connoted job product as the more important criterion.

The conflict between skill and responsibility is best explained by an illustration drawn from the characteristic results of changes in technology. Commonly these changes involve a transfer of skill from the worker to the machine with a consequent increase in output and a dilution of the skill involved in the process. A job evaluation plan which gives a high evaluation to skill decreases the total worth and therefore the total compensation for the new work operation, notwithstanding the increase in output which results. A job evaluation plan which places its emphasis on responsibility is much more likely to reflect the increase in product. (In this connection note the shift toward responsibility incorporated in the job evaluation plan negotiated by the United Steelworkers of American with the United States Steel Company.)

Even when, as at Boeing, a union with strong craft traditions and a high regard for skill, like the IAM, is the bargaining representative, the conflict is not avoided. For neither the workers nor the unions that represent them are abstract in their approach to wages. The results are not measured by the principles governing nearly so much as the principles are measured by the results. Consequently, when work is simplified and the level of performance required of the worker is lowered, the attempt to adjust the wage downward in accordance with the reduced requirement of the job meets indignant resistance.

The problem was clearly illustrated in a case arising at Boeing in October 1944.[13] A change had been introduced in the engineering of the milling

12. *Aircraft Order 60* (WCAC — Region XII).
13. *Statement on Dispute Order 83* (WCAC — Region XII).

machine operation. Skilled operators capable of setting up their own machines were replaced by less skilled persons aided by a skilled mechanic who set up the machines.

The result of the change in operation was to increase the output and lower the cost. The union, therefore, demanded that the milling machine operators receive as closely as possible the same pay that the job had formerly carried and that the skill factor be raised from six months to one year to accomplish the change in rate, notwithstanding the fact that six months had proved more than adequate in which to learn to perform the task. The company rested squarely on the job evaluation plan and argued that productivity was irrelevant.

The arbitrator held with the company. The accompanying opinion pointed out that the history of industry since the industrial revolution has been continuously associated with just this kind of specialization and division of labor, and the high living standards of the American worker depended upon its continuance. Presumably the worker would share in the increased efficiency as he had always shared, through higher wage levels or through lower price levels and a higher standard of living.

Cogent as were these observations, the girls who ran the milling machines were not likely to buy many B-29's, nor were they likely to be able to trace the effects of increased efficiency on their living costs in any other way. The evident fact was that the company was getting a larger product and the employees a lower rather than a higher rate of pay.

The problem was explicitly recognized and, although not solved, was compromised in accordance with an agreement reached by the northern division of the WCAC, known as the "Washington Agreement."[14] One of the points of this agreement was incorporated into a provision that, where work simplification had occurred, there would be no decrease in the rate of pay unless the re-evaluation of a job reduced its point value by a sum sufficient to drop the job two labor grades or more.[15]

Postwar Changes — Once the war was over and governmental controls were removed, the parties were free to examine the job description and evaluation plan without the restraints earlier imposed by federal agencies. The most significant decision was to keep job description and evaluation.

At Boeing the major postwar change which had occurred by 1949 was the unilateral scrapping by the company of the plant-wide seniority system when it conflicted with administration of the job structure that had been built up.

14. Dated, January 15, 1945.
15. *Aircraft Order 62* (WCAC — Region XII).

A number of changes were made in Southern California. Early in 1944 a "Re-Study Committee," ordered into operation by the War Labor Board, began an overall study of the plan. Originally bipartite, the industry members of the committee completed the study when in the postwar period the union representatives withdrew. The recommendations of the Re-Study Committee, many of which were adopted when the committee was still operating in a bipartite fashion, became the basis for the postwar systems at all companies, except Ryan which continued to follow the original plan.

Each company developed its own variations on the recommendations of the Re-Study Committee. While some of these were major in the immediate postwar period, by 1949 substantial uniformity had again evidenced itself. The unions were accepting and living with the plan, although the UAW, in particular, still argued for a negotiated system of flat rates. The labor market was moderately loose, and the plan, with a considerable history behind it, was operating relatively smoothly.

The major postwar changes were these:

(1) Industry-wide job descriptions were dropped in favor of company-by-company descriptions.

(2) Jobs were defined in much more detail and with greater accuracy. An effort was made to distinguish jobs, rather than describe them. At Boeing, job duties were listed as "determining," "associated," and "incidental."

(3) Employees, as a result of the deliberations of the Southern California Re-Study Committee, were told that job descriptions did not confine their assignment; that they were normally expected to perform some work at both higher and lower levels than those of their own job descriptions; that, while an employee need not perform all tasks in a job to get the rate, performance of a few of the tasks did not warrant it either; and that job descriptions did not limit the right of a company to make assignments.

(4) The number of separately described jobs was raised from about 300 to 350. The step was taken to aid classification of workers. It also had the effect of somewhat reducing costs, since the narrower jobs, on the average, were evaluated somewhat lower. At Boeing, at the same time, an effort was being made to reduce the number of jobs below the wartime level of 735. A desire to broaden training of the workers, reduce the paper work, and simplify transfers encouraged this step.

(5) The number of labor grades at the Southern California companies was increased in most cases from 10 to 13 or 15, with spreads of 5 cents and 10 cents instead of 5, 10, and 15 cents. This, also, had some cost-reduction effects.

(6) The same factors were continued but the maximum weights given to physical application, job conditions, and hazards were raised about 20%.

(7) In 1949, separate titles were being given jobs in place of A, B, and C grades. There was great resistance to being classified as a B or C mechanic, and this exerted upward pressure on costs.

(8) Considerable attention in 1949 was being given the respective merits of continu-

ing or eliminating rate ranges. While they gave management an opportunity to reward, they led to many grievances and also gave the workers an opportunity to obtain higher rates of pay. Some of the companies felt there was a net cost in perpetuating the ranges.

(9) At one company in 1949, the SCAI plan was discontinued as a "plan" and made instead a "guide," with provision for consideration of market rates outside the confines of the plan.

SOME PRECEPTS AND CAVEATS

The observations that follow have been framed as generalizations. Technically, no more can be claimed for them than that they held true at Boeing or in the Southern California aircraft industry or in both places, and that the relative success during the war of the job description and evaluation plan at Boeing and its relative failure in Southern California may be largely explained by reference to them. (At Boeing, the plan was put completely into operation by the end of the war; it was administered with integrity; and it was the source of little controversy and few grievances, except for the postwar disturbances when plant-wide seniority and the job structure proved incompatible. In Southern California, the plan never was fully effectuated; it was administered very loosely; and many grievances arose under it, and many conflicts occurred over it.)

These precepts and caveats are offered for general testing because the environment in which the SCAI plan operated was for the most part not unique, and aspects of it will be widely duplicated at different times and different places, as will the administrative problems. Although there are evident dangers in generalizing widely from two experiences, confined to the Pacific Coast, many of the problems encountered in the career of the SCAI plan are the common problems of job description and evaluation under collective bargaining.

(1) The higher the wage level of the plant, both relative to the community and in absolute terms, the more successful will the plan be. If this appears to be an observation which is true of all systems of compensation and is by no means specific to job evaluation, then let it be taken as a general observation that job evaluation runs special risks from low wage levels because of the relative inflexibility of its response to market forces, changes in the cost of living, prevailing wages, and the other equitable considerations of wage compensation. Furthermore, a plan is likely to work more readily in a stable wage market than in a rapidly rising one; and in a loose labor market than a tight one.

(2) A job evaluation plan must be devised and administered with one eye always on the market. Here is a major dilemma faced by job evaluation. If the evaluated rate falls substantially below the prevailing rate for any job with a clear counterpart in the

community, the rate will fail to command the necessary supply of labor in a tight market. The entire history and progress of unionism are intimately bound up with the standardization of rates of pay over wider and wider areas and for more and more occupations. As unionism progresses, the number of jobs which may have their rates set by evaluation formulas becomes fewer and fewer.

(3) Pressures for uniformity of rates emanate from employers as well as unions. The employer lives in a business community. If a job evaluation plan yields rates which are significantly higher than those paid by other employers for the same kind of labor, many informal pressures will be brought to bear to bring the rates "into line," and this will mean "into line" with other enterprises and not with other jobs in the same enterprise.

(4) The better established the relations of the parties and the more peaceful their dealings, the easier it is to introduce and administer a job description and evaluation plan.

(5) In the administration of a job description and evaluation plan, the system of compensation cannot be separated from other provisions of the contract. The seniority provisions of the contract, the grievance procedure, and the plan of job evaluation need to be parts of a single apparatus, mutually consistent with one another as well as adequate in themselves.

(6) A job description and evaluation plan is more likely to survive when confined to a single company than as an industry-wide undertaking. For industry-wide job description and evaluation to succeed, the degree of job standardization within the industry needs to be so great and the cohesiveness of the several firms so strong that the industry acts virtually as a single firm not only in its wage policies but in its job engineering as well. A company isolated from the rest of the industry is likely to have more freedom to work out its problems after its own fashion than is one surrounded by others who are simultaneously competitors in both labor and product markets.

(7) If an industry-wide plan is undertaken, it is likely to be more successful with uniform job evaluation than with uniform job description.

(8) A single industrial union will prove more compatible with job description and evaluation than will several craft unions.

Any single craft union is likely to encompass too small a proportion of the plant workers, and its responsibilities are therefore too limited to offer much hope of genuine endorsement of the objectives of job description and evaluation. For a craft union to accept job description and evaluation wholeheartedly would amount to a concession that the rates of its members might be established, in part, by noncraft workers or workers in other crafts who were not members of the union and might belong to no union at all.

Rival unionism, whether between craft and industrial unions or between unions of a single type, is likely to prove fatal to the orderly administration and even the survival of an evaluation plan.

(9) If the employees of a plant are organized, it is highly desirable that any job description and evaluation plan adopted be agreed to and, if possible, jointly developed by the company and the union. In any establishment in which a strong union exists, one key to success or failure of a job description and evaluation plan lies with

the attitude the union takes toward it. A desire on the part of the union to make it work will prove a good deal more important than the technical perfection of the plan.

(10) The terms of a job description and evaluation plan will be better executed under conditions of universal, or nearly universal, union membership than will be true if substantial groups of employees do not belong to the union. The opportunities for manipulation of the plan by the union for the advantage of union members and by employers for the advantage of nonunion members will be many. Under these circumstances the plan may become primarily an instrument in the struggle over unionization, with consequent damage to the plan.

(11) Less distortion of the plan is likely to occur when the union official charged with responsibility for its administration is free from the political pressures inevitable in an elective office. There may be valid objection to an appointed union official, only indirectly responsible to the membership, but there can be no question that he will be better able to resist pressures which make for distortion of the plan. Unions with stable leadership will better be able to cooperate in the administration of a plan than unions whose leadership is insecure.

(12) On the management side, the plan is better administered by the industrial relations staff than by the wage or industrial engineers who may have designed it. The essence of successful administration is flexibility. This is better understood by those who practice the art of industrial relations than by those engaged in the science of industrial management.

(13) It is of major importance that the number of job titles and classifications be held to a minimum. The results of excessive elaboration of the job structure are many and unfortunate. They deprive management of flexibility of assignment, restrict the workers' training and competence to the narrowest of fields, make seniority systems burdensome and impractical, and turn each job into a narrow caste to which the worker clings because outside of it he is untrained and insecure. It is particularly important that this error be avoided at the outset; for, if it is not, efforts to correct the error are likely to meet strong·resistance from the workers themselves, who will have come to prefer monotony and security to the anxieties of the learning process.

(14) Anticipated re-engineering of jobs and work simplification should be undertaken, so far as possible, before a job description and evaluation plan is installed. A constantly changing job structure is an upsetting factor for a job description and evaluation system.

When work which formerly required a relatively high level of skill is re-engineered and is subsequently performed at a lower level of skill and, as frequently happens, a higher rate of output, a particularly searching light is thrown upon job evaluation as a method of wage determination.

Most job evaluation plans reward skill highly. Yet the relationship of level of skill to level of productivity is seldom very close. For the most part, the great increase in productivity in recent times has been associated with a transfer of skill from the worker to the machine. Work simplification, although reducing the qualifications of the worker and commonly reducing his compensation, nevertheless is likely to increase the efficiency of the process and presumably the company's profits. A wage cut under these circumstances, although consistent with the principles of job evaluation, is quite likely to appear to the worker as unjust.

(15) Unless the defects of the plan make it virtually inoperable, modifications should be resisted until the plan has become established. It will be of prime importance to the future success of the plan that it become the customary mode of compensation. Once the plan becomes customary, desirable modifications can more easily be made than if it undergoes constant changes from the outset and never becomes authoritative enough to gain acceptance.

(16) A plan which provides for single rates and for specific ratios of A, B, and C workers in job families is easier to administer than one which calls for rate ranges and sets no fixed ratios.

(17) The purpose of job description is not so much to produce a perfect account in words of the duties of a particular job. The object of a job description is to differentiate the job from other jobs and to set its outer limits. A good deal of time and misunderstanding would be saved if job descriptions dwelt more on what was unique about the job and less on its central core.

(18) It is sound practice for a limit to be set upon the total sum available for re-evaluations or other alterations in the plan. If this sum is set, both management and union know the outer limits of the adjustment and will make their specific positions correspond to it. In the absence of any limit on the magnitude of the total adjustment, the union is under no obligation to make any choices at all. Such a limit was set informally at Boeing, while there was none for the Southern California companies.

(19) In the administration of a job description and evaluation program it is difficult to avoid invidious comparisons between classifications of work and therefore between classifications of workers. Involved in these comparisons is not only the matter of compensation but also the important matter of status. A job description and evaluation structure is commonly graduated in detail. Often there are not only the variety of labor grades, but A, B, and C degrees for each classification. Job description and evaluation plans not only are compensation systems; they are social systems with each employee neatly ticketed as to his relative standing. The result is that status becomes exceptionally important. The sensitivity of the worker under a description and evaluation program is greatly aggravated by certain apparent contradictions. For purposes of morale and the general level of output, he is an essential cog in a great machine. For purposes of compensation, he is the lowest degree assembler in the next to bottom labor grade. Management operates under the mutually contradictory compulsion to inflate the importance of a job for the sake of the worker's productivity; and to deprecate its importance for purposes of his compensation.

(20) Over a period of time it will prove difficult to retain the heavy weighting which is given to skill factors in the SCAI and many other job evaluation plans. There are influences operating which will require that greater weight go to the disutility factors such as hazards, physical effort, and job conditions.

It seems probable that skill has much greater weight at the commencement of job evaluation plans than can reasonably be expected of their later phases. During periods of expansion, the most urgent employer demand is for skill. Many of the present job evaluation plans had their birth in such a period with the consequence that skill factors commonly account for half or more of the total rating points in a plan. But when the plant is constructed, the machinery built, the process installed and rationalized, the demand for skilled workers met, and relatively scarcity manifests itself in the semiskilled and unskilled classifications, tendencies toward the devaluation of skill will appear.

In the long run, the tendency may be even more pronounced. As the general educational level of the industrial worker rises and as the opportunities for skilled work decline relative to the semiskilled classifications (a clearly defined trend over several decades now), more weight will have to be given to the elements of disutility in a job rather than to those of skill.

(21) The operation of a plan highlights the impelling influence of power in the labor market. The jobs which tend to rate high as compared with the market are those of janitor, nurse, and typist; while craft jobs rate comparatively low. Weaker groups are better served by an evaluation plan than by the market; the former places the emphasis not on force but on equity. Ideally, for a system of factors to reflect accurately the market, it should give heavy weight to those considerations to which the market most responds: skill, job conditions, and bargaining power.

(22) Custom is a powerful force. The absence of historical practice in the case of SCAI greatly increased the original conflict over the location of jobs on the scale of compensation. In closing out the work of the WCAC (Region XII), the chairman noted the prospect of "increasing acceptance" of the job and wage structure by the employees "as they become more accustomed to it."[16] By 1948 they had become sufficiently accustomed so that efforts to change the plan were met with a strike. Careful development of the original plan becomes particularly important since it may become solidified in a comparatively short time.

CONCLUDING OBSERVATIONS

There is very nearly universal agreement with the moral propositions of wage compensation. If employers, unions, and from time to time arbitrators and the government had no need to apply these propositions, there would be no difficulty in securing ready assent by all parties to a clause which would provide that wages paid shall be "fair" and "equitable"; that an employee shall not receive less than his worth.

But the criteria of equity are many. The orthodox would hold that the market is the only measure of equity. The worker tests his wage against the cost of living and his aspirations for a higher standard of living. The union leader is strongly influenced in his judgments by the scales of competing unions and the temper of the rank and file. The employer is concerned with his labor costs of production and with rates paid in the community in which he produces and by competitors in the market in which he sells.

In a well-ordered world these several tests of equity might yield similar results. But in industrial society as it is they yield very different results. It is the essential task, if not always the achievement, of collective bargaining to compromise and moderate these differences.

16. *Statement on Aircraft Order 62* (WCAC — Region XII).

The selection of a single measure of equity, no matter how persuasive its logic, cannot meet all the demands upon it and cannot satisfy all the needs and interests which require satisfaction. Job evaluation faces its gravest threat from the monolithic character of the value system it assumes. For at base all job evaluation systems attempt to measure the relative worth of a job by ascribing given exponents of value to such characteristics of the job as skill, hazard, job conditions, and the like. The more fixed, definite, and self-executing the formula, the less will it allow for the other and perhaps more important pressures to which job rates respond.

Most job evaluation plans purport to set internal wage relationships only and not the wage level itself. Most plans explicitly provide that the level of rates shall be set by fixing certain points on a wage curve with reference to which other jobs will be evaluated. These have nonevaluated rates, or fixed points, commonly represent jobs which have a well-established rate in the community, ordinarily craft jobs often supplemented by a negotiated common labor rate.

Yet it must be obvious that, in communities where the level of union organization is high, the number of well-established rates will be large. In poorly organized communities, where only the crafts are well organized, the plan may need to reflect only established contract rates for craft unions. In communities such as those on the Pacific Coast, the community rate for warehousemen, truck drivers, and machine operators will be just as well established as the rates for electricians and machinists.

If a job evaluation plan operating in an organized community were to accommodate itself to every firm and well-established community rate, there would be little left of the plan. However, to fail to meet the competitive rate for any well-established classification of work is to invite dissatisfaction, turnover, loss of manpower — and rival unions developing within the plant for the express purpose of raising evaluated rates to community rates.

It will not do, therefore, to parry these problems with the observations that job evaluation is only a means of distributing the total wage bill of a plant with the amount of that bill determined by other considerations. The relative compensation of jobs will be directly affected by these "other considerations" and with it the internal logic of the plan. The more forceful are "other considerations," by and large, the less forceful is the plan.

Firmness and Flexibility — Clearly then, an element of contradiction does exist. Job evaluation as a system of rate setting tends to meet only one of many criteria of equity; and the more decisive the considerations of job evaluation become, the less likely is it that other criteria of equity will be met. Perhaps there is no logical resolution. However, if the logical contradiction cannot be resolved, it can at least be attenuated. Those who construct job description and evaluation plans should seek no greater precision than the plan can afford and still survive in the environment in which it must operate.

Unfortunately the tendency is to move in the opposite direction, to plug the loopholes, to ferret out each imprecision and make it precise, to define jobs more and more exactly. The administration of a job description and evaluation plan develops a strong tendency to substitute means for ends, to forget that the objective is simply the acceptable determination of wages for a group of employees and to lavish more and more care upon the production of a systematic end result which will be logical, polished, and final.

But if the job description and evaluation plan needs to be flexible, it also needs to be susceptible of authoritative interpretation. There will be many occasions on which conflicts can be resolved by authoritative reference to the plan. The very existence of a formula represents a predisposition toward settlement in terms of that formula and takes the burden of proof upon those who would reach a conclusion at variance with it. A job description and evaluation plan accepted by union and management alike places limits upon the area of disagreement. There are many disagreements which it will not settle precisely, but it will always narrow the scope of controversy.

There are positive advantages to both union leadership and management. A job description and evaluation plan permits a shifting of responsibility from the negotiators in any grievance to the plan by which they are presumably bound. Management representatives are not bested by their union counterparts or union representatives by management when a grievance is won or lost. Responsibility for the result may be laid directly to the presumably automatic functioning of the formula. It would yield no more, and so the political perils of representation, particularly union representation, are alleviated. Internal conflicts within management and within the union can better be resolved by reference to the authority of the plan.

These are the positive aspects of job description and evaluation, and their importance should not be underrated. When a formula is useful, the formula is at hand. When authority is needed, authority can be invoked. When the substantive area of disagreement is large, job description and evaluation may be expected to narrow the issues in dispute.

Narrowly construed, there appears to be conflict between the twin requirements of firmness and flexibility. Actually the discovery of the true compatibility between firm and flexible uses of job description and evaluation is the essence of sound administration of a plan. Job description and job evaluation under collective bargaining constitute a tool in the larger task of mutual agreement. It is not the end product. Skillfully used, the tool can be of great value. If it is mistakenly taken to be an end rather than a means, it will not prove adequate to the task assigned.

Job description and evaluation plans differ widely in their internal assumptions and their procedures. Some make substantial allowance for community wage rates and others relatively little. Some weight skill very heavily; others do not. Some distinguish small differences between jobs; others define jobs broadly. However, they all have one common characteristic. Every such plan represents an attempt to discover a system of analysis which can be described, transmitted, and repeated whereby a variety of jobs can be related to one another logically and equitably, and a series of appropriate wage rates can then be derived. Each attempts to develop an internally consistent, rational, and systematic plan for allocating the wage bill of a plant to the various claimants upon it in accordance with some scheme of relative value ascribed to the different claims.

The SCAI Plan in Retrospect — The concern of this study has not been primarily with the internal logic of the SCAI plan, or the equity of the relationships it established. The more important problems posed by job description and evaluation arise from different considerations and would in large measure remain no matter how exact, precise, and well engineered the plan itself might be. For job description and evaluation always in some measure represent an effort to substitute rational considerations for a variety of nonrational influences — market forces, the requirements of social status and union objectives, among others, which commonly influence the price of labor. (The term "rational" is used here in its industrial engineering meaning.) A rational wage plan, though its own internal logic be irrefutable, may have little survival value in a nonrational environment.

The SCAI plan, at least in its final form, was a reasonably good plan. At any rate the problems encountered in its administration would not have been eliminated or even much reduced by technical improvements in the plan itself. The issues of importance which arose from the adoption of a job description and evaluation plan by the aircraft industry were not primarily issues of the plan itself but rather of relationship to an environment dominated by other plans and other purposes.

It is of great importance to an understanding of the operation of the plan and to the problems that arose under it to recapitulate the circumstances surrounding the adoption of the plan. The labor market was tight and the aircraft industry expanding. Consequently the industry required a wage structure high enough to attract labor to the industry and well enough organized so that competitive bidding among the several firms making up the industry would be held to a minimum. The SCAI plan served this purpose well.

The ordinary operations of both management and labor were seriously limited by the existence of the War Labor Board and the control which the Board held over wage changes. In addition, in Southern California the War Labor Board had denied a general wage increase. The SCAI plan offered an opportunity for considerable flexibility of operation. The principles laid down in the plan were not so clear, objective, and self-executing that there was not a large area for movement within. The approval of the plan returned to labor and management a broad area for self-determination of wage rates and, as it developed, a substantial opportunity for wage increases despite the apparent prohibition of such increases.

The several unions, seemingly deprived of their principal economic role — the demand for increased wages — came to see in the manifest flexibility of the job description and evaluation plan an opportunity to substitute individual grievance claims for contract bargaining. The SCAI plan in its administration became a permanently open contract under which constant negotiation took place around problems of classification, upgrading, merit rating, and the like; each with its opportunity for retrieving some part of the chance for economic gain lost when the War Labor Board denied a general increase to aircraft workers. In addition, the political necessities of the unions were well served by the plan. The unions had representation on the WCAC, their business agents were skilled in the mysteries of the plan, and it was reasonably obvious to the rank-and-file worker that there were important benefits from union membership even though the government had denied aircraft workers any increase in wages.

Notwithstanding the many evident departures from the plan, the manipulation that took place, and the pressures responded to, the plan was successful. Labor disputes were at a minimum, labor was recruited, airplanes were produced in larger and larger numbers. Labor and management had a framework within which to operate and a set of rules which, although not entirely governing, were nevertheless very influential.

The plan was less successful from the point of view of wage stabilization. The War Labor Board largely nullified its denial of a general wage increase by its approval of the SCAI plan. As mentioned, the operation of the plan in Southern California resulted in a wage increase averaging more than 15 cents per hour.

It is a reasonable surmise that had the SCAI plan been more exact, less subject to manipulation, it would have been less successful in preserving labor peace. There are important elements of conflict and even contradiction between technical criteria, on the one hand, and economic and institutional criteria, on the other. The area for manipulation was also the area of indeterminateness of the plan. This area of indeterminateness provided the necessary scope for the satisfaction of economic and institutional objectives.

Thus an observation suggests itself which, though cast in the form of a paradox, is nonetheless true: The more exact, consistent, and rigid a job description and evaluation plan, the less its survival value under collective bargaining. The more self-executing the plan, the more it is self-defeating.

A job description and evaluation plan is not self-enforcing, and it does not live in a vacuum. It must exist in an environment, and it must be administered. If environment and administration were accorded the careful attention customarily devoted to the plan itself, failures and disappointment, while not eliminated, would be greatly reduced. The wider view is the sounder view.

PART II — The Limits of Union Power over Wages

Labor's Income Share and
the Labor Movement

$\mathbf{O}$ VER THE PAST century generally, but particularly in recent decades, the industrialization of the world has given rise to organized labor movements.[1] These labor movements have varied greatly in their ideological orientations and in the environmental contexts in which they operate. But, almost universally, they have promised a redistribution of income, at the least in favor of their members, and at the most of the total working population. Nevertheless, labor's share of national income has remained more nearly constant than almost any other economic variable in society; Keynes thought this stability was "a bit of a miracle."[2] If Keynes and the statistics are right, the world has probably seldom seen so much expenditure of effort, emotion, and invective with so little result.

What has happened to labor's share, and — to the extent that anything has happened at all — what effect has the labor movement had? These are not easy questions to answer. First, there must be adequate statistics covering long enough periods in a sufficient number of countries before entirely definitive conclusions can be reached, and this information is clearly lacking. One has to rely on statistical data primarily for the United States and Great Britain. Second, so much more is changing in a dynamic economy than just the

Reprinted from George W. Taylor and Frank Pierson, editors, *New Concepts in Wage Determination*, (New York: McGraw-Hill, 1957).

1. Melvin K. Bers and Donald J. Blake, of the staff of the Institute of Industrial Relations, University of California (Berkeley), were helpful in the development of this chapter. This chapter contains some ideas developed by the author in an earlier paper, "Trade-Unionism and Distributive Shares," which appeared in the *American Economic Review* (May 1954).

2. J. M. Keynes, "Relative Movements of Real Wages and Output," *Economic Journal* (March 1939).

amount and the direction of the power of the labor movement that it is impossible to single out with any great degree of precision the impact of this factor alone. Third, theoretical convictions or class prejudices have often stood in the way of realistic approaches to these questions; some answers were desperately desired in advance. Fourth, as we shall see — and it is the central theme of this chapter — great difficulty has arisen out of the way the question has usually been phrased: Can trade unionism increase labor's share or can it not?

THE CONTROVERSY OVER UNION EFFECTIVENESS

A great confusion of tongues has resulted. Some economists have taken one position and equally reputable ones another. Trade unionism both can and cannot, or so it is said. This controversy starts a long way back — in fact, with the rise of economics as a separate and respectable discipline — and has involved a great many people during the intervening century and a half or more. But it is really not such a complex and confusing controversy as it might at first seem. The different theorists can be placed in four categories according to whether they believe the basic forces at work are "natural" or social laws and whether they feel that the problem should be approached as one involving economic classes or individuals (and small groups). Certain consequences for the assumed impact of the labor movement on labor's share flow from each of these orientations.

Natural-Class Theorists

The first group in point of time formed the "classical school" of Smith, Ricardo, and Malthus, among others. They thought there were certain "natural" laws at work which governed the income shares of large functional classes — landowners, laborers, capitalists. The real share of the laborers was determined by the goods and services necessary for subsistence times the number of laborers; it could never rise much above this or fall much below this in the long run. The money share was set by the cost of these goods and services, mainly by the cost of food. This is why Ricardo, in particular, was so opposed to the corn laws which held up the price of food in Great Britain and why he so favored free trade. If the price of food could be reduced, labor's share would be smaller; then the share of profits would rise, and this would mean more investment and thus more progress. This greater progress might lead to a temporarily higher "market" than the "natural" rate of wages, and this higher "market" rate might even become enough of a custom to establish a higher "natural" rate.

Combinations of laborers could only have a negative effect. By raising wages, they would reduce profits and thus impede progress; and in the long run labor's absolute share would be lower. Social policy should be directed toward reducing labor's relative share so that, over the course of time, its absolute share would be greater; the abolition of tariffs on food (mostly grain) was the means to accomplish this. In the world today, perhaps the Russians have most closely followed this social policy: cheap food (grain) permits low wages, which make possible heavy investment in industrial and military progress; the cheap grain, however, has been obtained not through low tariffs but forced collectivization of farmers.

Social-Class Theorists

Marx accepted the class-share approach of the classical economists, but he believed that "social laws" relating to the class structure of society, rather than natural laws, were the fundamental force fixing the rates of rent, wages, and profits. Wages were held at subsistence levels, in fact, by the impact of the "reserve army" of the unemployed. As society progressed, more and more "surplus value" became available to the capitalists, exploitation of the workers increased, and labor's relative share was constantly reduced. Trade unions could achieve little, if anything. The entire social structure had to be changed before the workers could get their fair share of national income, which Socialists have tended to identify as the "whole product."

Among more modern approaches are some which resemble that of Marx. Kalecki wrote that "the distribution of the product of industry is at every moment determined by the degree of monopoly,"[3] and he believed that the degree of monopoly tends to increase in the long run. In the United States and Great Britain, labor's share failed to fall only because raw material prices were falling to offset the rise in monopoly power; but if basic raw material prices do not continue to fall, "the relative share of manual labor will tend to decline."[4] Labor's share remains stable over the business cycle because changes in raw material costs are offset by variations in the degree of monopoly. Trade unions can gain a bit in a depression by holding wages rigid and thus reducing monopoly profits, but this is a minor factor; and any advantage through governmental redistribution efforts is likely to be minimal in a capitalist system.[5]

3. Michal Kalecki, *Essays in the Theory of Economic Fluctuation* (New York: Farrar and Rinehart, 1939), p. 24.
4. *Ibid.*, p. 34.
5. *Ibid.*, p. 92.

Dobb also holds that trade unions can increase labor's share to the extent that they can reduce the degree of monopoly, but he believes that their power to do this will probably not be very great "short of more sweeping institutional changes in the economic system itself."[6] Boulding, somewhat similarly, though much more mildly, has written that "distribution depends on decisions, and mainly on the decisions of capitalists" and that "the history of trade unionism, and the evident impotence of trade unions in increasing the share of labor in the national income, are telling tributes to the accuracy of this insight."[7]

Kalecki, Dobb, and Boulding all hold to the "class-share-determined-by-the-actions-of-capitalists" approach to income distribution, and thus to a largely negative view of trade union influence, but none of them, contrary to Marx, contends that capitalists will decide to hold wages at minimum subsistence levels. The "actions-of-capitalists" theory of distributive shares would seem to find its realistic expression most readily in an economy where one or a few very large employers have effective control, as in certain Central American "banana" countries or Middle East oil economies or in the Belgian Congo or South Africa; and in South Africa Douglas did find labor's share substantially below what the marginal-productivity theory would indicate.[8] In all these instances there is substantial independence of action for the "capitalists" in both the product and the labor markets, and thus quite a degree of "free will" in what they do.

Natural-Individual Theorists

Natural-individual theorists are at the opposite extreme from those who speak of class shares determined by capitalists. They see an atomistic world where the decisions of all participants affect supply and demand and thus determine individual income. They are interested in personal distribution rather than in class shares, although personal incomes can be added together by their major source to get functional shares. Certain "natural laws" or, perhaps better, physical relationships, primarily the law of supply and de-

6. Maurice Dobb, *Wages* (New York: Pitman, 1952), p. 152.

7. Kenneth E. Boulding, "Wages as a Share in National Income," in David McCord Wright, editor, *The Impact of the Union* (New York: Harcourt, Brace, 1951), p. 148. Boulding considers his approach to constitute a revival of the classical theory, but he places so much emphasis on the "decisions of capitalists" that he seems to belong more properly in this second classification, although it should be noted that Ricardo did think distribution depended in part on human decisions, as in the case of the corn laws.

8. Paul H. Douglas, "Are There Laws of Production?" *American Economic Review* (March 1948). Douglas relied for his information on G. W. G. Browne, "The Production Function in South African Manufacturing Industry," *South African Journal of Economics* (December 1943).

mand, govern income distribution among individuals. This is the world of the neoclassical economist — of Walras, Clark, Marshall, Pigou, and Hicks. A worker, like anyone else, receives in wages the value of his net contribution to production. The concept of functional shares is rather foreign to this approach; but it is brought in through the notion of "elasticity of substitution."[9] If the elasticity of substitution of capital for labor (the ease with which capital can take the place of labor) in a society with an increasing amount of capital is less than unity (and thus it is relatively difficult to replace labor with capital), then labor's share will tend to rise, and vice versa. The relative stability of labor's share, in fact, would seem to indicate that the elasticity of substitution of capital for labor and labor for capital has been about unity, so that an increase in either one or both has not affected distributive shares.

While the neoclassicists were little concerned with class shares, they did consider the effect of group action, as well as of individual contributions, on rates of reward. In regard to trade unions, as well as other special-interest groups, they were convinced that, while restrictive practices could aid the special group — at least under some circumstances in the short run — such practices were at the cost of total product (as, for example, through reduced employment) or at the cost of some other related group, perhaps another group of workers, or both. They were not impressed with the ability of trade unions to raise labor's share and even less with the desirability of their trying to do so.[10]

The study by Douglas would indicate that actual developments in a number of countries (with a few exceptions, including South Africa as noted) are consistent with this marginal-productivity theory.[11] However, it has been pointed out in more recent times that because of short-run possibilities and of certain imperfections in product and labor markets, trade unions presumably could raise labor's share slightly or even moderately within a "range of indeterminateness,"[12] although efforts to do so continue to be viewed with substantial alarm in some quarters.[13]

9. See J. R. Hicks, *The Theory of Wages* (New York: St. Martin's, 1935), p. 117.

10. See, for example, *ibid.*, Chapters 9, 10.

11. "Taken in the large, there is an almost precise degree of agreement between the actual share received by labor and that which, according to the theory of marginal productivity, we would expect labor to obtain." Douglas, *op. cit.*

12. For example, by exploiting employers in the short run through forcing them to neglect rewards to fixed costs or by eliminating monopsonistic possibilities in the labor market or by taking advantage of "kinked" demand curves in the product market. See, for example, William Fellner, *Competition Among the Few* (New York: Knopf, 1949), Chapters 10, 11; and L. Reed Tripp, "Labor's Share in the National Income," *Annals of the American Academy of Political and Social Science* (March 1951).

13. See, for example, Charles E. Lindblom, *Unions and Capitalism* (New Haven: Yale University Press, 1949).

Social-Group Theorists

A more optimistic view was introduced into popular thinking by Mill. He came to believe, after abandoning the "wage-fund" doctrine, that unions could raise wages to a new "common level" and even raise labor's share, that "the distribution of wealth is a matter of human institutions only." Carey and Walker, among early American economists, held that labor productivity could increase and in increasing would raise labor's share; and Walker believed that unions could raise wages and that higher wages would mean greater productivity — the doctrine of "efficiency wages." The Webbs and other "bargaining" theorists contended that unions, through effective "higgling" of the market, could advantage labor. In more recent times, Golden and Ruttenberg have argued that organized labor should and could get for its members "a larger share of the nation's annual income."[14]

The essence of this approach is that social relations do affect distribution and that individual and group actions, including bargaining, can be effective; but there are no "natural laws" or "class shares," nor is there any monopoly of influence in the hands of the capitalists. The rates of exchange among groups and individuals are not set by any inexorable compulsions, but are subject, within limits, to control by man; leeway exists for effective individual and group bargaining. Out of this philosophy has grown much of the *raison d'etre* of non-class-conscious trade unions; and also of employers' associations, farmers' organizations, and other special-interest bargaining groups. These theorists have asserted the effectiveness of group action within certain socially set limits.

These, then, are the main answers given by the theorists over the past century and a half. Which of them is more nearly correct? Now it might be held that this is a question of little importance for, it is said,[15] individuals are concerned, not with the distribution of the national income among economic and social classes, but with the personal distribution of income. This is no doubt true, particularly in the United States, but distribution by aggregate functional shares does interest economists and policy makers, nevertheless. It was with this problem that classical economics first started, and it is one which has come to the fore again in recent times. It is part of the deathless issue of the comparative influence of eternal "laws" and of men on economic

14. Clinton S. Golden and Harold J. Ruttenberg, *The Dynamics of Industrial Democracy* (New York: Harper, 1942), p. 151. For a much more conservative view of the limits to union action in affecting labor's share see Sidney C. Sufrin, *Union Wages and Labor's Earnings* (Syracuse: Syracuse University Press, 1950).

15. See comments of Kenneth E. Boulding, Milton Friedman, and Paul A. Samuelson, in Wright, *Impact of the Union, op. cit.,* pp. 352-355.

events. An examination of the behavior of labor's share may also illuminate the policies of the trade union movement and indicate which of these policies, if any, may raise, or perhaps reduce, wages as a share of national income and under what circumstances. An investigation of changes in labor's share can also help indicate how productivity gains are shared,[16] how employers respond to increases in money wages under different environmental conditions, how wage-price-profit relationships are structured, and how governmental fiscal policies affect broad segments of the economy. Finally, aggregative distribution has implications for personal distribution; an increased share for wages and a decreased share for interest, for example, may result in a more equitable distribution among individuals.

And so we ask the question: Can trade unionism affect distributive shares? Now, the term "trade unionism," instead of "collective bargaining," is used deliberately. Unions can and do affect actions of both employers and governments, and some of both kinds of actions have potential or actual consequences for distributive shares. To explore the impact of unionism in only the economic sphere and not also in the political sphere is to tell but half the tale. It should be noted, also, that attention here is directed to the percentage share of labor in national income, not its absolute share, although a few comments about the latter will be made occasionally since relative and absolute shares can and sometimes do move in opposite directions. When the term "labor's share" is used, it means, unless otherwise specified, labor's relative share.

It was noted above that the confusion of tongues may stem, in part from the apparent simplicity of the question as customarily phrased: Can trade unionism increase labor's share or can it not? An affirmative or negative answer seems required. A more fruitful phrasing of the question might be: Under what circumstances, if any, can trade unionism affect distributive shares and in what fashion? Trade unionism is more than one thing and it operates in more than a single environment. It is the thesis of this chapter that a certain kind of trade unionism under certain conditions will have no effect, that a certain kind of trade unionism under certain conditions will increase labor's share, and that a certain kind of trade unionism under certain conditions will reduce labor's share.

We shall discuss, first, several kinds of trade unionism; second, the results they are likely to have in the environment or environments appropriate to each; and third, the American and British and certain other experiences in relationship to this analysis.

16. It can also indicate the relationship between real wages and productivity. A constant share for labor implies a constant relationship between real wages and productivity, and vice versa.

SIX TYPES OF UNION POLICY

Unionism may be categorized in many ways and for many purposes. For our purposes it is useful to distinguish among types of unionism in accordance with their broad economic purposes and their methods. We distinguish here among six types of unionism, or union policy, according to their attempted depth of penetration into economic processes and to the principal approach they have chosen to take to their assigned tasks. The various degrees of penetration include efforts to affect money wages, real wages, money and real wages after governmental redistribution of income, distributive shares, and the overall operation of the industry or the economy. The approaches can be primarily economic, through collective bargaining, or political, through party action. By considering both depth of penetration and method of approach, the six types of policy are identified.

Before presenting these six types, certain qualifications are in order. First, we are primarily concerned with unionism in democratic, capitalistic nations in an advanced state of industrial development, where the economic order is generally accepted by the workers; not with the "agent-of-the-state" unionism of a Communist or Fascist nation, nor with the quasi-revolutionary unionism of an unstable system, as in France or Italy, nor with the volatile unionism of a newly developing economic order, although reference will be made to some of these situations.

Second, our six types and their subtypes are something of caricatures. They exaggerate certain characteristics of unionism rather than draw a full picture, but this is inevitable in the presentation of analytical types. Particularly, several of the types tend to overlap in actuality, and some of them may never occur at all in pure form. Moreover, in these caricatures, we largely ignore the internal variations within each type.

Third, the six types do not necessarily occur historically in the same order set forth here, although the first types listed do tend to come earlier in the historical process than do the others. The latter types generally result from more sophistication about economic processes and from the accumulation of greater power, and usually also from more ideology and more ruthlessness.

Fourth, the different types and subtypes are of quite unequal importance. Some of them may occur so infrequently in fact as to be considered freaks.

Fifth, we shall not concern ourselves very much with the origins of these different types, though each has its own environmental womb, but rather accept each as given to us full-grown.

It should not be taken as implied in any way, however, that a union or a union movement is offered these six alternative economic policies from which to pick and choose, rationally or irrationally, according to its own free will. In large measure, each union or union movement has its economic policy virtually given to it by the changing nature of the society in which it develops and lives. And once the policy is given, certain possibilities almost automatically follow from it. The union in this area of activity is a mechanism, often an important one, that links largely uncontrolled cause with well-nigh inevitable effect. Understanding of the situation comes more readily than its control; consequently, realization that a policy lacks effectiveness does not assure its abandonment. Free will, in the sense of self-determined actions unrestricted by imposed social necessities, must usually find its scope of expression within quite closely circumscribed confines, within the generally narrow limits set by the situation. Consequently, the righteous assessment of personal blame and personal praise for the effectiveness or ineffectiveness of each policy rests on but a slight foundation.

The six types of unionism, or perhaps better, the six economic programs of unionism, follow:

(1) *Pure and simple unionism* — Here the emphasis is on collective bargaining to raise the money wage without benefit of theories or formulas.

(2) *Wage-policy unionism* – This type of unionism takes several forms, depending on the dominant policy being followed. One illustration is what might be called the "improvement unionism" of the United Automobile Workers, where the union bargains with the employer for a real wage (the escalator clause) and a share of increased productivity (the improvement clause). It is unionism which is still pure but no longer so simple. "Pure and simple unionism" will, of course, also react to changes in the price level and in productivity but in a more informal manner. As we shall see, there are several alternative policies, in addition to "improvement unionism," which have been adopted.

(3) *Managerial unionism* — Unions adopting this approach try to affect distributive shares at the plant or industry level through such devices as Bronfenbrenner has set forth[17] the "all-or-none" contract, profit-sharing schemes, union-management joint control of the industry with the union participating in price-setting, control of entry of firms, and so forth. This might be called "not so pure and not so simple unionism." On a larger scale this is, in fact, the Israeli economy.

(4) *New Deal unionism* — The essence of this type is a political alliance with other forces also concerned with securing a full-employment economy

17. Martin Bronfenbrenner, "Wages in Excess of Marginal Revenue Product," *Southern Economic Journal* (January 1950).

through governmental action, while bargaining for a higher money wage under the improved economic conditions.

(5) *Labor-party unionism* — Here the effort is to control distributive shares, but through influencing governmental action instead of through collective bargaining, by means of progressive taxation and various forms of subsidies.

(6) *Direct-controls unionism* — Direct governmental controls on a temporary or permanent basis are sought, particularly over prices. In Norway, the unions and the Social Democratic party have sought and secured a permanent price-control law,[18] and unions in the United States and Great Britain have been more favorably disposed to direct controls, under certain conditions, than have been most other elements in the population. The Swedish trade union federation seeks permanent price control on "monopoly products." At a more sophisticated level, there may be a national bargain at the parliamentary level over "class shares," involving wages, prices, taxes, government benefits; and, at the extreme, a fully planned economy.

PURSUIT AND ESCAPE

Each of these types of unionism is engaged in a grand pursuit — a pursuit mainly of the employer. And the employer is always trying, with more or less success, to escape. Now I do not wish to conjure up a picture of poor Eliza being chased across the ice by bloodhounds. Our Eliza is by no means always poor; nor do the bloodhounds always pursue very aggressively (they are often quite gentle creatures). They may even agree to stay a certain distance behind her, or to care for and protect her if she will be nice to them, or they may help arrange for better ice so that both Eliza and they can run faster. However, they may also try to get somebody else to hold Eliza one way or another so that they can catch up with her, which does not, offhand, sound very fair, though it may be quite effective. And, in our little drama Eliza does not always get across the river in time, although she usually does remarkably well and at times even turns around and chases the bloodhounds back again. Beyond that, the bloodhounds sometimes catch somebody else while chasing Eliza. They may even, inadvertently, catch themselves. In the extreme case, they may liquidate Eliza and start chasing each other, and this can turn out to be the bloodiest drama of all.

It is to this pursuit of employers by unionism that we now turn our attention. The end conclusion will be that only through quite deep penetration into

18. See Walter Galenson, *Labor in Norway* (Cambridge: Harvard University Press, 1949).

economic decision making, either directly or indirectly through government, can unionism increase labor's share more than temporarily, that unionism must approach the problem of distributive shares directly and consciously if it is to attain the goal of a higher relative share for labor. In the discussion which follows we shall relate type of program to degree of change in labor's share. This assumes, of course, that unionism has the power to make each program effective. We shall be taking power for granted and concentrating on the program and its likely results, but it should be understood throughout that the results will depend on power as well as on program.

The "likely results" we will be examining are the effects on labor's share and not either the possible economic consequences of a change in labor's share or the internal or external costs to unions and their members incurred in effecting the change. Our focus thus will be on the impact and incidence of unionism, i.e., with the initial effect of a certain program on the share of labor and with the effect on other shares if labor's share is raised or lowered. We shall not consider, except occasionally, the effects of such initial shifts in shares on employment, the inducement to invest, the propensity to consume, productivity, and the like, although the impact of the initial shifts on each of these economic variables may well lead to a secondary shift in shares. Nor shall we consider the costs to unions and their members of certain of the programs, costs such as increased internal factionalism or the introduction of external control.

Pure and Simple Unionism

It is relatively easy for employers not to be caught by the economic program of "pure and simple unionism." To begin with, union wages may not be raised above the rates which otherwise would have prevailed. If they are, there are two important links between wages and profits, and employers may elude pursuit at either or both of these two points. First, they may raise prices (and this is particularly easy to do if the union covers the whole industry); and, second, they may introduce laborsaving devices[19] or otherwise raise productivity. Thus one would expect this kind of program to result in a higher

19. Slichter believes, however, that collective bargaining can cause the share of property to drop and the share of labor to rise. The elasticity of substitution of capital for labor is less than unity, he argues, and thus by forcing up wages, with capital not being easily substituted for labor, unions can raise labor's share. The validity of his conclusion depends on whether the elasticity of substitution of capital for labor is less than unity and whether unions can and do force wages above the levels which would exist in their absence. One can only speculate, however, about the relative elasticity of substitution of capital for labor. See Sumner H. Slichter's contribution to *The Economics of Collective Bargaining* (Berkeley: University of California Press, 1950), pp. 36-38.

share for labor only when unionism is particularly aggressive, as perhaps in its organizing period; when the market is "hard," to borrow the phrase of Phelps Brown and Hart,[20] i.e., when it is pressing down on prices; and when laborsaving innovations or other improvements in the use of labor are not available. Presumably such gains in labor's share at the expense of profits would be only temporary, although Phelps Brown and Hart have suggested that employers, once having had their margins cut, may be content to leave them at lower levels for substantial periods of time and, perhaps, also the reverse.

Pure and simple unionism may, under some circumstances, actually reduce labor's share and raise the share of profits; recognition of this possibility, however, does not imply that it is a normal occurrence. With the introduction by unionism of what the Webbs called the "standard rate," the natural spread of rates over a wide range from firm to firm[21] is greatly reduced, or even eliminated. Within this range, in the absence of unionism, firms are distributed in the wage rates they offer largely in accordance with their ability to pay. The more efficient firms, in effect, share their larger profits informally with their employees.[22] "Good" behavior by an employer consists of paying in excess of the "going rate." Under the "standard-rate" policy, however, it consists of paying the union rate. Given any substantial degree of union sensitivity to the volume of employment, the "standard rate" will be set well below the capacity to pay of the more efficient firms. Some firms may be forced out of business, although this seldom occurs, and others may have their profit margins reduced, but for others the "standard rate" preserves for the firm itself that portion of profits it otherwise would have shared with labor. Whether the profit share will be larger more than temporarily, if at all, will depend, of course, on many things, including what happens in regard to the entry of new firms, prices, the volume of employment, and the incentive for efficiency of the supramarginal firms.

This tendency to protect profits and minimize the wage bill is seen in an exaggerated form in Germany, where wages are set on an industry-wide basis

20. E. H. Phelps Brown and P. E. Hart, "The Share of Wages in National Income," *Economic Journal* (June 1952).

21. See, for example, Richard A. Lester, "Results and Implications of Some Recent Wage Studies," in Richard A. Lester and Joseph Shister, editors, *Insights into Labor Issues* (New York: Macmillan, 1948); also, Richard A. Lester, "Wage Diversity and Its Theoretical Implications," *Review of Economic Statistics* (August 1946).

22. Note in this connection Douglas' observation: "Quasi-monopolies and oligopolies which may have shared with their workers the excess gains they have made at the expense of consumers." Douglas, *op. cit.* See also comments on the behavior of the "good" employer in Joseph Garbarino, "A Theory of Interindustry Wage Structure Variation," *Quarterly Journal of Economics* (May 1950).

in accordance with the dictates of a "dictatorship-of-the-last-bench" approach, that is, where wages are set for a whole industry at a sufficiently low level so that not even the most marginal worker becomes unemployed. So long as the discipline of the industry holds firm, this can give rise to very high profits for the more efficient firms. In Germany, this discipline has broken down in two ways: first, by the provision of more complete paternalistic benefits by the supramarginal firms — a practice of long standing in Germany; and, second, by breaking the solid employer front and bidding up wages above contract levels. The latter has happened in recent years, particularly during the great boom in the Ruhr metalworking industries. The greater the obsession with the fear of unemployment, which has been unusually intense in Germany, and the greater the respect for adherence to laws and rules, again quite pronounced in Germany, the greater the tendency for the standard rate to be set at low levels and widely followed.

But this phenomenon is not confined to Germany. In the United States the United Automobile Workers, for example, cannot have too wide a dispersion among rates paid by passenger-car producers; thus the rates for General Motors are in part set with an eye on the survival of certain smaller companies. This evidences not only a concern for unemployment if the smaller companies go out of business but also for the structure of the industry; the standard or nearly standard rate if raised to higher and higher levels could end in only one, presumably the most efficient, producer surviving. So the standard rate, to the extent that it is set with an eye on unemployment and the structure of the industry and to the extent that it is followed, can raise the profit share of an industry.

There are at least two ways out of this predicament. First, the union can fail to set a standard rate at all or can set it for only restricted segments of its membership at a time (as the teamsters' union sets separate rates for drivers of ice, coal, oil, and beer trucks in accordance with the ability to pay of each industry), thus acting like a discriminating monopolist with a separate wage policy geared to the capacity of each separate market. Second, the employers can escape from the standard rate by paying above-contract rates (which is often frowned upon) or, more commonly, by providing more favorable fringe benefits or better conditions — an increasingly available escape hatch now that substantial wage supplements are more common. The customary history seems to be that the more efficient employers, originally, share their extra profits with their employees, since this is one of the more pleasant and less embarrassing ways of getting rid of them; then the union introduces the standard rate; and, finally, either the union finds some way to allow the more efficient firms to spend more money on their employees or the firms find a way of their own. It is very difficult to keep the employers indefinitely from giving away their profits in part to their employees, in one way or another.

A further aspect of "pure and simple unionism," and one of more than theoretical significance only, is the policy of the "rigid money wage." Keynes believed[23] that money wages were quite rigid throughout the business cycle, partly because of union policy, except in periods approaching full employment or under conditions of full employment. If money wages were so rigid, it would mean that labor's share would rise in a depression because aggregate wages would fall in proportion to the decline in employment while profits would fall more than proportionately, both because of some decline in prices and because of the fixity of overhead costs. Labor's share would fall in times of prosperity because, with larger volume and perhaps higher prices, profits would rise and not be recaptured for the workers through wage increases. Actually money wages are not so rigid in a depression as Keynes suggested, and certainly not in a period of recovery,[24] but pure and simple unionism does tend to lead to rather rigid money wages in depression,[25] thus holding up labor's share during such a period, and to some lag of wages behind prices in times of prosperity — through delays in negotiations among other reasons — thus holding down labor's share during such a period.

Wage-policy Unionism

Pure and simple unionism is largely pragmatic and bereft of doctrines, except for the concepts of the standard rate and of wage rigidity in depressions. Aside from these policies, which relate to quite fundamental beliefs of their members, pure and simple unions approach wage setting without much more of an orientation than the idea of getting as much as they reasonably can under the circumstances. Under certain conditions, usually when they have an ideological framework for their actions or when they are a specially active force in their national economy or both, unions tend to move away from their pragmatic predilection toward reliance on an explicit policy or even a formula — the policy serves both to guide action and to rally support over a wide area. Such policy generally takes one of three forms: (1) it may be oriented within the working force to some concept of proper relationships — the "just wage

23. J.M. Keynes, *The General Theory of Employment, Interest and Money* (New York: Harcourt, Brace, 1936), and also, "Relative Movements . . .," *op. cit.*

24. See John T. Dunlop, "The Movement of Real and Money Wage Rates," *Economic Journal* (September 1938).

25. See Joseph Shister, "The Theory of Union Wage Rigidity," *Quarterly Journal of Economics* (August 1943).

structure;" (2) it may be concerned with external relationships toward other elements in the population — the "fair share" of national income; or (3) it may be directed toward the effective operation of the national economy — the "responsible general wage level."

The just-wage-structure view is illustrated by the policies of the unions in Sweden,[26] Holland, and Israel,[27] for example, where they have quite firm ideas about the proper relationship of wages to each other, but perhaps best by the Australian approach. There the basic wage is tied to certain views about a minimum standard of life and the cost of living, and wages above the basic wage are all related to each other in quite a fixed fashion. The system is not an entirely rigid one, of course, and there is much more to it than this,[28] but ethical views about the right relation of one wage to another are a controlling factor in wage setting. Wootton has recently suggested that "justice," which means mainly the equalization of wages and salaries, should be the central purpose of the wage-setting process.[29] Such an approach to wage policy has some repercussions on labor's share. First, the whole structure will tend to move slowly and to resist the impact of changing market forces; and, second, the wages for the more skilled may not be as high as the market would bear. Consequently labor's share will tend to rise more than otherwise in a depression, to fall more than otherwise in prosperity, and in the long run, perhaps, to be slightly lower than would normally be the case.

The "fair-share" policy is more outward-looking toward other economic groups in the economy and seeks to assure at least parity of treatment with them. "Improvement unionism" in the United States illustrates this philosophy. It seeks to tie wages closely to the cost of living and to the increase in physical productivity.[30] Wages tend to follow the cost of living and productivity in any event; but this policy, by calling for quick and automatic adjustments, reduces the lag. Thus labor's share would tend to fall slightly less than it otherwise would on the upswing and to rise slightly less (assuming the escalator clause is allowed to work downward as well as upward) on the downswing. Assuming, however, a full-employment economy without inflation, the net results, as compared with what otherwise might happen, would probably be negligible.

26. See, for example, Lloyd G. Reynolds and Cynthia H. Taft, *The Evolution of Wage Structure* (New Haven: Yale University Press, 1956), Chapter 9.

27. See, for example, *The Economist* (March 10, 1956).

28. For a recent discussion of the wage setting process in Australia, see Mark Perlman, *Judges in Industry*, (Carlton: Melbourne University Press, 1954).

29. Barbara Wootton, *The Social Foundations of Wage Policy* (New York: Norton, 1955).

30. Escalator clauses adjusting wages to the cost of living alone are, of course, very common, but they give a much more partial and temporary version of "fair shares."

The policy probably, on balance, slightly favors chronic inflation by reducing lags, although Ross and Reder have suggested that it will make the swings in both directions more violent.[31] It certainly favors inflation if unions obtain provisions calling for overcompensation for cost-of-living rises and increases in physical productivity. If such a policy of overcompensation becomes generalized over the whole economy, as it did in Finland,[32] and is effectively enforced, the share of labor will have to rise at the expense of some other segment.

The policy of improvement unionism may also result in a heightened public consciousness of inflation and thus in greater public measures to control it or to reduce the customary effects on the distribution of real income obtained through the introduction of the universal escalator.

More generally, however, this is a policy designed not so much to catch employers as to prevent them from running farther away. Individual employers, of course, can run away farther by having their prices advance faster than prices generally or by raising the productivity of their workers more than the general rise in productivity, but employers as a whole cannot.[33]

The "fair-share" policy may go beyond an effort to keep up with the general advance of the economy and become a rather rigid program for distributing "class shares." The postwar agreements in Austria are a good example of this attitude.[34] Since 1947, agreements between representatives of labor, management, agriculture, and government have determined wage and price levels, tax rates, subsidies, rationing provisions, and pension and family-allowance benefits. Each group has sought to gain at the expense of the others, and in totality they have tried to share out more than was available. Somewhat the same course has been run in France, although the arrangements have been less formalized.[35] Low-income workers and salaried employees,

31. Arthur M. Ross, "The General Motors Wage Agreement of 1948," *Review of Economics and Statistics* (February 1949), and M. W. Reder, "The Significance of the 1948 General Motors Agreement," in the same issue.

32. The arrangement grew out of negotiations between the trade union federation and the federation of employers but was effectuated by government. It lasted from 1947 to 1951. See U.S. Bureau of Labor Statistics, *Notes on Labor Abroad*, No. 7 (April 1948), and No. 19 (March 1951). Labor's share in Finland rose from 59.6 to 61.2 percent from 1947 to 1948. See United Nations, *National Income Statistics of Various Countries, 1938-1948* (United Nations, 1950), p. 217.

33. Related to improvement unionism in intent are those contracts which tie wages, in part, to the price of the product (like copper, wool, lead). The purpose is to share prosperity (and, to a lesser extent, poverty) with the employer. The area of attention is the industry instead of the economy.

34. Murray Edelman, *National Economic Planning by Collective Bargaining* (Urbana: University of Illinois Press, 1954).

35. See, for example, Jean Marchal, "Wage Theory and Social Groups," in John T. Dunlop, editor, *The Theory of Wage Determination*, (London: Macmillan, 1957).

peasants, and tradesmen have, in particular, sought to maintain or raise their "class share"; a gain by one has resulted in counteraction by others. The total result, as in Austria, has been more inflation and less economic progress than might otherwise have occurred. In Finland, the general strike in the winter of 1956 was caused by a rise in the price of milk which resulted in a gain for the farmers and a loss to the workers, and the latter were determined to make good their loss. The Brannan Plan for fixing farm incomes in the United States is based on the assumption that there is a fair share of national income for the farmers and that they should be guaranteed its receipt regardless of what else may be happening in the economy. The class-share approach may be said to be quite sophisticated, but it certainly contributes to the attitude of class warfare out of which it partially originates. To the extent that it is effective, it tends to assign relatively fixed shares to labor[36] and the other groups and to protect them from cyclical and secular changes.

The "responsible-general-wage-level" policy is normally best expressed when the union movement shares responsibility for running the country, as has been the case in Sweden, Great Britain, and Holland, among other nations. The policy is usually geared to the maintenance of a reasonably stable price level under conditions of full employment, and perhaps also to foreign-trade possibilities (as in the case of Holland) and to the development of a high rate of investment (as in Germany). Beveridge has been a great exponent of such a policy;[37] and the Swedish trade union movement has given particular attention to its development.[38] To the extent that such a policy is effective, and the "wage slide" above contract rates in Sweden and Germany demonstrates its limits, the general level of wages is somewhat reduced in a period of prosperity to the advantage not only of profits but also of rent and interest, because of the lessened tendency toward inflation; thus labor's share is below what it might otherwise be.[39]

None of these three "wage-policy" approaches is aimed specifically at catching the employer. The first, the just wage, is aimed at enabling workers to keep up with each other; the second, fair shares, at enabling them to keep

36. In France, labor's share remained fixed at 46 percent from 1947 to 1950, but this can only be considered indicative, not conclusive. For statistics, see *National Accounts Studies: France* (Paris: United Nations Economic Commission for Europe, 1952).

37. William H. Beveridge, *Full Employment in a Free Society* (New York: Norton, 1945).

38. See Swedish Confederation of Trade Unions, *Trade Unions and Full Employment* (Stockholm: 1953).

39. Labor-share statistics for Holland and Sweden may be somewhat indicative. In Holland the share went down steadily from 55.0 percent in 1946 to 48.3 percent in 1949. See *National Accounts Studies: Netherlands* (Paris: United Nations Economic Commission for Europe, 1950). In Sweden it went from 64.9 percent in 1947 to 60.7 percent in 1951. See *National Accounts Studies: Sweden* (Paris: United Nations Economic Commission for Europe, 1953).

up with everybody else, including the employer; and the third, the responsible general wage level, at maintaining the well-being of the total economy. The first and third may generally reduce labor's share a bit from what it otherwise might be; the second holds out promise of at least maintaining it and possibly increasing it, but the success of the latter depends very much on the comparative economic and political strength of the opposing interests.

Managerial Unionism

The program of managerial unionism is designed to control the distribution of income within the plant or, more usually, within the industry. The specific method may be an all-or-none bargain which obligates the employer to a certain specified wage bill (a given number of employees at a set wage rate) if he is to operate at all. This certainly can cut into profits, as compared with the customary rule of flexibility in the number of employees. The employer, however, may be able to escape the impact of the all-or-none bargain by raising prices or by increasing the output of his labor force.

A second method is direct profit sharing. Here the employer can regain the original amount of profit he obtained only by increasing the total amount, since some of the profit must be shared with his employees. A third device is partial or complete participation in the direction of the industry — the determination of prices and output and the distribution of the gross returns. There are even instances where the employers are given a general ceiling on their incomes and, if this ceiling is pierced, the compensation of employees is raised in one fashion or another. The incentive for efficiency, under such arrangements, lies more with the employees than with the employers.

This kind of policy is very limited in its actual application, but there is no doubt that under it, assuming the union has enough power, shares can be affected; labor can receive more than its marginal revenue product.

New Deal Unionism

Under a program emphasizing the achievement of full employment through governmental policy, unions can chase employers faster and win higher money wages than in periods marked by less than full employment; but employers can run still faster. The profit share rises and, even though the shares for rent and interest are reduced, labor's relative share of national income falls. In a depression, exactly the reverse happens and labor's share rises. Within this share, the salary share rises more than the wage share but, contrary to Kalecki,[40] the wage share also increases.

40. John T. Dunlop, *Wage Determination under Trade Unions* (New York: Augustus M. Kelley, 1950), pp. 174 ff.

Thus, over a period of time, a permanent full-employment economy will show a lower average share for labor than one in which prosperity and depression alternate. The permanent full-employment economy, however, may show a higher share for labor than the prosperity period of a less stable economy, particularly since continued full employment and its associated conditions bring a shift away from debt and a relative reduction in interest charges, and also a shift away from rent. Also, continued full employment may reduce profit margins; competition will even them out over time and generally reduce them, and employers may be satisfied with lower margins if prosperity is considered a permanent condition. An economy with continuing full employment without inflation may also show a higher share for labor than one rapidly approaching full employment, since wages will not be lagging behind prices as they tend to do in an expanding economy. But, if permanent full employment is accompanied by constant inflation, lags will tend to hold the wage share down and the profit share up. Consequently, continuing full employment without inflation will result in a higher share for labor than will occur in an occasional period of full employment or one where permanent full employment and constant inflation go hand in hand. While we are inclined to agree with Morton[41] that union wage pressures are not usually the basic cause of inflation, still the governmental policies associated with New Deal unionism may cause inflation, and inflation does cut labor's relative share.

Full employment yields the unions a more favorable environment in which to bargain for money wages but one in which, while they are given an opportunity to chase, they cannot catch the employers. They must be content with catching, in terms of shares, the recipients of rent and of interest, and perhaps also some of their own members. In fact, the chief beneficiary of New Deal unionism in terms of shares (unless one separates out the share of the previously unemployed which, of course, goes up enormously) is entrepreneurial income. With their policies of the standard rate and full employment, unions of the American type — which in recent years have typically combined pure and simple unionism at the level of the plant and industry with New Deal unionism at the level of the national economy — might be viewed as the protectors of profits and the defenders of the faith.

The relative share, of course, is less important than the real, absolute share and the latter rises for labor with the movement from less-than-full employment to full employment, although it may fall slightly with inflation.

41. Walter A. Morton, "Trade Unionism, Full Employment and Inflation," *American Economic Review* (March 1950).

Labor Party Unionism

The policy of "labor-party" unionism relies on taxation and on subvention to affect, not the income received in the primary distribution, but rather the income retained after secondary distribution has taken place.[42] Through progressive taxation and subsidies the real income available to labor can be raised as compared with that of other segments of the population who were originally more highly rewarded. Here at last the employer can really be caught, although perhaps not to the extent that might first appear. Goods and services are taken out of the market place and given to wage and salary earners with the cost financed by taxes bearing heavily on other elements in the population.

Direct-controls Unionism

The essence of this policy is direct price control by government. At least in the short run, profit margins can be held steady in an inflationary period or even squeezed, if enforcement is adequate, and the share of labor consequently maintained or raised. By holding down rents, the share of labor can be further advantaged. Under this policy, with the government holding on to the employer, unionism can catch him and take some of his profits, although there may be some cost in volume of employment or amount of total output.

Direct controls may be spread to include rationing, subsidies, etc., which brings this approach very much in line with the class-share strategy discussed above, except that it is developed largely through government rather than collective bargaining, but at this level of penetration the distinction between them loses meaning. Beyond this lies the fully planned economy which has control over investment, foreign trade, manpower allocation, and the like. The greater the control, obviously, the greater the ability to affect distributive shares, as we shall see below in the case of Russia, and the more important becomes the intent of the government in affecting shares. Generally, a fully planned economy will be related either to a large-scale military or industrialization effort with some inevitable effect on the share kept by labor; such an economy has usually been related either to an external or internal war.

THE HISTORICAL EXPERIENCE

The historical experience — particularly the American and British experience, for which the best statistics exist — is consistent with the probable impacts of these several different union approaches as outlined above. It

42. Efforts to control secondary distribution may, of course, also change the pattern of primary distribution. See Geoffrey H. Moore, "Secular Changes in the Distribution of Income," *American Economic Review* (May 1952).

should be noted in advance of reviewing this experience that it is inherently difficult to separate out the impact of unionism on labor's share since so much else is usually happening, aside from the application of union policy, which affects distributive shares. Also, the basic statistical data are far from satisfactory and there are many inconsistencies and imperfections in the definitions relating to distributive shares.[43] We shall review, first, the American statistics; second, the British; and third, those for certain other countries, including Russia; we shall then make some general comments about the apparent effectiveness of the several union approaches.

United States

The experience in the United States may be summarized as follows:

1. Employee compensation as a share of income originating within the business sector of the economy, after allowing for interindustry shifts in weights, has been quite stable over substantial periods of time. It was virtually unchanged from 1929 to the early 1950's (see Table 1). When viewed from other less meaningful vantage points, however, it has gone up. Employee compensation has risen significantly as a per cent of total income (column 2), but this is true, in part, because of the great shift of employees into government, where employee compensation is calculated as 100 per cent of income in that sector. It has also risen as a per cent of total private income (column 3), leaving out government, but this is the case, in part, because industries (like construction) with a high wage and salary component in the income that they add to the economy have become relatively more important in our national productive effort. The really important question is whether the percentage of employee compensation has increased after allowances are made for such shifts in the industry mix as the increased importance of government and construction. When the "industry mix" is held constant (column 4), there is little apparent increase since 1929 in labor's share; and it is since 1929 that the great growth in trade unionism has occurred in the United States.

What happened prior to 1929? This is difficult to answer because the statistics become progressively less adequate as we go farther back, but to the extent that any generalization is meaningful, it appears that over the past century labor's share has risen primarily as employed persons have become a more important component in our population. In other words, employees are not comparatively better off as individuals; there are, however, many more of

43. For an excellent discussion of the importance of the definitions used see Dunlop, *Wage Determination under Trade Unions, op. cit.,* Chapter 8.

Table 1. United States: Compensation of Employees
as Percent of Income 1929-1954

Year (1)	Percent of Total Income (2)	Percent of Total Private Income (3)	Percent of Total Private Income Adjusted for Interindustry Shifts* (4)
1929	58.2	56.1	56.1
1930	61.9	59.6	59.0
1931	66.6	63.9	64.7
1932	73.0	70.0	74.1
1933	73.6	70.2	73.8
1934	70.0	66.1	65.2
1935	65.4	61.3	61.8
1936	66.1	61.6	60.0
1937	65.1	61.3	60.0
1938	66.6	62.2	61.7
1939	66.1	61.9	60.4
1940	63.8	59.8	57.5
1941	61.9	57.8	54.9
1942	61.9	57.0	53.5
1943	64.3	57.8	53.4
1944	66.4	59.0	54.7
1945	68.0	60.0	56.9
1946	65.5	60.8	59.2
1947	65.3	62.0	59.3
1948	63.6	60.4	57.8
1949	65.2	61.6	58.5
1950	64.3	60.8	57.4
1951	65.1	61.2	57.7
1952	67.2	63.1	59.0
1953	68.5	64.8	60.1
1954	69.4	65.7	61.5

*Weighted on the basis of each industry's contribution to total private income in 1929.
SOURCE: Data for 1929 to 1953 from *Survey of Current Business, National Income*, 1954, Tables 13 and 14; data for 1954 from *Survey of Current Business*, July 1955.

them. There has been no substantial shift of income to labor, as compared with the other income recipient groups put together; employees are better off to the extent that all income recipients are better off. In a review covering the period since 1870, Kuznets[44] makes the following observation:

44. See Kuznets' chapter "Long-Term Changes in the National Income of the United States of America since 1870," in Simon Kuznets, editor, *Income and Wealth*, Series II (London: Bowes and Bowes, 1952), p. 140. "Service income" is nonproperty income.

We may conclude therefore that, by and large, the decline in the share of entrepreneurs in service income, and the rise in the share of employees . . . paralleled the movements in the share of numbers in the total labor force.

Budd comes to much the same conclusion. No secular increase occurred from 1850 to 1900, although labor's share went up somewhat after the abolition of slavery and down somewhat with the introduction of mass immigration; but there has been a slow secular increase since 1900 in labor's share within the total economy, although labor's share in manufacturing has apparently remained constant or even fallen a bit. This increase has been, at least in more recent times, at the expense of interest and rent shares, and not at the expense of corporation profits or the income of unincorporated business, including the self-employed.[45] The reduction in the shares of interest and rent can be ascribed to several factors, including secular inflation.

2. The share of labor was higher in times of depression (1931 to 1934) and recession (1938) than in more prosperous periods.[46] The shares of interest and rent rise the most under depression conditions because they are made up of relatively fixed payments. The shares of corporations and unincorporated businesses, including farms, fall the most, and their fall more than offsets the rise for interest and rent. This set of adjustments leaves a larger share for labor, although in absolute terms, of course, labor is worse off. It should also be noted that the inclusion of salaried employees in "labor" gives labor a component with relatively stable employment; also, both salaries and wages tend to be rather "sticky" when the cycle is moving downward. As an extreme illustration of the effect of a depression on labor's share, there is the situation that arose in mining during the Great Depression. At that time labor's share was more than 100 per cent of the income of that sector of the economy because of the large losses sustained by the mines; the amount being paid out in wages was greater than the total income of the industry.

3. During the World War II inflation, labor's share sank a bit at first but later rose, particularly in the one area where price control was most effective:

45. Edward C. Budd, *Labor's Share of National Income*, unpublished dissertation, University of California, Berkeley, California (1954), p. 295. For a discussion of this same period, see also D. Gale Johnson, "The Functional Distribution of Income in the United States, 1850-1952," *Review of Economics and Statistics* (May 1954).
46. It was also higher again in 1954, a year marked by a recession that started in 1953 and that particularly affected farm income. It may be, however, that labor's share in the United States is moving to a somewhat higher plateau because of the continued effect of full employment in reducing the shares of rent and interest, but not of profits, so that at relatively full employment labor's share will be higher than it was during intermittent periods of full employment in the past, such as 1929. Twenty-five years' experience — the length of time for which reasonably reliable statistics are available — is, after all, hardly a sufficient basis for firm and final conclusions.

nonfarm corporations.[47] In World War I, also, labor's share went down at first and then rose again toward the end.[48] The wartime pattern seems to be for prices and profits to make the greatest gains at first, and then for labor's share to recover as the government imposes more control over prices and as unions (and labor-market stringencies) put greater pressure on wages.

4. Labor's share rose after World War II, from 1945 to 1947, when corporation profits were depressed by reconversion and when unions were unusually aggressive. This repeats the experience of World War I.[49] A reconversion period tends to be marked by a depression, although perhaps a special kind of depression, and so it would be expected that labor's share would rise; but it is different from the usual depression in that, as a result of wartime stimulation, unions are specially aggressive and thus particularly able to put pressure on employers from which they cannot readily escape.

5. After adjustments for allocable taxes on income, compensation to employees rose more, comparatively, from 1929 to 1950, than did other shares. The great loser, after taxes, was the share going to corporate profits.[50] The redistribution, however, has been comparatively modest in amount;[51] and not so great as in Great Britain, chiefly because in the United States the governmental taxation and expenditure programs are proportionately considerably smaller than in Great Britain.[52]

6. Labor's share of income, industry by industry, has generally fared no more favorably in unionized industries than in nonunion industries. Contrary conclusions have been reached, but they have been based on the results obtained from the chance selection of a terminal year. Looking at certain terminal years, it appears that labor's share within unionized industries has been increased more (possibly as a result of union action) than in nonunion industries; but looking at other terminal years, it has increased less (and this could hardly be the result of union action); and looking at both sets of terminal years, the conclusion seems obvious that the selection of the terminal year is quite important because what was happening to the two sets of industries in the terminal year is quite important. It is, of course, a little artificial to divide

47. Edward F. Denison, "Distribution of National Income," *Survey of Current Business* (June 1952).

48. Budd, *op. cit.,* p. 295.

49. *Ibid.*

50. Denison, *op. cit.*

51. See Budd, *op. cit.,* p. 269, for a summary of studies relating to this point. See also Alfred H. Conrad, "Redistribution through Government Budgets in the United States, 1950," in Alan T. Peacock, editor, *Income Redistribution and Social Policy* (London: Jonathan Cope, 1954).

52. Allan Murray Cartter, *The Redistribution of Income in Postwar Britain* (New Haven: Yale University Press, 1955), Chapter 8.

the economy into a "union sector" and a "nonunion sector," for unions are of varying strength in the former and not unknown in the latter. However, it is helpful to look at the economy in this way in an endeavor to answer the question of whether or not unionization of industry tends to shift income within that industry toward employees and away from other factors.

Stigler notes that "it is possible that the unions succeeded in increasing the share of labor income in total income."[53] He shows that wages and salaries as a percentage of income originating in selected manufacturing industries went up slightly from 1929 to 1947 in those which were unionized while they went down slightly for all manufacturing. However, had he taken the period from 1929 to 1950, he would have found both figures declining substantially and in about the same amount, which would have implied a different conclusion. The pertinent figures follow:

Year	Labor's Share in Unionized Industry	Labor's Share in All Manufacturing
1929	69.1	73.1
1947	70.1	71.5
1950	61.7	66.1

Labor's share in 1947 in unionized industry was comparatively high, partly because unionized industry was caught more by reconversion problems involved in durable-goods production — with specific negative effects on profits — than was manufacturing as a whole. In 1950, both in unionized industry and in all manufacturing, labor's share went down as a result of the inflation in prices and profits due to the Korean War, but this inflation was particularly great in the unionized durable-goods segment because consumers, profiting from World War II experience, undertook to stock up in the fear of a full-scale war.

Levinson may have been misled, twice, by his selection of a terminal year. First, he found that the union industrial group showed a gain in the share of employee compensation (excluding compensation of corporate officers) while the nonunion industrial group remained approximately unchanged from 1929 to 1947. Later, he found much the same results for the period 1929 to 1952.[54] Yet had he taken the period from 1929 to 1950, he would have found exactly the reverse situation; and from 1929 to 1951 the share for employees in the

53. George Stigler, *The Theory of Price*, Revised edition, (New York: Macmillan, 1952), p. 259.

54. Harold M. Levinson, *Unionism, Wage Trends, and Income Distribution, 1914-1947* (Ann Arbor: University of Michigan, 1951), p. 106, and also his "Collective Bargaining and Income Distribution," *American Economic Review* (May 1954).

Table 2. Compensation of Employees as Percent of Private National Income
by Sector 1929-1947, 1929-1950, 1929-1951, 1929-1952, 1929-1953, 1929-1954

Year	Nonunion Sector (Agriculture, Trade Finance, Service)	Union Sector (Mining, Construction, Manufacturing, Transportation, Communication)	Combined Sectors
1929	21.8	34.2	56.0
1947	22.4	36.5	58.9
1929-1947	0.6	2.3	....
1950	23.1	34.3	57.4
1929-1950	1.3	0.1	....
1951	22.7	34.7	57.4
1929-1951	0.9	0.5	....
1952	22.9	35.9	58.8
1929-1952	1.1	1.7	....
1953	23.6	36.5	60.1
1929-1953	1.8	2.3	....
1954	24.4	37.3	61.7
1929-1954	2.6	3.1	....

SOURCES: Data for 1929, 1947, and 1950-1953 from *Survey of Current Business, National Income*, 1954, Table 13 (Income) and Table 14 (Compensation of Employees); for 1952-4 from *Survey of Current Business*, July 1955; Table 13 (Income) and Table 14 (Compensation of Employees).

nonunion sector also showed a greater gain than for the union sector (see Table 2).[55] We have already commented on 1947 and 1950 as terminal years. The year 1951 continued to be a good one for corporation profits in the durable-goods sector, although not quite so good comparatively as 1950, and this had an adverse effect on labor's share in the union sector.[56] The year 1952 was a poor time for corporation profits in the union sector, partly because of the prolonged steel strike, and this had the effect of raising labor's share in that sector. Thus the selection of 1947 and 1952 as terminal years gives rise to the conclusion that unionization has raised labor's share. Similarly, the selection of 1950 and 1951 might give rise to the conclusion that unionization has had an adverse effect on labor's share. Neither conclusion would seem warranted. A more adequate conclusion might be that in the United States to

55. Table 2 is calculated according to the method used by Levinson but with the most recent figures available for each year, and some have been corrected since they were available to Levinson. The industry mix is held constant throughout the periods used.

56. For a similar conclusion to that presented here for the period from 1929 to 1951, see Paul E. Sultan, "Unionism and Wage-Income Ratios: 1929-1951," *Review of Economics and Statistics*, February 1954; and for a similar conclusion for the period 1929-1950, see Budd, *op. cit.*, p. 252, and Denison, *op. cit.*

date unionization has had relatively little measurable effect on labor's share, industry by industry, and, further, that the special circumstances of each terminal year must be closely scrutinized in attempting to evaluate the impact of the unions. Parenthetically, it might be noted that the recession which started in the second half of 1953 and continued into the first half of 1954 may have helped to raise labor's share somewhat in both sectors.

7. The degree of unionization by metropolitan areas appears not to be significantly related to labor's share of manufacturing income in these areas (see Table 3). If any conclusion can be reached from these statistics, it is that complete or nearly complete unionization of an area has a tendency to shift income toward wages, at the expense of the other income-recipient groups; but before this conclusion could be reached, a very careful study would need to be made of the effect of the industry mix in highly, as compared with less highly, unionized areas — and this is difficult to do because the mix varies so much from one metropolitan area to another. It should be noted in analyzing Table 3 that Salt Lake City and Worcester, which are relatively little unionized, match Detroit and Pittsburgh, which are highly unionized, in wages as a per cent of value added by manufacture.

The conclusion from this record is that trade unionism in the United States to date has had no important effect on labor's share except as (1) it has encouraged an employee-oriented national economic policy with heavy emphasis on full employment and some tendency toward inflation — which by increasing corporation profits has served both to reduce the percentage share of labor as compared to what it would be in less prosperous periods, such as the 1930's, and also to shift income in the longer run away from interest and rent to the benefit of labor's share; (2) it has supported effective price control; (3) it has put wage pressure on employers temporarily unable to recapture profits — the special case of the reconversion period, where output was limited and the "administered prices" for durable consumer's goods were rising comparatively slowly; and (4) it has furthered progressive income taxes and thus raised the share after taxes. There is no evidence of any significant permanent effect through normal collective bargaining, except possibly in highly unionized metropolitan areas, where employers are caught between a higher-than-average wage and salary scale all-around and a roughly equalized national price structure. There may have been some slow secular shift toward labor over the half century since 1900, but most of it occurred before 1920[57] (thus before the rise of the modern trade union movement), and in non-manufacturing sectors.

57. Johnson, *op. cit.*

Table 3. Wages of Production Workers as a Percent of Value Added by
Manufacture in 1947 for Standard Metropolitan Areas by Degree of Unionization

Proportion of Workers Covered by Union Agreements (by Standard Metropolitan Area)	Wages as a Percent of Value Added
90 *percent or more of plant workers*	
Albany, Schenectady, Troy	45.4
Buffalo	41.6
New York-Northeastern New Jersey	37.5
Cleveland	41.8
Detroit	49.9
Milwaukee	40.8
Pittsburgh	47.3
St. Louis	37.9
San Francisco-Oakland	37.5
Seattle	48.9
Weighted average	41.1
75-89 *percent of plant workers*	
Allentown-Bethlehem-Easton	49.2
Birmingham	38.7
Boston	38.2
Cincinnati	35.3
Hartford	47.5
Indianapolis	41.0
Kansas City	33.3
Los Angeles	38.8
Louisville	29.5
Minneapolis-St. Paul	33.5
Philadelphia	40.7
Phoenix	26.5
Richmond	24.5
Trenton	42.4
Weighted average	38.4
50-74 *percent of plant workers*	
Chicago	39.4
Columbus	37.9
Denver	36.3
Houston	34.1
Jacksonville	29.6
Memphis	31.4
New Orleans	35.1
Norfolk-Portsmouth	34.3
Providence	45.1
Sale Lake City	33.7
Scranton	49.2
Weighted average	39.1

Table 3. Wages of Production Workers as a Percent of Value Added by Manufacture in 1947 for Standard Metropolitan Areas by Degree of Unionization

Proportion of Workers Covered by Union Agreements (by Standard Metropolitan Area)	Wages as a Percent of Value Added
20-49 *percent of plant workers*	
Atlanta	34.1
Oklahoma City	28.5
Worcester	47.3
Weighted average	39.6

SOURCE: *Census of Manufactures*, 1947, and *Monthly Labor Review*, January 1953.

Great Britain

The British experience is different in details but not in essentials from the American experience. The available data are, however, much more adequate for analytical purposes and, in a really usable form, cover a far longer period. The British history may be summarized as follows:

1. The share of wages (not employee compensation) has risen slightly since 1870, from a little under to a little over 40 per cent (see Table 4), but the proportion of wage earners among the gainfully employed has gone down substantially. As a result, the average income of wage earners has gained more than that of the rest of the population. This comparative gain has not been at the expense of profits in the long run but rather of rent and more recently of salaries. Some of the gain relative to salaries may be due to the rising skill level of manual workers and the declining skill level of salaried workers; also, occupational differentials in highly developed economies gradually shift to favor manual workers increasingly over salaried workers, largely because of the provision of better educational facilities which serve to augment greatly the supply of salaried workers.

The most substantial gains in the share of wages took place during World War I and World War II, when full employment raised wages but inflation cut the shares of rent and salaries. This rearrangement of shares was no doubt inevitable in the long run anyway, but wartime conditions facilitated its introduction into the British economy. Rent as a share fell from about one-sixth of national income in 1870 to one-twentieth in 1950. Its share was cut in half in World War I and halved again in World War II. Salaries weathered World War I much better, partly because it was followed by a depression; but their

Table 4. Great Britain: Wages and Wages and Salaries as Percent of Home-Produced National Income; Wages' Share for Constant Proportion of Wage Earners, 1870-1913 and 1924-1950

Year	Wages as Percent of National Income	Wages' Share for Constant Proportion of Wage Earners*	Wages and Salaries as Percent of National Income
1870	38.6	34.0	54.8
1871	39.1	34.5	54.2
1872	42.0	37.2	56.4
1873	42.6	37.8	55.9
1874	41.2	36.7	54.6
1875	42.4	37.8	56.5
1876	41.8	37.4	55.7
1877	41.5	37.2	55.5
1878	40.3	36.2	54.7
1879	41.3	37.2	56.5
1880	39.8	35.9	54.6
1881	39.6	35.8	54.5
1882	40.7	36.9	55.9
1883	40.0	36.4	55.4
1884	40.0	36.5	56.6
1885	39.8	36.4	57.2
1886	39.0	35.7	56.9
1887	40.2	36.9	58.5
1888	40.2	36.9	58.0
1889	41.5	38.2	58.9
1890	41.5	38.4	58.8
1891	41.7	38.6	59.6
1892	41.8	38.8	60.5
1893	42.7	39.8	62.3
1894	41.7	39.0	61.1
1895	40.6	38.0	59.7
1896	41.3	38.8	60.6
1897	40.7	38.3	59.7
1898	40.6	38.4	59.3
1899	40.4	38.3	58.7
1900	40.7	38.7	58.6
1901	41.1	39.1	59.8
1902	40.0	38.2	59.0
1903	40.8	39.2	60.4
1904	39.0	37.6	58.5
1905	38.3	37.1	57.5
1906	37.5	36.5	56.1
1907	38.2	37.3	56.4
1908	38.3	37.5	57.9

Table 4. Great Britain: Wages and Wages and Salaries as Percent of Home-Produced National Income; Wages' Share for Constant Proportion of Wage Earners, 1870-1913 and 1924-1950

Year	Wages as Percent of National Income	Wages' Share for Constant Proportion of Wage Earners*	Wages and Salaries as Percent of National Income
1909	37.8	37.2	57.3
1910	37.8	37.4	57.0
1911	37.8	37.5	56.7
1912	37.0	36.9	55.7
1913	36.6	36.6	55.1
1924	41.9	42.5	66.6
1925	41.8	42.5	66.1
1926	42.0	42.8	67.7
1927	41.3	42.1	65.7
1928	39.8	40.7	64.3
1929	40.1	41.0	65.2
1930	41.0	42.0	66.6
1931	41.7	42.8	69.1
1932	41.5	42.7	68.7
1933	40.7	41.9	67.6
1934	41.0	42.3	67.5
1935	40.3	41.6	66.5
1936	39.8	41.2	65.3
1937	39.3	40.7	64.1
1938	39.2	40.7	64.4
1939	38.3	....	62.3
1940	38.2	....	60.3
1941	38.3	....	59.8
1942	39.1	....	59.3
1943	39.3	....	59.4
1944	39.7	....	60.5
1945	39.3	....	61.3
1946	40.5	....	63.6
1947	40.8	....	63.2
1948	41.7	46.5†	64.5
1949	42.3	47.3†	65.8
1950	41.9	46.9†	65.3

*Proportion of wage earners to total occupied population for 1913 used as base. This column calculated from data in Phelps Brown and Hart but does not appear in article. The next column is likewise calculated from the data given but does not appear in the article.

†Based on provisional data on proportion of wage earners among gainfully employed.

SOURCE: E. H. Phelps Brown and P. E. Hart, "The Share of Wages in National Income," *Economic Journal*, June 1952, pp. 276-277.

relation to total wages paid dropped as a result of World War II conditions from about two-thirds in 1939 to under three-fifths in 1946 and subsequent postwar years. It may be expected, however, that over the course of time they will be restored, in part, to their earlier relationship, if there is no continued inflation. Even though the long-run tendency is against them and no depression occurs, steady, although not spectacular, adjustments may carry them back toward their earlier relationship to wages.[58]

2. The share of wages over the cycle has not varied much; sometimes it has gone up slightly and sometimes down slightly. In the depression of the early 1930s, it rose only very moderately. The relatively steep rise in labor's share in the United States during a depression may be due largely to the inclusion of salaried workers (who are separated out in the British statistics), whose rates are probably cut less and whose employment most certainly is. The wage-and-salary share has risen in Britain in depressions more than the wage share alone — for example, in the early 1890s, 1926, and 1931. One would expect that the wage share itself rose less in Britain than in the United States during the early 1930s, not only because the capital-to-labor ratio is lower there, but also because the amplitude of the fluctuation was not so great. Cyclical activity in Britain during that period neither started from so high a level nor fell so low as in the United States. Also, agriculture, with its wider fluctuations in income, is not as important in the British economy as in the American.

3. Unionism, according to the excellent study of Phelps Brown and Hart,[59] has forced the share of wages upward only when the unions have been aggressive and the employers at the same time faced a "hard" market, so that they could not escape easily and quickly through higher prices. Phelps Brown and Hart note that in the United States the market is more protected from foreign competition and thus more likely to be "soft," allowing employers to escape. Perhaps, also, British unions have been comparatively more aggressive historically (although they curbed their aggressiveness after World War II with a policy of wage restraint), particularly in times of hard markets. In the United States, strong trade unionism has existed usually only when markets have been soft and not always even then, as in the 1920s. The American employer may also have had a greater chance to evade wage advances through laborsaving innovations in what has been a more progressive economy. Hard markets are likely to be particularly hard for agricultural products; thus some of the gain for wage earners under such conditions has been at the expense of

58. These observations are based on data contained in Phelps Brown and Hart, *op. cit.*
59. *Ibid.*

agricultural producers, although labor's share has risen in times of hard markets even within the nonagricultural segment of the economy taken by itself.

Phelps Brown and Hart believe that once employers are squeezed between aggressive unions and hard markets, they tend to go along at the new and lower profit margins more or less indefinitely until some new adjustment takes effect. But the new "normal" has never yet become a permanent convention of the economy. "Home profits," which is a residual figure after taking rent, wages, and salaries out of national income, were about one-third of national income in the period before World War I; they dropped to one-fourth in the 1920s, and to one-fifth in the 1930s; but they rose again to one-third in the 1940s, which is the more remarkable since they include interest. The employers finally escaped after twenty years of "capture," caused more by the depression than by the unions. As we have seen, unions can catch the employer to a degree in the case of hard markets, which characterized the 1920s and 1930s in Great Britain; but he can escape again in soft markets, which prevailed in the 1940s.[60] Since full employment, in the absence of price controls, means generally soft markets, the new "normal" share for profits may become more or less permanent.

4. The share of wages remained constant at first and then rose somewhat in Britain during World War II, probably, in part, because of the earlier and more effective price control and the absence of formal wage controls. The salary share, however, was cut at the start, for wages and salaries taken together behaved very much as did employee compensation in the United States, falling early in the war and then rising again.

5. A substantial increase has taken place, as compared with the period before World War II, in the real income of wage earners, after direct taxes, relative to the real income of other elements in the population.[61] Social expenditures for food and health, however, have been largely offset by higher taxes on beer, tobacco, and other purchases, so that the wage earners have

60. Four situations are possible: (1) hard markets and hard unions; (2) hard markets and soft unions; (3) soft markets and hard unions; and (4) soft markets and soft unions. The share of wages tends to gain in the first case and the share of profits in the last, with the other two cases lying in between. The first case is illustrated by the period of "new unionism" starting in 1889; the second, by the period following the collapse of the union movement in 1879; the third, by the period after World War II; and the fourth, by the periods of 1903 to 1905, following the Taff-Vale decision, and 1926 to 1928, following the failure of the general strike.

61. See Dudley Seers, *The Levelling of Incomes since 1938* (Oxford: Blackwell, 1951); also *The Economist* (January 21, 1950). There may have been a slight reversal in this trend quite recently. See Dudley Seers, "Has the Distribution of Income Become More Unequal?" *Bulletin of the Oxford University Institute of Statistics* (February 1956).

made no net gain from these subsidies.[62] Cartter's careful study shows the net redistribution of income in Great Britain to have risen from 8.8 percent in 1937 to 13.1 percent in 1948-1949. During roughly the same period in the United States (1938-1939 to 1946-1947), the increase was from 5.4 percent of national income to 7.5 percent, a rate of increase quite comparable to that in Great Britain. The fiscal system was less effective in redistributing income in the United States than in Great Britain, but only because it bulks considerably smaller in comparison with total national income and not because it is less progressive.[63]

This British experience suggests three modifications of the conclusions drawn from the American record. First, wage earners may gain at the expense of salaried workers. Second, full employment reduces the share of wage earners much less than the share of all employees, and unions are particularly concerned with the share of wages. Third, the redistribution effect of governmental programs depends not only on how progressive they are but also on the share of national income channelled through government.

Selected Other Countries

Data on labor's share are available for a number of countries besides the United States and Great Britain, but they are usually either so inaccurate or cover so short a period, or both, that they are largely useless for our analysis.[64] Data for four countries, however, are set forth in Table 5. The cases of Australia and New Zealand show the effect on labor's share of an economy geared to the international market and exporting one or more commodities with highly unstable prices. In 1950-1951 the share of labor dropped drastically in both countries. The explanation is quite simple. The price of wool rose very rapidly on the world market as a result of the Korean War, and this greatly raised agricultural incomes and lowered labor's share. When the price of wool quickly dropped again, labor's share assumed its normal level. Agricultural prices generally are not so subject to violent change in the United States and Great Britain, nor is agriculture so prominent a sector of the economy. However, in the United States the labor share and agricultural share also tend to move in opposite directions. Labor's share gained at the expense of

62. Findley Weaver, "Taxation and Redistribution in the United Kingdom," *Review of Economics and Statistics* (August 1950).

63. Cartter, *op. cit.*, p. 84.

64. See *National Income Statistics of Various Countries, 1938-1948, (op. cit.)* for data on Belgium, Chile, Czechoslovakia, Finland, France, Netherlands, Norway, Peru, Puerto Rico, Southern Rhodesia, and Switzerland. See also Paul Jostock, "The Long-term Growth of National Income in Germany," in Simon Kuznets, editor, *Income and Wealth*, Series V (London: Bowes and Bowes, 1955).

agriculture's in the Great Depression and agriculture's share at the expense of labor early in World War II. The experience of Brazil (coffee), of Chile (copper), and of Malaya (tin and rubber) might be expected to follow the Australia-New Zealand pattern.

The behavior of labor's share in Canada follows the United States' pattern in a rather exaggerated fashion — a sharp rise in the Great Depression and a sharp decrease at the start of World War II. The greater importance of agriculture and mining in the economy helps explain this more drastic variation. The rise in labor's share in 1953 followed substantial wage increases, due in part

Table 5. Labor Income as a Share of National Income (in Various Years) for Australia, New Zealand, Canada, Russia

Years	Australia* Income as Percent of National Income	Year	Canada‡ Labor Income and Military Pay as Percent of National Income
1910-1911	56.8	1926	56.5
1915-1916	53.2	1931	72.2
1920-1921	57.2	1936	64.1
1923-1924	61.5	1941	60.3
1938-1939	60.1	1946	57.7
1945-1946	62.4	1951	57.1
1950-1951	48.8	1953	63.0
1952-1953	57.9		

Years	New Zealand† Salary and Wage Payments as Share of National Income Received	Year	U.S.S.R.§ Wages and Salaries as Share of National Income
1938-1939	57.4	1928	32.3
1943-1944	43.3	1937	36.3
1948-1949	54.1	1940	33.6
1950-1951	45.9	1944	32.7
1952-1953	53.5	1948	35.7

*J. T. Sutcliffe, *The National Dividend* (Melbourne: Melbourne University Press, 1926); and *Yearbook of Labor Statistics* (International Labor Office, 1954).

†*Monthly Abstract of Statistics*, Special Supplement, July 1953.

‡Emile Bouvier, *Le Revenu National au Canada,* (Montreal: Editions Ballarmin, 1952); and *Yearbook of Labor Statistics,* (International Labor Office, 1954).

§Oleg Hoeffding, *Soviet National Income and Product in 1928,* (New York: Columbia University Press, 1954); and Abram Bergson and Hans Heymann, Jr., *Soviet National Income and Product, 1940-1948* (New York, Columbia University Press, 1954).

to rapid industrial expansion and to more aggressive unionism, at a time of stable prices.

The Russian experience demonstrates the role of governmental policy under conditions of a massive concentration of power and a heavy commitment to national survival and industrialization. The level is, of course, quite low for an industrialized nation, and it did not rise significantly over a twenty-year period despite a great increase in the relative numbers of nonagricultural workers; the figures do not hold the industry mix constant. The reduction of labor's share in advance of and during Russia's involvement in World War II is quite noticeable. The statistics indicate what can be done by a ruthless government dedicated to forced-draft industrialization and development of military power. The level of investment in new plant and equipment has been so high largely because labor's share has been kept so low. This must be the greatest case of "exploitation," in the sense of denying the individual worker the just fruits of his toil, in the history of any industrialized nation. But even with all its power, the Russian state has not been able fully to control the size of labor's share, for in order to be able to meet their quotas managers have "pirated" labor or hoarded it by adjusting piece rates and in other ways.

A few additional observations can be drawn from the experience of these four countries: (1) a large foreign-trade component in national income based on the export of commodities with highly flexible prices can cause erratic fluctuations in labor's share; (2) the more substantial the agricultural sector of the economy, the more likely it is that labor's share will change substantially over the cycle; and (3) an all-powerful government can drastically reduce labor's share.

SUMMARY OF EXPERIENCE BY TYPE OF POLICY

We may now turn to a summary of this historical experience as related to the six types of union policy set forth earlier:

1. Pure and simple unionism, with its defensive policy of rigid money-wage rates during a depression, can raise labor's share under conditions of a hard market, and, perhaps, also where a metropolitan labor market is highly unionized but the commodity price level is largely set by national markets, *i.e.*, in what might be termed a "hard" area.

2. Wage-policy unionism has different consequences depending on the policy. There is no useful experience in evaluating the just-wage program, but almost certainly a policy of wage restraint can lower labor's share somewhat

and a policy of class shares can hold it steady or even raise it at least temporarily.

3. There is no trustworthy evidence on the effect of managerial unionism.

4. New Deal unionism reduces labor's share, but probably more in the short run than in the long run. It aids profits but hurts the rent and salary shares.

5. Labor-party unionism clearly increases labor's share of redistributed income, and the effectiveness of this policy depends not alone on the progressiveness of the resultant program but also on its size.

6. Direct-controls unionism enhances labor's share. When carried to the length of a fully planned economy, however, this governmental power can be used as well, and perhaps more likely, for the opposite purpose.

While labor's share may rise for other reasons, unions can only really catch profits in a depression, which they hardly want, or through price controls, which are usually deemed a quite unpleasant or even impossible method, or through governmental distribution, which carries them into an area of activity which the Webbs termed "legislative enactment" and which, as they pointed out, generally works better with a labor movement than with just labor unions; but a labor movement, with its labor party, may give up through wage restraint some of what it gains through redistribution policy. In addition to wage restraint, a policy of full employment can reduce labor's share, but both policies may be considered quite valuable or even indispensable for other reasons.

Labor's share, except in the more advanced types of policies (class shares, managerial unionism, labor-party unionism, and planned economy), is not approached as a "decisional" matter; no one decides that labor's share should be at one level or another. In all other cases, any effect on labor's share is more or less inadvertent. For labor's share to become a decisional matter, the unions or their political allies must have a great deal of decision-making power.

CONCLUSION

Samuel Butler once observed that "life is the art of drawing sufficient conclusions from insufficient premises." This is too often the task of the economist. He seeks answers to important questions which lend themselves to no sure response. So it is here. We have, however, ventured a reply to our question: Under what circumstances, if any, can trade unionism affect distributive shares and in what fashion? Part of the answer is that, under certain conditions, it can affect distributive shares. It can reduce labor's share through the furtherance of a policy of continuing full employment, particularly if combined with a policy of wage restraint, and perhaps also through the application of the standard rate. It can raise labor's share, in particular, through standard collective bargaining when employers cannot quickly escape; or through support of the application of effective price controls; or, in terms of "kept" income, through the encouragement of progressive taxation and subventions.

The other part of the answer is that, while it can raise labor's share, it cannot raise it by very much. In the United States, to date, the impact has been minimal. The power of trade unionism, to use Galbraith's terminology, has been apparently "countervailing" and not "original."[65] One can only speculate about what might have happened if this "countervailing" power had not developed; but the American worker, in its absence, certainly would not have been condemned to a share so grossly below what one might expect as are the poor South African workers, as reported in the previously noted study by Paul Douglas. In Great Britain, on the other hand, through what might be viewed as "original" political power, a significant redistribution has taken place.

Now it might be concluded that the union pursuit of the employer through collective bargaining is much ado about very little, that unions are relatively powerless institutions in a market which responds to other, more persuasive, forces. This may well be. However, this could not be known surely in advance, and it is worth knowing. Workers could not be expected to accept the broad allocation of income among distributive shares without having their organizations explore the possibilities of major shifts. The probing of the situation by the unions gives the workers a greater assurance of the equity, or at least the inevitability, of the distributional pattern. Thus the pursuit of the employer may be of worth even if he is never caught at all.

To the extent that distributive shares are affected at all substantially, this comes about permanently only from a significant shift of decision-making power away from the employer to the union or the government or to both. Boulding has written, as previously noted, that "distribution depends on decisions and mainly on the decisions of the capitalist." As more decisions are made by trade union leaders and government representatives, they too can affect distribution, but this requires that they enter a long way into the direction of economic processes at the plant or industry or national level. The

65. John Kenneth Galbraith, *American Capitalism* (Boston: Houghton Mifflin, 1952), p. 143.

avenues for escape by employers must be narrowed or closed if labor's share is to rise at the expense of profits. Knowledge of this fact may, of course, sharpen labor's desire to deepen its control, directly or indirectly, and management's desire to resist.

This brings us up against the problem of absolute shares. As we noted at the start, they may move in an opposite direction from relative shares. For example, in moving toward full employment, the absolute share of labor (whether in real or money terms) will rise with the expansion in the number of jobs; yet the relative share will fall. If the policy of the standard rate has any effect in lowering labor's share, it may, at the same time, by penalizing the inefficient and rewarding the efficient producer, raise the absolute share of labor.

Similarly, price controls or progressive taxes could so reduce efficiency and retard investment that the absolute share of labor in the long run would be lowered even though the relative share would be increased. It is the size of the absolute share which is the more important, even in the short run; consequently the significance of what is happening to relative shares can be understood only by reference to the much greater significance of the trend in the magnitude of absolute shares.

But functional shares, whether relative or absolute, may be a rather dated way of looking at distribution, at least in the United States — a hangover from the classical economists and the Socialists. In the days of Ricardo and Marx, there was a close correspondence between function and class, between the supply of labor and the worker, and between the supply of property and the capitalist. But today there is an increasing percentage of employee compensation in the top 5 percent of income recipients and more dividends in the lower 95 percent;[66] the president of the company may get a large share of his income in the form of employee compensation and the worker a significant share of his in the form of rent or interest. What does it mean to talk of labor's share when the president of the company is labor and the worker a small-scale capitalist? Also the clear-cut distinction between the managers and the managed is breaking down with the subdivision of managerial tasks and the great growth of clerical and technical employees. The painfully evident divergence between worker and capitalist is disappearing both in source and amount of income,[67] and in possession of authority. We stand a long way from a society

66. Kuznets, "Long-term Changes in the National Income of the United States since 1870," *op. cit.,* p. 150.
67. It would be interesting to examine how income distribution could have been equalized as much as it has been with so little effect on labor's share; or, put the other way, how labor's share

based on two sharply differentiated classes. Transfer payments through government are also much more important than they were at the time of Ricardo and Marx. It is therefore probably becoming much more important to measure and to discuss size distribution than share distribution; and this has the added advantage that it is less likely to lead to a class-conflict approach to income distribution organized around functional groups. From the standpoint of social peace, it is better to discuss the share of, say, the bottom 25 percent of income recipients than to deal in terms of the farmers' share or of labor's share.

Returning, however, despite these hesitations, to the concept of labor's relative share, we may ask again and finally: Which of the four theories given at the start is more nearly correct? The answer given here has been, in effect, the fourth — the "social-group" theory — within limits.[68] Labor can change the pattern of distributive shares by its economic and political efforts, but there are confines to what its efforts can accomplish. It can remold this sorry scheme of things only somewhat closer to its heart's desire; this is one of the great lessons of industrial society since the utopianism of a century ago and its Socialist aftermath.

---

could have remained so steady at the same time that it was possible to equalize personal incomes substantially in both the United States and Great Britain.

68. Or it might be put another way around, the third (marginal-productivity) theory — with exceptions.

The Impacts of Unions
on the Level of Wages

INFLATION AND INDUSTRIALIZATION have marched together for the past two centuries. Rising prices and growing industrial output have characterized much of the economic history of this period, with the notable exception of the second half of the nineteenth century. While they have marched together, they have not marched closely and evenly in step until the past few years. The alternations of war and peace and prosperity and depression have variously affected the course of both inflation and industrialization. The pace of both has been subject to great variations.

The past few years, since World War II, on the other hand, have been marked in Western Europe and North America by more nearly constant, rather than sporadic, inflation and industrialization. And, while a little less than a decade and a half constitutes a great deal less than an everlasting trend, a spectre is haunting Western capitalism— the spectre of constant inflation. Many, although not all, of the powers of society have been allied to exorcise this spectre — government officials and editorial writers, monetary authorities and economists, financiers and ministers — but it still exists.

It is a real spectre though it is not new and it need not make society tremble. It is a real spectre because constant inflation could become constantly greater inflation; because it redistributes income often in an inequitable fashion; and because policies to combat it may also combat progress.

Constant inflation presumably should have a constant source. Several new or relatively new developments have accompanied constant inflation and are, consequently, the most likely causes. One of these is the growth of the trade

Reprinted from *Wages, Prices, Profits and Productivity,* Background Essays for the Fifteenth American Assembly, Columbia University, June 1959. The author acknowledges the assistance of Marjorie Galenson in the preparation of this paper.

union movement and of its power over the wage-setting process. But it is not the only companion. Other companions have been governmental commitments to full employment, policies and practices leading to unbalanced budgets and low interest rates, rapid industrial expansion, new supply conditions in labor markets and new patterns of mobility and immobility, and new mechanisms for price control by private agencies; and several of these companions are closely related to each other.

The question here is the responsibility of one of these companions — the trade union — for constant inflation. This is not an easy question to answer, partly because of the intermingling of ideology and group self-interest with analysis in so much of the discussion, but particularly because with so many things happening it is almost impossible to state precisely the force of any one development by itself. For example, what would be the effect of the trade union if there were no industrial growth or if there were no administered prices to go along with administered wages? Consequently, reliance must be placed on individual judgments rather than any universally accepted analysis; and judgments have differed.

The Split Jury

The jury which has sat most constantly on this case has been composed of economists; and almost any conceivable verdict can be obtained by picking almost any conceivable economist.[1] To illustrate:

To *Lindblom*[2] the union is a "monopoly" and also a "body politic." As a body politic, under the urging of political pressures, it uses its monopoly power to force wages higher and higher. This leads to "unemployment or inflation" and, with government guarantee of full employment, to inflation. As a result, "unionism and the private enterprise system are incompatible."

To *Chamberlin*[3] the unions introduce a "monopoly element" into the labor market and, whether or not they try to maximize the wage bill, they do try to get "more" and this leads to "wage-push inflation." "Unions today do have too much economic power."

To *The Economist*[4] the real cost of trade unions is not so much the loss in productivity per man-hour they cause but rather that they turn full production

1. For a summary of the recent literature see George H. Hildebrand, "The Economic Effects of Unionism," in Neil W. Chamberlain, Frank C. Pierson, and Theresa Wolfson, editors, *A Decade of Industrial Relations Research* (New York: Harper, 1958).

2. Charles E. Lindblom, *Unions and Capitalism* (New Haven: Yale University Press, 1949).

3. Edward H. Chamberlin, "The Economic Analysis of Labor Union Power," in American Enterprise Association, *Labor Unions and Public Policy* (Washington, D.C., 1958).

4. August 2, 1958.

into full inflation; and to avoid the latter, the former must also be forgone. This is one of the great economic tragedies of our age and our type of society.

To *Hicks*[5] the "Labor Standard" has replaced the Gold Standard. Governments will adjust their policies to maintain full employment at whatever wage levels the unions choose to set; and price levels follow along. But the unions, or at least British unions, may not be so unreasonable that this "Labor Standard" is much more "dangerous" than other monetary systems.

To *Lerner*[6] the problem is not "wage-cost inflation" alone but "seller's inflation." For there is also "profit inflation" as well as "wage inflation," and it is very difficult and even impossible to untangle the two. Wherever there are administered prices and administered wages, and they seem to be nearly everywhere, "seller's inflation" is a possibility, and it must be dealt with as a unitary phenomenon.

To *Slichter*[7] the unions are only one of several causes of inflation, and the others include the reduced availability of new sources of labor and the policy of government; but they are a significant cause. He concludes that, between 1933 and 1953, unions pushed up the general wage level "at least 25 cents per hour and probably more." This is one-fifth of the total increase that occurred during that period.

To *Reynolds*[8] "collective bargaining does not have as much impact on the money-wage level as has sometimes been suggested. My judgment would be that between 1945 and 1955 the money-wage level rose little, if any, more than it would have risen under nonunion conditions."

To *Morton*[9] unions are a minor factor affecting inflation and may retard it as well as augment it: retard it in a boom period; increase it in certain industries, where government regulation relates prices to costs, like public utilities and railroads.

To *Friedman*[10] unions have both a "rigidity effect" and "upward-pressing

5. J. R. Hicks, "Economic Foundations of Wage Policy," *Economic Journal* (September 1955).

6. Abba P. Lerner, "Inflationary Depression and the Regulation of Administered Prices," United States Joint Economic Committee, *The Relationship of Prices to Economic Stability and Growth* (March 31, 1958).

7. Sumner H. Slichter, "Do the Wage-Fixing Arrangements in the American Labor Market Have an Inflationary Bias?" *American Economic Review* (May 1954).

8. Lloyd G. Reynolds, "The General Level of Wages," in George W. Taylor and Frank C. Pierson, editors, *New Concepts in Wage Determination* (New York: McGraw-Hill, 1957), pp. 255-256.

9. Walter A. Morton, "Trade Unionism, Full Employment and Inflation," *American Economic Review* (March 1950).

10. Milton Friedman, "Some Comments on the Significance of Labor Unions for Economic Policy," in David M. Wright, editor, *Impact of the Union* (New York: Harcourt, Brace, 1951).

effect." The former holds down wage levels in a period of expansion; the latter forces them up in a period of stability. The two largely offset each other; but, of the two, the rigidity effect may be the more important under recent circumstances.

To *Boulding*[11] it is a certainty "that the main effect of unionism is to hold down money/wages and to prevent them from rising faster than they otherwise would . . . Unions are the opiate of the people under capitalism. That is why you have got to have them."

From the destroyer of "private enterprise" to the "opiate of the people," from the source of disastrous inflation to a bulwark of price stability, from a powerful monopoly to a minor or even negative force — the judgments vary. Economics is not yet a science; but economists are certainly free thinkers.

As a very part-time economist, I should like to suggest that all of them are right and all of them are wrong. All of them are right to the extent that they suggest that some kinds of unions could have the suggested effects under some kinds of circumstances. All of them are wrong, to the extent they suggest (and some of them do not) that their conclusions are the universal rule. The only universal rule is that there are all kinds of unions operating under all kinds of circumstances and they can have all kinds of effects. But it should also be added that kinds and circumstances and effects can be related — at least to a certain degree. Truth is more likely to emerge from studying the impacts of the unions, than "the impact of the union."

TYPES, CIRCUMSTANCES AND IMPACTS

Types

When talking about unions, it is helpful to specify the kind of union one is talking about. In terms of their approaches to price stability, unions can be broadly divided into the following general types:

Agent of the State — The "agent of the state" union, as in Russia or China, is the willing tool of the national administration. It serves its policies. It has no policies of its own. It is a weapon of social discipline, and the only variation of which it is capable is in the degree of its effectiveness.

Partner in Social Control — Some unions serve as "partners in social control." They may be formal partners, as they have been in Holland, assuming joint public responsibility for the economic welfare of the nation; or they may be informal partners, as they have been in Germany, almost equally

11. See Kenneth E. Boulding's comments in "Selections from the Discussion of Friedman's Paper," in *ibid.*, p. 245.

committed with the government to reasonably full employment and reasonable price stability at the same time. In Britain and in the Scandinavian countries, the unions have served as such informal partners when Labor or Social Democratic parties were in power. Here again there can be degrees of effectiveness as "social partner."

Sectional Bargainer — The union, as "sectional bargainer," is concerned not with the national impacts of its actions but with the consequences for its members and for its industry or segment of an industry. Its responsibility is relatively narrowly defined. The United States and Canada are representative of this type of unionism. The "sectional bargainer" union may be found in two major phases — (a) a state of excitement and (b) a state of normality. A state of excitement is most likely to exist in a new union, a union subject to the challenge of a rival union or a union undergoing internal political upheaval; and bargaining is likely to be much more aggressive in a state of excitement than in a state of normality.

Class Bargainer — The union, as "class bargainer," endeavors to get a "fair share," which usually means a larger share, of the national income for labor as a whole. It is usually matched by other "class bargainers," as in France, who seek "fair shares" for agricultural producers, the commercial classes, the civil servants, and so forth; and the total of these "shares" is almost certain to add up to more than the national output of goods and services. The "class bargainer" union usually has or develops a class ideology.

Enemy of the System — The "enemy of the system" union is devoted to the destruction of the surrounding economic and political structure. Among its techniques are the sabotage of production and the encouragement of excessive consumption aspirations. Such unions have been really effective only when a society is in the process of disintegration.

These above types suggest more uniformity and stability than is the actuality. Some societies have mixtures at any one moment of time — as in France with Communist, Socialist and Catholic unions. In some societies, the union movement shifts from one "type" or policy to another. The "agent of the state" union will remain an "agent of the state" so long as the state needs an agent. But the "social partner" union may be a partner only when the nation faces an emergency or when a government it favors is in power and then turn to a "sectional" or "class" approach under other circumstances. The "enemy of the system" union may in non-revolutionary periods follow a "class bargainer" policy instead of open full-scale opposition, or even be a particularly belligerent "sectional bargainer."

Each of these types has its own most natural habitat — the "agent of the state" union in an authoritarian society; the "social partner" union in a "social democratic" context; the "sectional bargainer" in a free enterprise system; the "class bargainer" in a semi-class or semi-feudal society; and the "enemy of the system" union in the latter type of society in the course of its decay. A society does not just conjure up the kind of unionism it would like to have after looking at the different models theoretically available; some kinds fit some societies and not others.

But we are concerned here not with the ultimate cause of a certain type of unionism, but with its impact on inflation. In general, unions — if they may all truly be called unions — will make a contribution to economic stability in the following descending order:

> Agent of the state
> Partner in social control
> Sectional bargainer
> Class bargainer
> Enemy of the system

The merest glance at this list indicates that a society usually cannot pick its type of unionism on the basis alone of its impact on stability; and that its effect on the price level cannot be the only proper test of the desirability of a union movement.

Theoretically, however, it might be expected that unions, from the top of the list to the bottom, would vary from strong supporters of stability to effective agents of instability.

Circumstances and Impacts

Unions, of whatever type, operate within an environment, and their potential impacts on the general level of money wages may be almost as much related to the environment as to their type.[12] Among the environmental situations with which we shall treat are those relating to the policies of other institutions (government and employers), to employment conditions, and to labor market conditions.

The standard for comparison will be "what would otherwise have happened" had there been no union; and this nobody really knows. The standard will not be the absolute increase in money wages; for unions may sometimes

12. We are discussing here only the impact on the general level of money wages and not the impact on prices. That depends also on changes in the level of productivity and in labor's share of income. Also we are discussing the economic impact of the unions within a given environment and not their political or economic impact in their efforts to change the surrounding environment.

do most when they seem to do the least, and do least when they seem to do the most. For example, in a depression a union may hold up wages which would otherwise go down and we can say they "raised the level"; while in a boom period they may belatedly negotiate a substantial wage increase which would have come earlier under nonunion conditions through the operation of market forces, and we can say they "reduced the level."

We shall consider first the policies of other institutions. Guaranteed full employment places the unions in an advantageous position, and two types of unions — "enemy of the system" and "class bargainer" — are in a particularly good position to take advantage of it. Administered prices by employers create a special opportunity for the "sectional bargainer" union, for administered wages can be passed on through administered prices and turn up in administered inflation.[13] With pattern bargaining, high settlements in an area of "administered prices" are likely to be imitated in other areas and thus spread the high "key" settlement. When the government is fearful of strikes and enters the collective bargaining arena to settle disputes, this again creates a favorable environmental situation for each of the three types of unions just mentioned. However, were the government to undertake a critical public review of wage settlements, this would have the opposite effect, and the "sectional bargainer" and particularly the "social partner" unions would be sensitive to such review. Government wage controls create an unfavorable condition for union impact on the general level of money wages and especially for the "social partner" of the union; the "agent of the state" union is, of course, always subject to wage controls.

In terms of employment conditions, unions probably have the greatest upward impact on money wages in a depression, when their attachment to past levels and the lags inherent in collectively bargained wages work toward stability. Next, in the downswing, particularly the early phases, they may not only be able to hold wage levels but actually increase them, contrary to "normal" tendencies. In a period of stable full employment, union pressure may well keep wages rising at some "standard" rate, say five percent a year, when under other circumstances they would have risen more slowly. In an upswing, particularly its later stages, and in "overly full" employment, however, unions with their term agreements and formal approaches may cause a lag behind the adjustments which would otherwise occur. A general rule might be: the smaller the wage adjustment, the greater the true impact of the union; and the greater the wage increase, the lesser the real impact.

13. Also, administered prices can create profit margins which lure the unions to make higher wage demands.

Labor market conditions may also relate to union impact. In a period of rapid accessions to the labor force — women, migrants from rural areas, young people — the unions can protect wages from the depressing effects. But when a labor force has become immobile, due to pensions or seniority rules or excessively specialized training or for other reasons, the union may reduce the upward impact on wages of this immobility. In the absence of unions, employers would tend to respond to individual scarcity situations with selective adjustments; and the impacts of these would spread. Unions, with their more formal wage relationships, tend to dampen this tendency and force employers to make other adjustments than the bidding up of individual classes of skills. This may possibly serve to lower, somewhat, the general level of money wages.

Putting together the variety of types of unions and the variety of environmental settings results in a variety of potential effects. Unions raise the general level of money wages greatly; or perhaps only a little. Unions reduce the general level of money wages substantially; or perhaps only a little. Or perhaps they have no effect at all. It all depends. And it all depends on type and circumstance, as the summary table suggests (see Table 1).

Table 1. Factors Relating to Union Impact on General Level of Money Wages

	Type of Union	Policies of Other Institutions	Employment Conditions	Labor Market Conditions
↑ Raise level	"Enemy of the system"	"Guaranteed" full employment	Depression	
				New recruits
	"Class bargainer"		Downswing	
		Administered prices		
	"Sectional bargainer"		Stable full employment	
(As compared with what would otherwise prevail)	a. State of excitement	Government settlements to avoid strikes		
	b. State of normality		Upswing	
		Government review of wage settlements	"Overly full" employment	Immobile labor force
	"Partners in social control"			
Reduce level	"Agent of the state"	Government wage control		
↓				

THE VARIETY OF EXPERIENCE

Experience is different from experiment. There have been no conscious experiments, and in the nature of the case there cannot be, through which a determination could be made with accuracy of the impact of the union on the general level of money wages. There is only experience; and the knowable reality from this experience is little more than conjecture. To speak with full assurance in this area is to speak from prejudice or from ignorance or both. Yet some things can be said.

Possible Tests

There are at least four ways in which one might try to test the impact of the union.

1. *How have union wages risen as compared to nonunion?* One might find here the true impact of the union not only on interindustry and inter-occupational differentials but also on the general level of money/wages.

But union and nonunion wages are not in water-tight compartments and what happens to one set of wages may affect the other. If it were found that union wages went up only as fast as nonunion wages, this might mean the unions had no impact; however, it might only mean that nonunion wages were playing "follow-the-leader" and thus that the unions were having an even greater effect on the general level of money wages. Also, if union wages were found to be going up faster, this might imply the unions did have an impact; but it might only reflect the fact that the wages of unionized manual workers, under the impact of broadly available educational opportunities and the breakdown of class lines, were rising faster than those of nonunionized white collar workers who had come into relatively greater supply — the important comparison might be manual and non-manual, not union and non-union.

2. *How has recent history, when strong unions existed, compared with earlier history when there were fewer unions?* Here again it might be discovered how the introduction of unionism has affected the course of the general level of money wages.

But the statistics, on any really comparable basis, do not go very far back. And if they did, it would still be true that more has happened in the course of intervening events than the rise of a union movement. Even adjusting for the amount of unemployment, there is still the question of what effect the expectation of generally lower rates of unemployment would have had on the behavior of employers in any event. Also, since employers, whenever they can, tend to share their profits one way or another with their workers, what would have been the effect of administered prices even without administered wages? And what has been the consequence of the drying up of the old sources of cheap labor on the general level of money wages?

3. *How has labor's share of national income behaved?* If there is evidence that the unions have really "squeezed" profits below their "normal" levels, then it might be said the unions were pushing wages up against profits and thus against prices.

But labor's share is one of the mysteries of economic analysis. And it is also affected by other developments than union pressure alone. There may be implications to be drawn from the analysis but little or no proof.

4. *How has experience varied from one country to another?* If one country has had a different course of money/wage levels from another, this different course might be related to the presence or absence of unions, or the different types of unionism; and we might find our answer.

But each country varies from the other in more ways than the presence or absence of unions, or the nature of union policy. Also, each type of union policy, as we have noted, is so related to its surrounding environment that it is difficult to say what is the real cause of a different behavior of money wages — the type of union or the type of economy.

With all their imperfections, these are four possible tests and their application to the actual course of events should give us some indications of how much and under what circumstances unions have had an impact on the general level of money wages.

Actual Tests

The application of actual or presumed facts to our problem is fraught with a number of perils, some of which have been mentioned earlier. However, their application may indicate a reasonable range of answers to our questions.

The United States — (1) The various studies which have been made of the course of union and nonunion wages offer no clear conclusions. Their results depend, to a substantial extent, on the dates taken for the studies and the definitions used. It may be fair to conclude, nevertheless, that, except for periods of active new unionism (as 1936-1937) and for situations with a closed shop (building trades), there is little evidence of a definite upward push by unions on wages.[14]

14. For summaries and comment on the literature see Lloyd G. Reynolds, "The Impact of Collective Bargaining on the Wage Structure in the United States," in John T. Dunlop, editor, *The Theory of Wage Determination* (London: Macmillan, 1957), and also the author's contribution to *The Theory of Wage Determination*, "Wage Relationships — The Comparative Impact of Market and Power Forces."

(2) The history of wage movements in the United States provides some additional evidence. Real compensation per man-hour dropped less from 1931 to 1932 (less than 2 percent) when unions had strong influence in a few industries than from 1893 to 1894 (3 percent) or 1920 to 1921 (3 percent).[15] Compensation in the 1931 to 1932 period held steadier, as compared with consumer prices, than in the two earlier periods, possibly, in part, because of union influence.[16]

Money wages held much steadier in 1944 to 1945 than in 1917 to 1918. In 1944 to 1945, wage controls were in effect by government as against 1917 to 1918, when there was great freedom in wage adjustments. But it should also be noted that the unions in 1944 to 1945 accepted and even cooperated in the imposition of wage controls, and also that the contractual mechanisms which had grown up since 1917 to 1918 helped make it possible to exercise control over the great mass of wage rates that comprise our national wage structure.

In 1936 to 1937, with new and rival unionism, money wages and real wages jumped much more rapidly than one would normally expect in a period marked with as much unemployment as then existed.

Taking two longer periods, 1900 to 1910 and 1947 to 1957, both eras of quite sustained growth, it is noticeable that money wages rose faster than productivity in both periods. From 1900 to 1910, wages rose by one-third and productivity by one-fourth; from 1947 to 1957, by one-half and by one-third. It would appear that there may be an inflationary tendency, with wages rising faster than productivity, in a period of sustained growth under both largely nonunion and largely union conditions. However, the excess gains of wages over productivity were somewhat greater in the second period and this may be due, in part, to unionism. Wages rose roughly one-third faster than productivity in the earlier period and one-half faster in the later period.

At a productivity rate of increase of 2.5 percent a year and assuming that price rises reflect the comparative changes in wages and productivity (in other words, that there is no change in labor's share of national income), the price impact of the greater comparative wage increase would be about one-half of one percent a year.[17] But it should be remembered that in the period 1947 to

15. For the basic statistics for this and the immediately succeeding comments, see Albert Rees, "Patterns of Wages, Prices, and Productivity," in Fifteenth American Assembly, *Wages, Prices, Profits and Productivity* (Columbia University: June 1959), Table 1, pp. 15-16.

16. For other evidence on the increasing rigidity of wages in business contractions, see Daniel Creamer, *Behavior of Wage Rates During Business Cycles* (New York: National Bureau of Economic Research, 1950).

17. 2.5 plus one-third equals 3.33; 2.5 plus one-half equals 3.75; the difference between 3.33 and 3.75 is 0.42.

1957, as compared with 1900 to 1910, there was much less of a labor reservoir of foreign immigrants, rural migrants and women, that administered prices were more widely prevalent, that government had created the expectation of continuing full employment and thus less risk for the employer who raised wage rates, and that there was the Korean War. Consequently, unionism, by itself, cannot be held responsible for the full one-half of one percent a year.

Several years ago Garbarino concluded, on the basis of a study of the period 1899 to 1929, that, under nonunion conditions, money wages and productivity kept pace with each other with unemployment rates of around 5 to 6 percent.[18] Most recent experience with unemployment rates above 5 percent has shown money/wage rates rising faster than long-term productivity rates. In 1958, with unemployment at nearly 7 percent, hourly rates in manufacturing went up about 3.5 percent over 1957, as against the 2.5 percent which might be considered "normal" (the long-term rate of increase in productivity), but then productivity seems to have risen faster than normal also. However it should be noted that wage rates rose only about two-thirds as fast in the second half of 1958 as in the second half of 1957.

(3) Labor's share of national income has tended to be quite constant in the long run after adjusting for changes in the proportion of wage earners and in the interindustry mix. But there have been occasions when the profit share has been "squeezed" and the wage share increased, perhaps partly due to union pressure on wages. These have been periods of depression (1931 to 1934 and 1938), periods when prices were held by price controls or the slower movement of administered prices in an inflationary period (1944 to 1947) and, most interestingly, a period of sustained full employment without substantial inflation, as in 1954-1957.[19]

Perhaps it could then be said that wages were really "pushing" on profits and thus on prices under these three circumstances. When there is no change in the profit share, it is harder to say who or what is "pushing" or "pulling"; and, when the profit share is rising, it would seem to indicate a "pull" rather than a "push." "Wage inflation," or wage pressure on the price level without

---

18. Joseph W. Garbarino, "Unionism and the General Wage Level," *American Economic Review*, December 1950. For comment on the relationship of changes in employment and changes in wages, 1947-57, see Otto Eckstein, "Inflation, the Wage-Price Spiral and Economic Growth," in *Relationship of Prices to Economic Stability and Growth, op. cit.*

19. For a review of the literature, see Clark Kerr, "Labor's Income Share and the Labor Movement," in Taylor and Pierson, *New Concepts in Wage Determination, op. cit.* See also Richard and Nancy Ruggles, "Prices, Costs, Demand, and Output in the United States, 1947-1957," in *Relationship of Prices to Economic Stability and Growth, op. cit.*

inflation, would seem most likely to have occurred when labor's share had risen above "normal."

Great Britain — (1) A recent study in Great Britain, by Phillips,[20] relating wage increases to volume of unemployment, as Garbarino has done for the United States, shows some interesting parallels and variations. Working with three periods, 1861 to 1913, 1913 to 1948, and 1948 to 1957, the first marked by relatively weak and the latter two by relatively strong unionization, Phillips found a very close correspondence between the related behavior of money wages and unemployment. The 1913 to 1948 period particularly followed the expectations based on the 1861 to 1913 period with only one major exception. Money wages went up faster in the years 1935 to 1937, a time of active union revival after the depression and also of rising food prices, than the general relation of money wage changes to the volume of unemployment would suggest. Taking the years 1948 to 1957, the "wage restraint" period of Trades Union Congress policy showed a lower than "normal" wage advance, but the years immediately following the end of the policy were noted for an unusually rapid increase, although they were also years of a rapid rise in import prices. As compared with the United States, lower levels of unemployment were found to be associated with the same wage behavior. For example, wages and productivity have seemed to march hand in hand with 2.5 percent unemployment in Great Britain rather than 5 percent in the United States.

(2) British experience also shows the importance of the divergence between actual rates and nominal rates — the rates paid in fact and those provided for by collective agreements and other formal documents. This divergence, or "wage drift," varies from one situation to another, but it was particularly great during periods of wage restraint, World War II and 1948 to 1950.[21] Actual rates drifted away from control through local action of employers and unions.

(3) The history of labor's share in Great Britain suggests no different general conclusions than does the history for the United States. Wages have squeezed profits when product markets were "hard" but not when they were "soft."[22]

20. A. W. Phillips, "The Relation between Unemployment and the Rate of Change of Money Wage Rates in the United Kingdom, 1861-1957," *Economica* (November 1958).

21. H. A. Turner, "Wages, Industry Rates, Workplace Rates and the Wage-Drift," *Manchester School of Economics and Social Studies* (May 1956). See also B. C. Roberts, "Trade-Union Behavior and Wage Determination in Great Britain," in Dunlop, *The Theory of Wage Determination, op. cit.*

22. See E. H. Phelps Brown and P. E. Hart, "The Share of Wages in National Income," *Economic Journal* (June 1952).

Western Europe — A review of postwar experience in selected Western European countries, including, for the sake of comparisons, the United Kingdom and the United States, is instructive (see Table 2). France, with its "class bargainer" approach and the type of economy associated with it, has witnessed the greatest increase in the general level of money wages in manufacturing. Italy, however, with a somewhat similar approach, has had a relatively small increase. This emphasizes the point that other things are happening to an economy aside from union action. In Italy, over this period, unemployment has averaged 9 percent, while it has been at quite low (but unmeasured) levels in France. Norway, Sweden, and the United Kingdom have all undertaken "responsible" wage policies during part of the postwar period, and when responsibility was most in practice, up to 1950 and the Korean War, wage increases may have been slowed down a bit; but their records are not much different from that of the United States, where no such policy was in effect. In fact it was in Sweden during this early postwar period that the term "wage drift" was invented.[23]

Holland and Germany have had stronger policies of wage restraint in the postwar period, for the sake of the restoration of their economies, but wages have gone up only somewhat less than in Norway and the United Kingdom, and more than in Italy. In Germany, wage restraint was particularly in force

Table 2. Indices of Hourly Money Earnings in Manufacturing
in Selected Countries, 1946-57

	1946	1947	1948	1949	1950	1951	1952	1953	1954	1955	1956	1957
					(1950 = 100)							
France	37	53	81	91	100	128	148	152	162	174	187	202
Italy	—	71	94	99	100	110	115	118	122	129	138	—
Norway	79	87	92	94	100	114	127	133	140	148	159	169
Sweden	74	85	93	96	100	121	144	150	156	168	183	—
United Kingdom	79	87	93	96	100	110	118	125	132	143	155	165
Germany	70	73	82	94	100	113	122	127	130	139	152	166
Holland	81	87	92	92	100	108	110	113	132	136	150	—
United States	74	84	92	95	100	108	114	120	123	130	135	141

SOURCES: *International Labor Review, Statistical Supplements;* and United Nations, *Statistical Yearbooks.*

23. For an early use of the term, see Swedish Confederation of Trade Unions, *Trade Unions and Full Employment* (Stockholm: 1953).

from 1949 (after currency reform) to 1955 with some apparent effect, but this was also a period of great absorption of refugees into the economy. In Germany, with wage restraint by the unions, a "wage drift" began to show up in pronounced form by 1954 particularly in the metal-working industries of North Rhine-Westphalia. And it might be noted that a "wage drift" above contract rates becomes increasingly embarrassing to unions and undermines a wage restraint policy.

Finally, the United States, without wage restraint and with a sectional bargaining approach, has demonstrated a comparatively high degree of wage stability, as Table 2 shows.

Russia — Russian statistics on a comparable basis are not readily available. However, some comparisons can be made. From 1948 to 1952 money wages are said to have risen 8 percent in Russia as against 24 percent in the United States;[24] and from 1953 to 1956 the figures are 7 percent and 12.5 percent.[25] Also, it should be noted, productivity, as an offsetting force, has been rising faster in Russia (though it is at a much lower absolute level) than in the United States. But even in Russia, with an "agent of the state" union movement and authoritarian control, money wages have been rising; and piece rates have been particularly resistant to controls.

OBSERVATIONS

The record, inadequate as it is, does permit some conclusions.

1. The "class bargainer" (or "enemy of the state") union movement, in the type of economy in which it develops, may well add to inflationary wage pressures.

2. The "agent of the state" union movement, in the type of system where it finds its natural habitat, is compatible with a comparatively slow rate of increase in the general level of money wages.

3. The "partner in social control" union movement may join in keeping wage increases somewhat below their normal levels for relatively short periods of time. But the "wage drift" and the internal pressures which develop under a wage-restraint policy make it unlikely that this effect will be long lasting. The results of wage restraint have been modest at best, although useful under the circumstances where they have been applied.

24. Janet G. Chapman, "Real Wages in the Soviet Union, 1928-1952," *Review of Economics and Statistics* (May 1954).

25. United Nations, *World Economic Survey, 1957* (New York: 1958).

4. The "sectional bargainer" union movement presents a more mixed situation. When in a state of excitement, as around 1937 in both the United States and Great Britain, it may push wages up beyond "normal." In a depression, it may well hold them somewhat higher than they otherwise would be. At the plateau of a period of prosperity or in the early downswing, it may continue rates of wage increases experienced in the recent and more favorable past into the new situation. But in the upswing or a period of demand inflation, it may, as Rees has argued for the basic steel industry in the United States from 1945 to 1948, actually retard wage increases.[26]

Generally, the "sectional bargainer" union movement will probably lead to a steadier advance of the general wage level, neither as fast nor as slow as might otherwise occur. Also, through pattern bargaining, wage increases may be spread more uniformly and more broadly throughout the economy than under nonunion conditions. Thus the total long-term effect is likely to be moderately inflationary; for the postwar period in the United States, a net impact (after allowance for the influence of other factors) on the price level of somewhat less than one-half of one percent as compared with "normal" or nonunion conditions.

The real question might be why, as compared with the havoc it might wreak as seen by Lindblom, it has had so little effect? The answer must lie, in part, in the general reasonableness of the unions and their leaders in the context of the type of society in which they evolve; and thus in the nature of this kind of union as an institution.

In fact, two reversals of common statements come closer to illuminating the truth. Instead of asking why unions have so much inflationary effect, it might be more pertinent to ask why, as "monopolies," they have so little. Instead of accusing unions of an effective upward pressure on wage levels in a period of expansion and inflation, it would be more pertinent to make the accusation about them in periods of depression and deflation. The wrong question is asked; and the wrong accusation made.

5. The volume of unemployment is closely related to changes in the general level of money wages. In general, the level of employment must be considered the most important single factor. Its influence is over and beyond that of the trade union.

6. A period of expansion in a capitalist economy is normally a period of some inflation. Expansion and inflation are common traveling companions, whether a union movement travels with them or not.

26. Albert Rees, "Postwar Wage Determination in the Basic Steel Industry," *American Economic Review* (June 1951).

7. Government wage controls can have an effect in holding down wage levels, perhaps more in the short run than in the long run, except in an authoritarian economy like the Russian.

8. Administered prices most certainly can make it easier to pass on administered wages without affecting profits.

The type of union and the character of the environment together determine the impact of the union on the general level of money wages. To view either one alone is to view but part of the scene. Taken together, in Western capitalism, the combination has probably become a somewhat more inflationary one than in earlier times. The union has often become more insensitive to the pressure of unemployment because of seniority rules protecting its older members and unemployment compensation for its newer members; but offsetting this has been the general growth in reasonableness and a sense of responsibility. The major changes are in the environment which is more permissive — full or more nearly full employment, the spread of administered prices and the drying up of pools of readily available labor.

If the unions secure greater wage increases than in the past, it is not so much because they want "more, more and more," which they do, but rather because it is easier to get "more, more and more." The environment is more conducive, rather than the unions more insatiable. The source of the trouble, to the extent there is trouble, is more that there is less pressure on the wage fixers than that the wage fixers are less sensitive to it; is more that there is less power in the environment and less that there is more power in the unions.

If remedies are to be sought, they would seem to lie, first, in strengthening the pressure of the environment toward stability and, second, in making unions more sensitive to that pressure.

REMEDIES

In considering remedies, in the context of the American economy, it may be well to contemplate these four points:

1. Some inflation may be a normal cost of growth.

2. The United States has had a comparatively good record on inflation in the postwar years.

3. Some mild inflationary pressures are inherent in the kind of unionism which evolves out of American society.

4. Certain "solutions" are not compatible with the character of this society
— "agent of the state" unionism, or even "social partner" unionism, or
permanent unemployment in excess (and possibly substantially in excess) of 6 percent, or, probably, permanent wage (and price) controls by
government.

Within the context of our society, however, several things may be possible:

1. To begin with, it would not be wise to guarantee full employment,
particularly sector by sector, regardless of wage and price behavior. There
should be some costs to irresponsible actions.

2. Next, administered prices are not fully socially accepted and their more
unreasonable excesses should be discouraged by all reasonably available
means, including antitrust action and freer trade.

3. Industries of great pattern-setting importance or otherwise crucial to the
economy should be made subject to *ex post* and *ad hoc* impartial fact-finding
review of their wage bargains (and price policies) to acquaint the public with
their consequences. This is one way to mobilize public opinion to bring
pressure for stability on the private wage and price fixers.

4. The government should not enter industrial disputes with a "peace-at-
any-price" approach except in a true national emergency.

5. All available action should be taken to increase the total supply of labor,
for example, by providing part-time jobs for housewives and older persons,
and to improve the mobility and adaptability of the labor force.

6. Unions should be open to all qualified workers. At the same time, rival
unionism and great internal union instability should be avoided since the
conflicts arising from them usually find their solution, in part, in wage
increases.

These are reasonable means and only reasonable results should be expected
from them. We are living in an age marked by uneven but rapid economic
growth, by a commitment to more-or-less full employment, by an exhaustion
of earlier available sources of new accessions to the industrial labor force, by
the great advancement of group initiative and group control over the
economy, by the substantial freedom of individuals and groups from the
imposed power of the state, and by mild inflation. Remedies for the last
phenomenon must be seen in the light of the other phenomena which surround
it. All things are not possible in all situations; and one thing which is not
possible in this situation is full price stability and the wage levels which are
consistent with it. The most successful case of wage control in an industrialized nation in the postwar period is also the most repugnant.

Wage Relationships — The Comparative Impact of Market and Power Forces

O<small>NE MODERN VERSION</small> of Adam Smith's famous observation (Book I, Chapter 8) might read: "Workmen are always in constant and uniform combination to raise the wages of labor above their actual rate."[1] Now this version would not be so true as Smith's about "masters" (as Smith himself noted), for their combination is less the "natural state of things." Workers, being more numerous and diverse, have less of a community of interest than masters and a greater need for formal bonds. These formal bonds, over the past century, have been supplied by labor unions in many trades and industries in those industrialized nations which are organized into pluralistic systems, and a major purpose of most of these unions has been to modify "market forces" by group decisions and organized power in setting wages.

A classic question in economics has been the extent to which this organized power has exerted its will over market forces. Some economists in recent times have judged the impact to be substantial[2] and even potentially disastrous;[3] others that it has been minimal or even virtually non-existent.[4] This

Reprinted from John T. Dunlop, editor, *The Theory of Wage Determination* (London: Macmillan, 1957).

1. Melvin K. Bers, Graduate Research Economist, Institute of Industrial Relations, University of California (Berkeley), was helpful in the development of this paper.

2. See, for example, Arthur M. Ross, *Trade Union Wage Policy* (Berkeley and Los Angeles: University of California Press, 1948), Chapter VI.

3. See, for example, Henry C. Simons, *Economic Policy for a Free Society* (Chicago: University of Chicago Press, 1948), p. 48 ff. and pp. 121-159; and Charles E. Lindblom, *Unions and Capitalism* (New Haven: Yale University Press, 1949).

4. See, for example, John T. Dunlop, Preface to *Wage Determination Under Trade Unions* (New York: Augustus M. Kelley, 1950), and his review of Lindblom's *Unions and Capitalism* in

chapter concludes, on our current state of knowledge, that no categorical answer can be given because unions have had varying degrees of impact on the five different types of differentials into which a nation's wage structure can be divided: (1) interpersonal, (2) interfirm, (3) interarea, (4) interoccupational, and (5) interindustry. The impact on the first two, it will be found, has been considerably greater than on the last two. We must then turn to an explanation of why the impact should vary so substantially; why there should be such a shift in the incidence of trade union power from one set of differentials to the other. The answer given is that a sharp downward plunge in motivation and an equally sharp upward surge of the power requisite to effect alterations in differentials occur as we move from the first three (and particularly the first two) to the last two.

The customary dichotomy of "market" and "power" forces lacks full precision. "Power forces" often work through the market as well as on price directly; and "market forces" themselves contain elements of power to the extent that persons or groups can and do directly influence the demand or supply side of the market. It might be more useful to speak of "individual responses" on the one hand and "institutional behavior" on the other.[5]

"Individual responses" are the expressed preferences of individual workers and unorganized employers in response to the environmental context in which they find themselves. While in totality their actions affect the result, their individual actions taken separately do not succeed in manipulating their environment. "Institutional behavior" is comprised of the policies and practices of groups of individuals in the dominant corporation, the employers' association, the trade union, or government.

When a market responds largely to the first type of action, it might be designated as a "natural" market, however imperfect it may be aside from collusive action itself; and when to the latter, an "institutional" market. Most actual markets will, of course, have characteristics of both of these types; and then some evaluation is in order of the comparative influence of these two

---

American Economic Review, June 1950. See also Milton Friedman, "Some Comments on the Significance of Labor Unions for Economic Policy," in David M. Wright, editor, *The Impact of the Union* (New York: Harcourt, Brace, 1951), p. 215; and Kenneth E. Boulding, *The Organizational Revolution* (New York: Harper & Brothers, 1953), p. 94.

5. Lester divides the forces at work into "competitive," "impeditive," and "anticompetitive." The first category includes competitive drives among companies but also among unions. The second includes the standard "frictions" of lack of knowledge, personal attachments, and so forth. The third includes a miscellany of practices such as pattern following by an employer and restriction of entrance to the trade by the union. Richard A. Lester, "A Range Theory of Wage Differentials," *Industrial and Labor Relations Review* (July 1952).

types of forces. Our question is then, to rephrase it, to what extent have wage differentials been affected by the entry of "institutional behavior," in addition to "individual responses," into the supply side of the labor market; and how may the varying extents be explained.

I. WAGE DIFFERENTIALS

Interpersonal Differentials

Institutional policy quite universally regularizes, when it does not eliminate, differentials among persons doing like work in the same plant — with one sometimes quite major exception. The differentials may be regularized by a piece-rate system, or by seniority increments, or by a formal method of merit recognition, if a flat rate for the work is not introduced. The union contract, the company job evaluation system, and government wage regulations all have the effect of banishing the purely personalized rate. Such personalized rates, reflecting the merit of the worker or the prejudices of the individual foreman or employer, are quite normal in the "natural market."

"Job selling" by foremen, wage discrimination by supervisors, and the secrecy of individual arrangements have given way to formalized rates for the job. The movement towards centralization of hiring by employers and the experience in several countries with governmental wage controls have aided this change, as well as trade union pressure. While statistical proof of union influence is largely lacking, at least one study in the United States indicates a close association between unionization and formal wage structures.[6] "Individual rates" are most common in those areas where unionism is not influential. Formalized wage structures were shown, also, to be closely associated with increasing size of the enterprise.

The one important exception is differentials between men and women doing the same work. These have been largely eradicated in the United States, particularly during the 1940s, but they are still customary in some other countries, such as Germany.[7] The degree of elimination may well relate

6. Otto Hollberg, "Wage Formalization in Major Labor Markets, 1951-1952," *Monthly Labor Review* (January 1953). See also comments in Richard A. Lester, *Company Wage Policies* (Princeton: Industrial Relations Section, Princeton University, 1948). In Denmark, however, some unions permit a system of "elastic" wages allowing for both individual and collective bargaining. See Walter Galenson, *The Danish System of Labor Relations* (Cambridge: Harvard University Press, 1952), p. 146.

7. They have, however, been regularized there in the sense of being made subject to contractual arrangements. See Clark Kerr, "Collective Bargaining in Postwar Germany," *Industrial and Labor Relations Review* (April 1952). In Germany and some other countries there are also established differentials for youths below the regular rates.

more to the general social status of women in the community than to union influence.

Interfirm Differentials

In the absence of unionism, the labor market normally displays a wide dispersion of wage rates for the same type of work among firms operating in the same product and labor markets.[8] Lester, on the basis of data for some sixty-odd cities in the United States, generalized that the high wage plant normally paid 50 percent more in rates, occupation by occupation, than the low wage plant.[9] The findings of Reynolds in his New Haven survey are consistent with this, although they relate to more than a single industry at a time.[10] The Lester data were taken from a period of turbulent wage movements during the second World War. But numerous wage surveys covering less unusual times demonstrate a normal dispersion, odd stragglers aside, of at least 25 percent from top to bottom.

While union policy does not always aim at full uniformity,[11] unionization is closely associated with increased uniformity. Two recent studies in the United States have noted this. One found a considerably lower dispersion of rates in the more highly unionized of two metropolitan areas.[12] The other concluded that within a single metropolitan area, namely Los Angeles, unions reduced and even abolished interfirm differentials in the industries they organized.[13]

This phenomenon is not limited to the United States. It occurs wherever unions are able to organize all the firms producing the same product in the same labor market area. In fact, it may be more manifest in other nations where the "master agreement" has met less employer resistance than in the United States. In some countries, as Germany, the "master agreement" is even extended by law to cover all employers. The achievement of this un-

8. See Lloyd G. Reynolds, "Wage Differences in Local Labor Markets," *American Economic Review* (June 1946), for an early emphasis on the significance of these differentials.

9. Richard A. Lester, "Wage Diversity and its Theoretical Implications," *Review of Economic Statistics* (August 1946).

10. Lloyd G. Reynolds, *The Structure of Labor Markets* (New York: Harper, 1951), Chapter 7.

11. See, for example, George Seltzer, "Pattern Bargaining and the United Steelworkers," *Journal of Political Economy* (August 1951). The cases to which Seltzer refers, however, are usually in different labor markets and partially differentiated product markets.

12. John L. Dana, *Wage and Salary Relationships in Los Angeles and San Francisco Metropolitan Areas – January 1952*, U. S. Department of Labor, Bureau of Labor Statistics (June 1953).

13. Frank C. Pierson, *Community Wage Patterns* (Berkeley and Los Angeles: University of California Press, 1953), p. 152.

iformity is an essential part of the union program of "taking wages out of competition." It flows also from the activities of employers' associations and the application of government minimum wage regulations.

Interarea Differentials

What are usually called "geographical differentials" are, in part, interindustry differentials in the sense that the industry mix varies from one area to another and for this reason alone the general average of wages would be expected to vary; and, in part, real geographical differentials in the sense that different rates are paid for the same type of work. The term "interarea differentials" is used here in the second sense of relative rates of pay for the same kind of work in the same industry but in different geographical areas. Here union policy has generally favored the reduction or elimination of differentials, particularly where there is an interarea product market.

In the United States, interarea differentials have been narrowing gradually, both overall and industry by industry.[14] This is probably largely due, as Reynolds notes,[15] to the increased dispersion of manufacturing industry around the nation and the reduced importance in some areas of a large localized supply of agricultural workers. In some industries with nation-wide markets, such as steel, automobiles, and meat packing, union agreements have brought a reduction or elimination of geographical differentials. In other industries with local product markets, like building trades and service trades, no similar result has been attempted or achieved.[16]

Oxnam describes a similar narrowing of differentials among the several states in Australia,[17] but does not relate this to union policy. In Germany, where highly formalized wage structures are subject to well-developed collective arrangements, interarea differentials (including urban-rural differentials) have either been eliminated or substantially narrowed and precisely prescribed.[18]

14. See Joseph W. Bloch, "Trends in Regional Wage Differentials in Manufacturing, 1907-1947," *Monthly Labor Review* (April 1948); Richard A. Lester, "Southern Wage Differentials: Developments, Analysis, and Implications," *Southern Economic Journal* (April 1947); Harry Ober and Carrie Glasser, "Regional Wage Differentials," *Monthly Labor Review*, (October 1946); and Pierson, *op. cit.*

15. Lloyd G. Reynolds, *Labor Economics and Labor Relations* (New York: Prentice-Hall, 1949), p. 332.

16. On a less spectacular level, unions have often raised wage rates for the same type of work in the same industry in labor market areas adjacent to the metropolitan districts where they first establish their organizational strength.

17. D. W. Oxnam, "Wages in Australia, 1913-14 to 1949-50," paper given before the Australian and New Zealand Association for the Advancement of Science, Brisbane (May 1951).

18. See Gerhard Bry, "Trends and Cycles in German Wages," *Proceedings of the Sixth*

Evidence about the impact of unionism on interarea differentials is less conclusive than for interpersonal and interfirm differentials. Union pressure generally is directed towards the narrowing and regularization of such differentials, but the overall effect certainly has been substantially less than in the case of the first two types of differentials.

Interoccupational Differentials

Occupational wage differentials have undergone a most significant narrowing in recent decades in the United States, Western Europe, Australia, and New Zealand, with one very important exception.[19] In the United States the margin for skilled workers has dropped over the past half-century from over two to under one and one-half times that of unskilled workers.[20] Since 1880, in the United Kingdom, the differential has also been cut in half, although it was not so great to begin with.[21] An almost equal reduction has occurred in Australia over the period since 1914.[22] In more recent periods, reductions have occurred in Austria, France, Germany, Italy, Netherlands, Norway, and Switzerland,[23] and also New Zealand.[24] The great exception, and a most interesting one, is Denmark (another possible one — although the evidence is less complete — is Belgium).[25] In Denmark the differential did not narrow

---

Annual Meeting, Industrial Relations Research Association, 1953 (Madison: 1954); Kerr, *op. cit.*

19. What has happened to "compensation" differentials (wages and "fringe benefits" taken together) is a different and more complex question, and an increasingly important one with the growth of "fringe benefits." The "compensation structure" is a more meaningful, if less tractable, concept than the "wage structure." On the currently available evidence it is almost foolhardy to estimate whether occupational "compensation" differentials are or are not behaving similarly to occupational wage differentials.

20. See Harry Ober, "Occupational Wage Differentials, 1907 to 1947," *Monthly Labor Review* (August 1948); and Toivo P. Kanninen, "Occupational Wage Relationships in Manufacturing, 1952-1953," *Monthly Labor Review* (November 1953).

21. See K. G. J. C. Knowles and D. J. Robertson, "Differences between the Wages of Skilled and Unskilled Workers, 1880-1950," *Bulletin of the Oxford University Institute of Statistics* (April 1951); and Jean A. Flexner, "Great Britain: Wage Trends and Policies, 1938-1947," *Monthly Labor Review* (September 1947).

22. See D. W. Oxnam, "The Relation of Unskilled to Skilled Wage Rates in Australia," *Economic Record* (June 1950); also Oxnam, "Some Economic and Social Consequences of the Australian System of Wage Regulation," paper given before the Australian Institute of Political Science, Sydney (July 1952). See also Sir Douglas Copland, "The Full-Employment Economy with Special Reference to Wages Policy," *Oxford Economic Papers* (October 1953).

23. "Changes in the Structure of Wages in European Countries," *Economic Bulletin for Europe*, Second Quarter (1950). On France, see also H. I. Cowan, "France: Wage Trends and Wage Policies, 1938-1947," *Monthly Labor Review* (August 1947).

24. International Labor Conference, *Wages: (a) General Report* (Geneva: International Labor Office, 1948), p. 95.

25. *Ibid.*, p. 96; Galenson, *op. cit.*, p. 179; and "Changes in the Structure of Wages in European Countries," *op. cit.*

over the period 1938-1948, nor from 1920 to 1949, although it did decrease substantially from 1914 to 1920.

This narrowing of occupational differentials has been an important massive and highly controversial social phenomenon. Turner views trade unions as a substantial causative force, as unions follow the policy of flat increases, as they seek to recruit to their ranks the unskilled, as they endeavor to avoid undue incentives to employers to break down skills and use machines, and as they pursue egalitarian policies to minimize internal strife.[26] Knowles and Robertson, however, see unions as having a relatively minor and largely unpurposeful effect as they support, for other reasons, flat increases and the simplification of wage structures.[27] Reynolds[28] and Samuels[29] consider the impact of unionism a temporary one as organization first spreads from the ranks of the skilled to the unskilled. Fisher[30] and Clark[31] find the explanation for reduced differentials lying almost entirely outside unionism in the spread of public education and its effect on the relative supply of skilled and unskilled workers. Among other explanatory factors have been listed the impact of full employment in raising the demand for the unskilled,[32] of mass technology which reduces the level of skill, of egalitarian tendencies generally, which are expressed in many ways, including state minimum wage regulations.

As to the weight to be given these several factors, there is little incontrovertible evidence. My own view, which will be set forth below, is that the impact of unionism is seldom the major factor involved; and that, in the long run, its influence is generally in the direction of maintaining, not reducing, occupational differentials.

Interindustry Differentials

Clay wrote that there was once a "system" of wages in Great Britain.[33] It might almost be said that there is a "system" of wages which operates in a

26. H. A. Turner, "Trade Unions, Differentials and the Levelling of Wages," *Manchester School of Economic and Social Studies* (September 1952).

27. Knowles and Robertson, *op. cit.*

28. Reynolds, *Labor Economics and Labor Relations, op. cit.*, p. 331.

29. Norman J. Samuels, "Patterns of Wage Variations in the United States, 1951-1952," *Personnel* (September 1952).

30. Allen G. B. Fisher, "Education and Relative Wage Rates," *International Labor Review* (June 1932).

31. Colin Clark, *Conditions of Economic Progress*, 2nd edition (London: Macmillan, 1951), pp. 458-483.

32. For a dissent from the customary view that occupational differentials widen significantly in depression, see Philip W. Bell, "Cyclical Variations and Trend in Occupational Wage Differentials in American Industry since 1914," *Review of Economics and Statistics* (November 1951).

33. Henry Clay, *The Problem of Industrial Relations* (London: Macmillan, 1929), p. 74. See comment in J. R. Hicks, *Theory of Wages* (London: Macmillan, 1935), p. 80.

recognizable form in a number of the industrialized nations — not an entirely uniform and constant system, it is true, but one according to which the several series of interrelationships are roughly similar. It is the variations, not the likenesses, which call for explanation. Lebergott found interindustry rankings, with a few major exceptions, to be much the same in six countries (United States, Canada, United Kingdom, Sweden, Switzerland, Russia);[34] and the Economic Commission for Europe study shows somewhat the same pattern.

A second general observation about interindustry differentials is that they are narrowing (in percentage terms) over time. Oxnam has demonstrated this for Australia,[35] Woytinsky for the United States,[36] and the Economic Commission for Europe study for Western European countries.[37]

Has unionism had an appreciable effect on these differentials?[38] Douglas thought it had not as between unionized and unorganized industries.[39] Ross at first challenged the observation of Douglas, but later agreed that, except in the case of new organizations (a point made also by Douglas), unionism has had little appreciable effect in the United States.[40] Essentially similar results to those of Douglas have been obtained by Garbarino, Rees (for the steel industry only), and Dunlop,[41] all also having analyzed American experience.

34. Stanley Lebergott, "Wage Structures," *Review of Economic Statistics* (November 1947).

35. Oxnam, *Wages in Australia . . . op. cit.;* see also Copland, *op. cit.*

36. W. S. Woytinsky and Associates, *Employment and Wages in the United States* (New York: The Twentieth Century Fund, 1953), pp. 507-509.

37. On Great Britain see also Flexner, *op. cit.*, and on Germany see also Bry, *op. cit.*

38. Actually there are two questions: (1) Has unionism been a source of comparative advantage to workers in unionized as contrasted with unorganized industries?; and (2) Has unionism changed the pattern of relationships among organized industries? The literature is almost solely concerned with the first of these two questions, partly because it has been the more debated point and partly because statistical evidence is more easily procured.

39. Paul H. Douglas, *Real Wages in the United States, 1890-1926* (Cambridge: Houghton-Mifflin Co., 1930), pp. 562-564.

40. Arthur M. Ross, "The Influence of Unionism upon Earnings," *Quarterly Journal of Economics* (February 1948); Arthur M. Ross and William Goldner, "Forces Affecting the Interindustry Wage Structure," *Quarterly Journal of Economics* (May 1950); Sumner H. Slichter considers this not yet fully proved: "Do the Wage-Fixing Arrangements in the American Labor Market have an Inflationary Bias?" *American Economic Review* (May 1954).

41. Joseph W. Garbarino, "A Theory of Interindustry Wage Structure Variation," *Quarterly Journal of Economics* (May 1950); Albert Rees, "Postwar Wage Determination in the Basic Steel Industry," *American Economic Review* (June 1951); John T. Dunlop, "Productivity and the Wage Structure," in Lloyd A. Metzler and others, *Income, Employment and Public Policy: Essays in Honor of Alvin H. Hansen* (New York: Norton, 1948). For a contrary view to Dunlop's (and Garbarino's) that a relationship exists between productivity differentials and interindustry wage differentials see Frederic Myers and Roger L. Bowlby, "The Interindustry Wage Structure and Productivity," *Industrial and Labor Relations Review,* (October 1953). Myers and Bowlby conclude that though such a relationship existed at one time, it has not in more recent periods. See also reply by Garbarino and rejoinder by Myers and Bowlby in the July 1954 issue of the *Industrial and Labor Relations Review.* See also Slichter, "Do the Wage-Fixing Arrangements . . .," *op. cit.*

Levinson essentially agrees, except that unions may hold up the level of wages in an organized industry in a depression when wages in unorganized industries are not faring as well[42] Sobotka, further, reached the judgment, after a study of the building trades, that craft unions may be a source of wage advantage to their members.[43] The three likely exceptions to the general rule that unionism has not been a source of wage advantage to workers in organized industries, then, are (1) new and thus aggressive unions (which may also be offsetting the prior monopsony power of employers); (2) unions in periods of substantial unemployment; and (3) craft unions with their restrictions on entrance to the trade.[44]

It is evident from this review of the literature and the available data (both of which relate more to the United States than to any other country) that the impact of unionism on wage differentials has not been uniform:

1. Personal differentials have largely been eliminated or brought under formal control in unionized sectors.

2. Firm differentials within the same product and labor markets have generally either been much reduced or wiped out.

3. Area differentials have been occasionally eradicated and frequently diminished, particularly where there is interarea product competition.

4. Occupational differentials have been much reduced, but there is little evidence that this is a result of union policies.

5. Industrial differentials have also been reduced, but have apparently not been greatly affected to date by unionism.

For the first two types of differentials the impact of unionism has been

42. Harold M. Levinson, *Unionism, Wage Trends, and Income Distribution, 1914-1947* (Ann Arbor: University of Michigan Press, 1951). See also Daniel Creamer, *Behavior of Wage Rates during Business Cycles* (New York: National Bureau of Economic Research, Inc., 1950). It should be noted, however, that wages in the construction and bituminous coal industries, once well organized, fell unusually far during the Great Depression in the United States. See Leo Wolman, "Wages in the United States since 1914," *Proceedings of the Sixth Annual Meeting, Industrial Relations Research Association, 1953* (Madison, 1954), pp. 40-46. The basic forces at work over the course of the cycle are probably what is happening to employment but particularly to prices from one industry to another, with very little reference to unionism. See Dunlop, *Wage Determination . . . op. cit.,* Chapter 7.

43. Stephen P. Sobotka, "Union Influence on Wages: The Construction Industry," *Journal of Political Economy* (April 1953). The construction industry in the United States, however, may be a special case. It stands somewhat higher in interindustry wage rankings than in several other industrialized countries on which information is available. See "Changes in the Structure of Wages in European Countries," *op. cit.*

44. This may be a finding largely related to American experience; and the factor in American experience which may most count for the special results of craft unions is their comparatively heavy emphasis on the closed shop and the partially closed union. In Denmark also, where the craft unions have close historical connections with the craft guilds of earlier times and their tight apprenticeship systems, they apparently have also been a source of differential advantage.

substantial; for the third (at least in the limited situation of interarea product competition), significant; and for the last two, minor.

The intrusion of unionism into labor markets does not present a clear-cut case of "market forces" versus "power." For the power of the union is sometimes ranged alongside the market forces and they work in the same direction. Also, the opposition to union power may not be market forces, or market forces alone, but the power of the employers or the government. We turn now to a general explanation of why union power had been more effective in transforming some aspects of the wage structure than others.

II. THE SELECTIVE IMPACT OF UNION POWER

Is there any general explanation of why union power has achieved so much rearrangement of some wage differentials and so little of others? The explanation offered here is that the impact of unionism on wage differentials has varied (1) directly with the strength of the motivation of workers and their organizations to exercise control, and (2) inversely with the amount of power requisite to effect such changes.[45] It would, of course, be surprising if this were not true. What, then, can we say about intensity of motivation and the magnitude of power requirements in each of the five types of differentials which constitute wage structures?

As we shall see, where motivation is most intense, power requirements tend to be least in magnitude. Were it otherwise, trade unionism would have to endure much greater frustrations; for what it could best achieve it would least want, and what it most wanted it could least achieve.

The Intensity of Motivation

The idea of the "just wage" has never died, although the meaning of justice in this regard is perhaps less clear than it once was and there are many more wage rates to be adjusted one to the other. The "just wage," it is often remarked, is largely an ethical rather than an "economic" concept. But one purpose of organization, as in the Middle Ages, is to make it both. Now this is not to suggest that this is the only purpose of organization in the labor market, nor that the customary appeals to justice are always sincere, but only that the achievement of justice, however defined, is a real and major goal. This is particularly true in the early days of unionism. The drive to end discrimination, to get "equal pay for equal work," to obtain the "standard rate," is behind the original organization of many, if not most unions."

45. It should be noted that power and motivation are not entirely independent factors. The degree of power required may affect motivation; and the intensity of motivation may affect the amount of power available.

This drive for the "standard rate" is particularly insistent at the level of interpersonal relationships in the same work place. Workers are physically close to each other and comparisons are easy to make. It is less forceful but still quite intense as it relates to interfirm differentials in the same labor and product markets. Here the incentive comes not from one worker eyeing another at the next bench, but from workers in low-wage plants thinking they are worth as much as those in high-wage plants and the workers in high-wage plants feeling uneasy about unfair competition possibly threatening their jobs. Considerations of equity for the one group and security for the other move hand in hand. The motivation is more a result of thought processes and less one of glandular response than in the case of interpersonal differentials for the same jobs in the same plant.

When we move out of the same labor market area, the strength of the inducements to uniformity subsides. Knowledge of the total situation is less personal and less complete, comparisons are made on a less individual basis, similarities are less striking — the cost of living may be different, market conditions diverse, and so forth. Particularly when produce market competition is less intense or even non-existent, the interest in uniformity is much reduced, although the equity of interarea relationships may still be a factor; but the coercion of wage competition is absent.

When we turn to occupational differentials, the character of the situation changes quickly. Dissimilarity is now the essence of the problem. Degrees of skill, of responsibility, of unpleasantness must be estimated and weighed, and this takes intimate knowledge and careful judgment. Equal pay for equal work gives way to equivalent pay for equivalent work; and there is little agreement on what is equivalent.[46] While workers may generally agree that there should be the same pay for the same type of work in the same plant, labor market area, or industry, motives become mixed within the work force in regard to appropriate occupational differentials. The unskilled wish equality or some close approximation; the skilled want to be differentiated on the grounds of their skill.

Thus, almost no unions in the United States have a general policy on skill differentials, as Bell notes,[47] although nearly all have definite policies, however imperfectly enforced, on interpersonal, interfirm, and interarea differentials. It is often said that craft unions favor the skilled workers and industrial

46. As skills become more diversified with the progressive division of labor, particularly at the semiskilled level, comparisons become increasingly difficult to make. See Robert L. Raimon, "The Indeterminateness of Wages of Semiskilled Workers," *Industrial and Labor Relations Review* (January 1953).

47. Bell, *op. cit.*

unions the unskilled. But this is certainly not universally true. Industrial unions must be sensitive to potential revolts of their skilled members, and skilled workers quite normally are influential in an industrial union beyond their relative numbers. The differential between skilled and unskilled workers in the construction industry (organized on a craft basis) in the United States has narrowed over recent decades much more than in the steel and somewhat more than in the automobile industries (organized on an industrial basis).[48] In the steel industry, a formal contractual job evaluation plan sets differentials, and in the automobile industry special adjustments for skilled workers have been made to offset the effect of flat cents-per-hour increases. Industrial unions too, with very few exceptions, are hierarchical organizations.

In Denmark the skilled workers, after a time, resisted further reductions in their differentials, although they had once supported a "solidaristic" wage policy.[49] In Norway and Sweden, the unions have maintained a policy of improving "the relative position of traditionally low-paid groups of workers";[50] but the statistical evidence does not indicate that this policy has had the effect of narrowing differentials more rapidly than was occurring in other comparable nations. In the Netherlands, the Foundation of Labor (a joint employer-union organization) has endeavored to maintain (not reduce) occupational differentials in the postwar period at their approximate pre-war relationship, but apparently without substantial success, for the wages of the unskilled have in fact risen much faster than those of the skilled.[51]

Unions may, however, unwittingly have had two effects on occupational differentials. First, the organization of the skilled may originally have spread differentials a bit and the subsequent organization of the unskilled narrowed them again;[52] and, second, across-the-board and pattern increases, particularly as applied by industrial unions, may have reduced them somewhat. But

48. Harry M. Douty, "Union Impact on Wage Structures," *Proceedings of the Sixth Annual Meeting, Industrial Relations Research Association, 1953* (Madison, 1954), pp. 61-76. Bronfenbrenner notes: "Robert E. Strain, 'Occupational Wage Differences: Determinants and Recent Trends,' unpublished Ph.D. dissertation, Wisconsin, 1953, . . . finds that skill differentials have narrowed as rapidly and to approximately the same extent in industries organized on a craft basis, or largely unorganized, as in industries where industrial or 'mass unionism' has been important." Martin Bronfenbrenner, "The Incidence of Collective Bargaining," *American Economic Review* (May 1954), p. 302.

49. Galenson, *op. cit.*, pp. 180 and 186. The laborers have a strong and separate union of their own.

50. "Changes in the Structure of Wages in European Countries," *op. cit.*; on Norway see also J. Inman, "Post-War Wages Policy in Norway," *Bulletin of the Oxford University Institute of Statistics* (July and August, 1950).

51. See P. S. Pels, "The Development of Wages Policy in the Netherlands," *Bulletin of the Oxford University Institute of Statistics* (July and August 1950).

52. See Sobotka, *op. cit.*

neither of these results generally has grown out of deliberate policy on occupational differentials *per se*.

Interindustry differentials confront unions with much the same problems of unclear motivation as do occupational differentials. New elements of dissimilarity enter in — different families of occupations, working conditions, product market arrangements, among many others. Here, also, the workers in the highly paid industries wish normally to maintain their relative superiority, however much those in the low-paid industries might wish to narrow the gap.

Thus, in summary, the unions speak with a distinct although decreasingly loud voice on interpersonal, interfirm, and interarea differentials; but in halting tones, if at all, on interoccupational and interindustry differentials. A great drop in strong and unambiguous motivation takes place as they move from "equal work" to "unequal work" situations. The "equal work" orbits are generally the most coercive.[53]

The Variation in Power Requirements

Group motivation to be effective must be expressed through the exercise of power, and this power may need to be exercised not only against "market forces" but also against the opposing power of organized employers or the state, and even against discordant factions internal to the union institution. Thus the power required to effect changes is not just the opposite of the strength of market forces.

At the level of interpersonal differentials the individual employer usually stands alone — and confused. On the one hand, he may like his prerogatives, including the right to reward those who gain his favor or whose work merits it; but, on the other, a formal wage schedule reduces grumbling, is easier to administer (particularly for the large firm) than a person-by-person rate system, and has some obvious ethical appeal to it. Moreover the employer, who is likely to pay more attention to personal differences in productivity than the union, can make some relatively easy adjustments to adapt to the "standard rate" by eliminating the poorer workers or by forcing them to raise their output.

Interfirm differentials are more difficult for a union to assault. Now it must organize similar firms in the entire labor market area. But the union is not without aid and comfort from the enemy. High-wage firms may accept or

---

53. This is not to suggest that political forces, like rival unionism, may not be of preeminent importance in individual situations. For an interesting discussion of such "orbits of coercive comparison" see Arthur M. Ross, "The Dynamics of Wage Determination Under Collective Bargaining," *American Economic Review* (December 1947).

even welcome union action to raise the wages of their low-wage competitors; and uniformity of wage levels is often a necessary prerequisite to uniformity of price in the product market — with or without union support. Moreover, uniformity of wage levels can be as essential to the internal harmony of an employers' association as it is to a union; and tactics in bargaining with an aggressive union dictate removal of the "whipsaw" approach of first raising the low-wage firms in the name of equality and then the high-wage firms in the name of preserving historical positions.

Once uniformity is achieved there is normally little to destroy it, at least at the "official" level. Effective rates, however, under conditions which favor the "wage slide" (to be noted below) may depart, even substantially, from the "official" level. The low-wage firms have either been eliminated or have become efficient enough to survive at the standard rate; and unions do not normally press for wage rates which would force unionized employers to cease operations or break with the union. A standard rate, too, and perhaps one at much the same level, might well be the result of market forces if the labor market were more perfect than it usually is. Unionization, instead of "distorting" the interfirm wage structure, may act instead as a substitute for greater labor mobility.

The reduction or removal of interarea differentials demands an additional accumulation of power by the union. To be effective the union now must organize beyond a single labor market area, even on a national basis. In a large country, such as the United States, this may be quite difficult, and peculiarly so if there are regions which are especially hard to organize, like the southern states; and, in the absence of complete organization, plants may be able to run away from one area to another. Also, the union must either negotiate contracts on an interarea basis, or be able to establish effective policy for its local branches negotiating area by area. Moreover, employers, if product market competition is confined to local labor markets, will normally uniformly oppose, even strenuously, the standardization of wages among different product markets. Also, wage differentials tend to be more widely dispersed over a series of labor markets than in a single market, and thus less tractable to standardization. But the state may enter here and range its power alongside that of the unions through minimum wage laws or laws on the extension of contracts; and wherever labor mobility is increasing and product markets are widening, "market forces" are also conducing toward uniformity.

As far as occupational differentials are concerned, something can be done about them quite readily at the plant or industry level, and in totality this can have some effect. This can be done consciously or almost inadvertently, as

Knowles and Robertson comment,[54] through policies of the flat increase and simplification of the wage structure which are intended to serve other purposes. But occupational differentials, given the occupational diversity among industries, are, in part, also interindustry differentials. Consequently, in order to control occupational differentials generally, as interpersonal and interplant and sometimes interarea differentials are controlled, would require a national union federation with considerable influence over its constituent elements. What is requisite is a single policy covering the building trades, the textile industry, and many others, all at the same time. Perhaps only in Norway and Sweden do the union federations have this much power, if they wish to use it.

A great social force is at work on occupational differentials. This force is, the changing nature of supply and demand in the labor market as industrialization progresses. The absolute demand for skilled workers is certainly larger in an advanced industrial state than in one entering industrialization; but the need for skilled workers is much more critical in a nation undergoing industrialization, and particularly in one where the process is rapid.[55] In percentage terms, the additional need for skilled men is much reduced as industrial societies mature. In Russia, for example, in 1928, skill differentials about matched those in the United States a quarter of a century earlier, and then widened as the first five-year plan speeded up the process of industrialization.[56] Concurrently with the smaller percentage increase in demand for skilled workers, as industrialization becomes well established, the supply of skilled workers greatly increases through the effects of public education,[57] and perhaps also a concomitant reduction of class or social discrimination, while the supply of unskilled workers dries up as agriculture becomes a smaller segment of the economy, as income and educational levels rise, and as the trade and service industries draw also on the ranks of the unskilled.

54. Knowles and Robertson, *op. cit.*

55. The general theorem advanced here is: The lesser the degree and the greater the rate of industrialization, the wider will be the occupational differentials and the greater the premium for skill; and the greater the degree and the lesser the rate of industrialization, the narrower will be the occupational differentials and the greater the premium for distasteful work.

56. Abram Bergson, *The Structure of Soviet Wages* (Cambridge: Harvard University Press, 1946). Bendix also notes a widening of skill differentials in the Russian Zone of Germany with the Russian emphasis on industrial expansion there after the second World War. See Reinhard Bendix, *Work and Authority in Industry* (New York: Wiley, 1956). Skill differentials are rather greater in the United States than one would normally expect for a country at its stage of development. Large-scale immigration undoubtedly held down the level for unskilled workers for a substantial time and the differentials are particularly wide in the South, which is industrially underdeveloped.

57. See Fisher, *op. cit.*, and Clark, *op. cit.* See also comment of Tinbergen on relation of educational opportunities to skill differentials. Jan Tinbergen, "Some Remarks on the Distribution of Labour Incomes," *International Economic Papers, No. 1* (New York: Macmillan, 1951).

We may, in fact, be witnessing currently a great social phenomenon of occupational differentials being turned partly on their heads. Already they have been greatly narrowed and in some cases reversed, as, for example, when common laborers come to receive more than skilled office workers.[58] If this is the social process at work, then we should not be surprised that the narrowing of differentials has not caused a shortage of skilled workers, for their comparative plenitude has, in fact, caused the narrowing.[59] Adam Smith's first wage-determining factor (Book I, Chapter 10), "the agreeableness or disagreeableness of the employments themselves" may come to be a most influential one once the "difficulty and expense of learning them" have been much more equalized; and, it should be noted, unskilled work is quite frequently more disagreeable than skilled.

Unions have probably not had much effect on the historical narrowing of occupational differentials. These differentials began narrowing in some countries before unions were effective and have narrowed since that time in non-union sectors as well as organized sectors. The government has not been at a uniform rate but has gone in spurts, particularly during the first and second World Wars. Once having narrowed under the pressure of full or overly-full employment, the differentials have not dropped back to their prior relationships in periods of less than full employment.[60] The long-run trend has worked itself out partly gradually and partly in these forward jumps.

In the future, however, unionism may well be an impediment to further narrowing, as it protects the position of skilled workers in particular and as it stands generally for a continuation of established and formalized differentials perpetuated through contractual arrangements and the development of conventional patterns. Already this has happened in Denmark, as noted above, where craft unions are particularly strong,[61] and for a substantial period of

58. For a discussion of the narrowing of the white-collar manual worker differential over the past century in the United States see Kenneth M. McCaffree, "The Earnings Differential between White Collar and Manual Occupations," *Review of Economics and Statistics* (February 1953). This differential has narrowed more rapidly in the United States than in some other countries, like Germany, where a "closed education" system based on class lines has protected white-collar employees just as the "closed shop" has craft workers in the United States.

59. See Allan Flanders, "Wages Policy and Full Employment in Britain," *Bulletin of the Oxford University Institute of Statistics* (July and August 1950). See also comment in Lester, "A Range Theory . . .," *op. cit.* It is sometimes argued that skilled workers must be in relatively shorter supply than unskilled workers because the unskilled in a depression make up a disproportionate number of the unemployed. But this can be explained by a general pushing down of workers and those on the bottom, the unskilled, go out.

60. This long-term trend explains why Bell, *op. cit.*, did not observe a widening of occupational differentials in depression periods. The standard statement is that the differentials narrow in prosperity and widen in depression. Because of the effect of this long-run trend, the former is true, but not the latter.

61. Galenson, *op. cit.*, also notes that ". . . nationwide bargaining on the Danish model

time (1920-1950) in Australia, where government wage setting is of pre-eminent importance;[62] and it has been attempted in the Netherlands.[63]

Interindustry differentials may well follow the same course as occupational differentials. They also are narrowing and a long-run reversal is taking place in interindustry relationships in favor of those industries, like mining, where the work has heavy disutility factors connected with it. Such a parallel development is to be expected because interindustry differentials are, in significant part, skill differentials.[64] This is particularly true at the extremes. The high-ranking industries historically have been industries with many skilled workers; the low-ranking industries have been industries with many semi-skilled and unskilled workers (and usually also a high proportion of women). The contribution of the skill mix to the wage levels of the several industries is also indicated by the similarity in interindustry wage differentials among countries where other potentially influential factors, like the organization of workers or the structures of product markets, are quite diverse. In addition, the narrowing and reversal of rank order of interindustry differentials can best be explained by the narrowing and reversal of rank order of occupational differentials.

The skill mix, while it is probably the basic underlying force in determining interindustry differentials, is not the only important factor. Ability to pay,

---

creates a propensity toward rigidity in wage structure. . ." (p. 186). It is my own view, albeit somewhat heretical, that, in the long run, industrial unions may often grant more protection to skill than craft unions, despite the early cry of industrial unions that they are the special benefactors of the unskilled. This is, first, because industrial unions gather within the same decision-making unit both unskilled and skilled rates and thus can subject them simultaneously to control; while craft unions usually leave the unskilled on the outside in other decision-making units less subject to control. Industrial unions thus can hold the rates for the skilled and the unskilled apart if they wish and usually they will, since the skilled workers are the long-service workers and the most influential members. Craft unions cannot really hold the rates apart because only one set of rates — those for the skilled — falls within their control. The width of the gap is the distance between two levels, only one of which the craft unions can control. Second, under the craft system, both the unskilled and skilled rates are "in the market" and the unskilled rate by itself must be high enough to permit adequate recruiting; while, under the industrial system, the combined rate structure does the recruiting. That is to say, unskilled workers are attracted not only by the unskilled rates but also by the skilled rates to which they may expect to advance through time and the operation of a seniority plan. Just as the unskilled rate can be somewhat lower because of the prospect of higher rates ahead, so also the skilled rates are "out of competition" in the sense that recruiting is usually from within and not from the open market and it can be "artificially" high without being very obvious.

62. However, the differentials were narrowed substantially before 1920 and have been again since 1950. See Oxnam, "The Relation of Unskilled to Skilled . . .," *op. cit.*

63. See Pels, *op. cit.*

64. See Lebergott, *op. cit.*, on the association between skilled and unskilled rates, industry by industry; Sumner H. Slichter, "Notes on the Structure of Wages," *Review of Economics and Statistics* (February 1950); Deneffe, "The Wage Structure of the Federal Republic," *Wirtschaft und Statistik* (July 1953).

influenced by many factors, including the concentration of production, is of very substantial importance.[65] So also is the secular expansion or contraction of employment for particular industries at particular times, the geographical location of different industries and their cyclical price sensitivity,[66] among other factors. Factors other than occupational differentials are probably particularly important for the series of industries between the extremes of those with a high skill mix and those with a low. Thus, just as occupational differentials affect interindustry differentials, so also changes in interindustry differentials (for reasons other than changes in occupational differentials) will, in turn, affect occupational differentials.

If the narrowing (and scrambling) of occupational differentials is to continue to cause a narrowing (and scrambling) of interindustry differentials,[67] what effect is unionism likely to have on this process? Probably the major effect is in the direction of preserving differentials, once established, because of the penchant for pattern following. Organizational price and leadership survival are often intimately linked to the preservation of established wage relationships. But the pattern is seldom followed exactly; the economic situations of industries do change over time; and so do interindustry wage differentials, whether through changes in negotiated wage levels or through the process of individual employers bidding for labor, particularly during high peaks or low troughs of the business cycle, despite union inclinations to formalize them.[68] What other effects may unions have on interindustry differentials? They cannot assure an advantage to organized industries over unorganized, because, among other reasons, nonunion employers can follow right along. Nor can they control differentials among organized industries except through very substantial centralized power over their member elements, and then only if they can also impose their will on the employers.

The amount of power requisite to control or even to influence differentials increases precipitously as we pass from the simple case of interpersonal differentials on through to the complex one of interindustry differentials. The purpose of the application of power changes also from highly consciously

65. See, for example, Garbarino, "A Theory of Interindustry Wage Structure Variation," *op. cit.*, and Slichter, "Notes on the Structure of Wages," *op. cit.* It appears likely that control of entrance into the labor market and reduction of competition in the product market raise wage rates more effectively above the "natural" level than does direct bargaining pressure; restriction and collusion open more doors for gain than the strike.

66. See Dunlop, *Wage Determination . . . , op. cit.*, Chapter 7.

67. The reduction of regional variations has also served to narrow interindustry differentials in the United States.

68. In Denmark, however, the unions have had remarkable success in maintaining almost unchanged for a substantial period of time intercraft (which in Denmark are also in large part interindustry) wage differentials. See Galenson, *op. cit.*, p. 181.

attempted elimination of interpersonal, interfirm, and interarea differentials to less consciously attempted stabilization of interoccupational and interindustry differentials, and, thus, from egalitarian reform to caste-conscious rigidity. The slogans associated with the former sometimes obscure the contribution to the latter. Appearance and reality go their separate ways.

As a union movement adds to its power it would be expected to penetrate effectively first into the control of interpersonal differentials (where the motivation is much reduced). The degree of effective penetration into control of wage differentials is one measure of the true power of unions.

We remarked earlier that what the unions and their members most wanted they could best secure. Where the unions are consequential, they are also largely beneficial (in that they help achieve results which would flow from full employment and more perfect labor and product markets); and where they are less beneficial (impeding the rearrangement of differentials encouraged by the equalization of opportunity which tends to accompany industrialization), they are also less consequential.

What effect, then, does unionism have on the overall distribution of wage and salary earnings among persons? The pattern of earnings distribution must change greatly as industrialization progresses, although statistics are largely lacking to demonstrate this. In Stage One there must be (assuming a substantial number of agricultural laborers) a heavy concentration of persons at the low end of the distribution. In Stage Two a second "hump" appears at the high end of the scale as skilled "aristocrats of labor" are recruited. In Stage Three, a third "hump" appears in the middle representing the semi-skilled; and this "hump" grows and grows. In Stage Four, only one "hump" is left — in the center — as the unskilled have their rates raised and the skilled their rates relatively reduced; and inside this "hump" some skilled jobs shift to the left of the distribution (like white-collar occupations) and some less skilled jobs (like coal mining) shift to the right. The effects of unions on this historical process are probably as follows: (1) to pull up the very low rates a bit (by eliminating the low-paying firms and areas or forcing them to pay more); and (2) to hold up the high rates a bit against the pressures for narrowing; and (3) within the "hump," to stand as an element of rigidity against the transposition of rates from one side to the other. But, in totality, they lack the influence to effect, through collective bargaining, a major redistribution of income among persons.

Böhm-Bawerk, forty years ago, as many had before and even more have since, discussed this same problem.[69] He set in opposition to each other

69. Eugen von Böhn-Bawerk, *Control or Economic Law* (1914), translated by John R. Mez

"power" and "natural economic laws" and posed the issue: "The great problem, not adequately settled so far, is to determine the exact extent and nature of the influence of both factors, to show how much one factor may accomplish apart from, and perhaps in opposition to, the other." His main illustration was from the labor market and his conclusion was that, with a few exceptions,[70] "there is, in my opinion, not a single instance where the influence of control could be lasting as against the gently and slowly, but incessantly and therefore successfully, working influence of a 'purely economic order'."

The problem is still not adequately settled and may never be, for we are working with a tangled web of forces. The answer offered here is that neither market forces (or what we have called "individual responses") have basically governed in fact nor is power, or perhaps more accurately "institutional behavior," the compelling force which has determined wage differentials.

The problem is too complex for a single reply. Union policies have often brought major, and presumably permanent, changes in two of the differentials we have examined— personal and firm; and have had some, and presumably also permanent, effects on area differentials. They have not evidently, however, been a dominant factor affecting the other two — occupational and industrial. The general explanation given here is that the degree of penetration of trade union influence into the establishment and maintenance of wage differentials is related directly to the intensity and clarity of the motivations of the workers and their organizations, and inversely to the amount of power requisite to the task.

(Eugene, Oregon, 1931). See also discussion in Erich Preiser, "Property and Power in the Theory of Distribution," *International Economic Papers, No. 2* (New York: Macmillan, 1952).

70. The main exception was where union power offset the pre-existing monopsony power of employers.

The Short-Run Behavior of
Physical Productivity and
Average Hourly Earnings

PRODUCTIVITY and wage rates,[1] thought by many economists to be a highly desirable match, do not appear to possess those characteristics of compatibility upon which the perfect marriage depends. Disconcertingly, in the short run, they display a clear tendency to move either in opposite directions or, if in the same direction, at quite different rates.

The postwar experience in this country and the possibility of continuing high levels of employment in the future, in an economy imperfectly protected from the raids of pressure groups, have caused intensified concern over the relationships of these two variables. We may appropriately inquire whether it is reasonable to expect man-hour output and money wages, from year to year or over moderately longer periods, to progress hand in hand.[2]

It is frequently suggested that they should move in close harmony over

Reprinted from *The Review of Economics and Statistics,* Vol. XXXI, No. 4 (November, 1949).

1. The term productivity will be used throughout to mean physical, not value, productivity; and wage rates to mean money, not real, wages.

2. Real wages per hour and man-hour output, unless there is some change in the wage earners' share of the national product, must change approximately together in the long run and in fact they do. See Jules Backman and Martin R. Gainsbrugh, "Productivity and Living Standards," *Industrial and Labor Relations Review* (January 1949).

This article is not concerned with the relationship of real wages to man-hour output, nor with long-run historical relationships between money wages and productivity in the economy at large, nor with long-run relationships in individual industries. Professor Hansen has noted, for example, that over a period of about seventy-five years prior to World War I money wages rose commensurate with improved productivity. A. H. Hansen, "Wages and Prices: The Basic Issues," *New York Times Magazine,* January 6, 1946. Professor Dunlop has discussed the long-run impact of productivity on interindustry wage differentials and demonstrated that it has had a pronounced effect. John T. Dunlop, "Productivity and the Wage Structure," in Lloyd A. Metzler and others, *Income, Employment and Public Policy: Essays in Honor of Alvin H. Hansen* (New York: Norton, 1948).

some period of time, since, if they did, price stability would be facilitated. Lord Keynes was particularly influential in popularizing this view.[3] Sir William Beveridge[4] and Professors Hansen[5] and Slichter,[6] among others, have added the weight of their support. These normative proposals of economists have been elevated to the level of a national policy by the Council of Economic Advisers which advocates "wage increases which are in line with productivity trends."[7]

This article is not concerned with whether this norm is a desirable one or not, but rather with a realistic appraisal of the likelihood of its being followed. The time period under consideration is the short run. Over relatively long periods — the three quarters of a century before World War I and the quarter of a century after it — man-hour output and wages increased by approximately the same amount. The short-run movements of the two variables, however, are also important and have an effect on the operation of the economic system — on costs, profits, prices, and real wages. Significant short-term departures from the pattern of the long-term movements will be shown to have occurred. It will be suggested that, given the business cycle and our present collective bargaining institutions and practices, the short-run gearing of wages to productivity in the future is unlikely to be achieved with any great precision. The distinct impact of the business cycle on productivity and on wages, a neglected consideration, and the realities of the wage setting process make implementation of the policy more difficult than commonly supposed. The two variables almost inevitably act diversely in the short run. The reasons for this are suggested below.

Comparative Behavior, 1920-48

Physical productivity and money wages in the manufacturing segment of the economy have not conformed to the suggested norm in the recent postwar period, despite the expectations, hopes, or arguments of various economists.

3. J. M. Keynes, *The General Theory of Employment, Interest and Money* (London: Macmillan, 1936), p. 271. See also Seymour E. Harris, "Keynes' Attack on Laissez Faire and Classical Economics and Wage Theory," in Seymour E. Harris, editor, *The New Economics: Keynes' Influence on Theory and Public Policy* (New York: Knopf, 1947), pp. 554-56. For a discussion of earlier suggestions along the same lines as Keynes's, see Arthur G. Pool, *Wage Policy in Relation to Industrial Fluctuations* (London: Macmillan, 1938), pp. 286 ff.

4. William H. Beveridge, *Full Employment in a Free Society* (New York: Norton, 1945), p. 200.

5. A. H. Hansen, *Monetary Theory and Fiscal Policy* (New York: McGraw-Hill, 1949), Chapter 8. He views "stability of efficiency-wages as the appropriate goal for wage policy."

6. Sumner H. Slichter, *The Challenge of Industrial Relations* (Ithaca: Cornell University Press, 1947), p. 89. See also his *Basic Criteria Used in Wage Negotiations*, Chicago Association of Commerce and Industry (January 1947), pp. 44-48.

7. *The Annual Economic Review, January 1949*, Report to the President by the Council of Economic Advisers (Washington: 1949), p. 45.

It was confidently expected in some quarters that productivity would rise substantially after the war was over.[8] This supposition influenced governmental wage policy, particularly during the first round of wage increases in 1945-46.[9] It was argued that output per man-hour would rise for a variety of reasons. The labor force would be qualitatively improved by the return of the veterans and the withdrawal of less efficient wartime recruits. New technological and managerial improvements would come into fuller utilization. Moreover, productivity had gone up by one-third after World War I, from 1919 to 1923, and there seemed no good reason why this experience should not be repeated. Accompanied by other cost reductions, through elimination of overtime premiums and the downgrading of workers, and by inroads into excess profits, substantial wage-rate increases were considered possible without raising prices.

Apart from what else went awry with governmental wage-price policy, man-hour output did not rise as anticipated. Productivity in manufacturing industries declined in both 1946 and 1947 and recovered in 1948, but not to the levels of 1945.[10] Average hourly earnings rose substantially,[11] as did, consequently, unit labor costs. Man-hour output in 1948 was about five percent less than in 1945, and average hourly earnings about thirty percent higher. Compared with 1939, output per man-hour in 1948 was up less than five percent while average hourly earnings had doubled.

These figures are based primarily upon the Federal Reserve Board index of production for manufacturing, and the reports of the Bureau of Labor Statistics on manufacturing employment, hours, and average hourly earnings, all of which sources are subject to many well-known limitations, but, while faulty, are the best available.[12] The figures, inadequate though they are, are considered to be somewhat more indicative of what has happened within the

8. See, for example, Robert R. Nathan Associates, Inc., *A National Wage Policy for 1947* (Washington: 1946), p. 5, and Hansen, *New York Times Magazine, op. cit.*

9. See, for example, Director of War Mobilization and Reconversion, *Third Report*, July 1, 1945, p. 39.

10. See Table 1, below.

11. Average hourly earnings are used since they are more directly related to labor costs and purchasing power than other measurements, such as straight-time hourly earnings or urban wage rates.

12. The Federal Reserve Board index of production is particularly open to question as a basis for these calculations. For a discussion of statistical methods and problems in developing data on man-hour output see National Research Project, *Production, Employment and Productivity in 59 Manufacturing Industries:* Part One, *Purposes, Methods and Summary of Findings* (Works Progress Administration, 1939), Chapter 2; U.S. Bureau of Labor Statistics, *Summary of Proceedings of Conference on Productivity, Oct. 28-29, 1946*, Bulletin No. 913 (Washington: 1947); and Solomon Fabricant, *Employment in Manufacturing, 1899-1939* (New York: National Bureau of Economic Research, 1942). Figures on output per man-hour are particularly suspect for the period beginning with 1940.

totality of manufacturing than are the studies, by the Bureau of Labor Statistics, of productivity in individual industries.[13] The latter cover industries with less than one-third of 1947 employment in all manufacturing. They are the most adequate data available for the industries they purport to cover but are not properly representative of manufacturing since they are heavily concentrated on food, leather and leather goods, and clay, glass and stone products.[14] The rubber, basic steel, apparel, automobile, and other important industries are either not covered at all or are covered very inadequately. The Bureau of Labor Statistics reports on productivity, which cover several non-manufacturing industries, show a more complete recovery, although a rather spotty one, than the figures set forth above.[15] This relatively minor divergence is an expected one. None of the industries covered by the Bureau of Labor Statistics had a major reconversion problem, although several experienced severely reduced man-hour output during wartime and had difficulty making a recovery.

The manufacturing segment of the economy is by no means the totality of the economic system, nor is it a valid sample of it.[16] Within this segment, however, where one-quarter of the employed labor force works, the evidence is clear that since the end of the war changes in output per man-hour and money wages have not conformed to the economists' norm. The performance of these two variables has been conspicuously unfortunate from the point of view of short-run price stability.

Nor does it appear more fortunate if the period 1919 to 1948 is examined. Table 1 shows that productivity and average hourly earnings moved in opposite directions during nine years,[17] and in the same direction but at substantially different rates during twelve years.[18] During only seven of the twenty-

13. The Bureau of Labor Statistics makes no claim that these studies are representative of all manufacturing. See Celia S. Gody and Allan D. Searle, "Productivity Changes since 1939," *Monthly Labor Review* (December 1946).

14. *Ibid*.

15. U.S. Bureau of Labor Statistics, *Output per Man-Hour Trends for 1947 Begin Upward Climb in Selected Industries*, mimeographed release (Washington: September 3, 1948).

16. While productivity increases were lagging in manufacturing from 1939 to 1946, other sectors of the economy were making good progress so that productivity for the total civilian economy went up three percent per year. Julius Hirsch, "Productivity in War and Peace," *American Economic Review* (May 1947). The gain in output *per worker* in agriculture was particularly rapid; see U.S. Bureau of Labor Statistics, *Productivity in Agriculture, 1909-1947*, mimeographed report (Washington: November, 1948). See also W.D. Evans, "Recent Productivity Trends and Their Implications," *Journal of the American Statistical Association* (June 1947).

17. 1921, 1922, 1923, 1930, 1931, 1933, 1937, 1946, and 1947.

18. 1926, 1927, 1928, 1929, 1934, 1936, 1938, 1939, 1941, 1942, 1943, and 1944. In 1925 average hourly earnings did not change at all while man-hour output went up substantially.

nine years, or about one-fourth of the time, did they move approximately together,[19] if "approximately together" is leniently defined as movement in the same direction with neither variable at a pace twice or more than twice the other. A year is often too short a time to observe the effects of disparate movements. The dissimilar trends, however, have often been reinforced from year to year. The period 1919 – 1948 may be somewhat arbitrarily broken down into a series of subperiods during each of which some fairly consistent tendencies are evident. The comparative movements, in each case the percentage changes from the first year of each subperiod to the last year taking the first year as the base, were as follows:

From 1919 to 1923, output per man-hour rose 31.3 per cent, much more than the normal rate, and average hourly earnings 9.4 per cent.

From 1923 to 1926, output per man-hour increased 16.8 per cent, and wages 4.9 per cent.

From 1926 to 1929, man-hour output went up 12.4 per cent and average hourly earnings only 3.3 per cent.

From 1929 to 1933, man-hour output increased slightly (4.9 per cent), and wages fell substantially (21.9 per cent).

From 1933 to 1937, both man-hour output and wages rose, wages by 41.2 per cent or more than four times the rate of man-hour output, 9.9 per cent.

From 1937 to 1940, man-hour output went up substantially (13.6 per cent), and wages only moderately (5.9 per cent).

From 1940 to 1945, wages increased much more substantially (54.8 per cent) than man-hour output (7.0 per cent).

From 1945 to 1948, output per man-hour went down somewhat (5.2 per cent), and average hourly earnings went up greatly (28.2 per cent).

Some of these periods were long enough and the dissimilarities in the movements great enough to have an impact on such variables as profits and prices.

Not a single one of these periods evidenced a closely articulated movement of productivity and wages. Yet if the statistics for the quarter century, 1919-45, are taken, they would seem to indicate, surprisingly, that all really was quite ordered and proper.[20] Both man-hour output and average hourly earnings approximately doubled. Productivity and money wages did, apparently, keep pace with each other. All the diverse movements between 1919 and 1945 are not disclosed.

19. 1920, 1924, 1932, 1935, 1940, 1945, and 1948.

20. Edward H. Chamberlin and Hans Staehle point out that in the seventy-five year period prior to World War I, while prices were stable and productivity and wages rose together for the period as a whole, the pattern of development in important subperiods was quite different. (In a letter to the editors, *New York Times*, February 3, 1946.)

Table 1. Year to Year Percentage Changes in Man-Hour Output and in Average Hourly Earnings for Manufacturing Industries in the United States, 1920-48*

Year	Man-Hour Output	Average Hourly Earnings	Year	Man-Hour Output	Average Hourly Earnings
1920	6.0	8.6	1935	5.7	3.4
1921	15.0	−2.3	1936	0.2	1.1
1922	9.6	−6.7	1937	−1.1	12.2
1923	−1.7	10.6	1938	1.8	0.5
1924	6.6	4.8	1939	9.2	1.0
1925	6.6	0.0	1940	2.2	4.4
1926	2.8	0.2	1941	2.2	10.3
1927	2.3	0.4	1942	2.4	17.0
1928	5.3	2.2	1943	1.1	12.7
1929	4.0	0.7	1944	0.6	6.0
1930	2.4	−2.5	1945	0.6	0.4
1931	4.4	−6.7	1946	−5.8	6.0
1932	−6.8	−13.4	1947	−4.0	12.6
1933	5.3	−0.9	1948	4.7	7.4
1934	4.9	20.4			

*Mr. William Goldner assisted in the preparation of this table and other statistical material.

Man-hour output is calculated from Table F-1, *Handbook of Labor Statistics* (1947 edition, Bureau of Labor Statistics, United States Department of Labor), for period ending with 1939. Methods comparable to those used in the preparation of Table F-1 have been employed here in developing the data for the period 1940-48.

Average hourly earnings are calculated from reports of the Bureau of Labor Statistics, United States Department of Labor. See particularly Table C-1, *Handbook of Labor Statistics* (1947 edition).

Differentiation of Factors Affecting Productivity and Wages

There is no obvious reason, *a priori,* why man-hour output and average hourly earnings should spontaneously progress *pari passu* in the short run. If left to their own devices, there is almost as much reason why they should not. The factors affecting the movement of each are not generally the same and, when they are, do not always have identical effects. Any analysis of the comparative behavior of productivity and wages requires that the immediate influences affecting each of them be examined.

Man-Hour Output — Some of the short-run proximate determinants of changes in man-hour output may be classified into six general categories.[21]

21. For a more detailed discussion of some of these factors see Ewan Clague, "The Facts of Productivity," an Address before the Society for the Advancement of Management, mimeographed by the U.S. Department of Labor, 1946. See also, Hiram S. Davis, *The Industrial Study of Economic Progress* (Philadelphia: University of Pennsylvania Press, 1947), Chapter 5; and Solomon Fabricant, *Measuring Labor's Productivity,* Studies in Business Policy, No. 15 (New York: National Industrial Conference Board, 1946), p. 4.

1. The contribution of the employed labor force depends largely on the skill and effort of the workers.[22] Skill generally varies with the average length of time on the job and in the occupation. Turnover of workers and recruitment of marginal workers — long-standing unemployed, housewives and newcomers to the labor force — reduce the general level of skill. Effort, virtually impossible to measure, is almost equally difficult to explain. It is affected by the formal policies of unions and the informal practices of unorganized groups, length of hours, morale, working conditions, the degree of incentive deriving from the "carrots" of piece rates, promotional opportunities and other rewards, and the "sticks" of demotion, discharge, or transfer, among many other factors. Abnormal absenteeism reduces output more than hours.

2. The contribution of the managerial factor varies primarily with the general level of experience of the supervisory personnel and requirements for learning new methods or products, and with the impact of competition on the necessity for examining costs.

3. The technical elements chiefly at work are the volume and quality of research and the effectiveness of plant, equipment, and methods. New industries tend to make unusually accelerated increases in productivity because of improvements in these elements.

4. The regularity of flow and the quality of raw materials have an effect.

5. The variety, quality, and variability of products are important.

6. Within individual firms, the level of capacity affects the proportion of fixed workers necessary to maintain the operation, compared with variable workers;[23] and within the economic system, the level of capacity affects the degree of efficiency of the firms which are able to survive. This factor is sometimes said to affect "volume productivity" as against "real productivity."

Average Hourly Earnings — Average hourly earnings are more directly related to both purchasing power and per unit costs than are basic wage rates. Changes in them are, however, even more difficult to elucidate than in basic rates, and the latter are puzzling enough.

The more evident factors altering the general level of average hourly earnings can be divided into five groups.

22. W. Duane Evans, "Productivity and Human Relations," *American Economic Review* (May 1947).

23. This is particularly important for an industry such as railroad transportation. "In railroad transportation, the depression years made impossible an increase in man-hour output because of the heavy burden of overhead labor when traffic was at a low ebb . . ." Witt Bowden, "Wages, Hours and Productivity of Industrial Labor, 1909 to 1939," *Monthly Labor Review* (September 1940).

1. The amount of payment of special premiums for overtime, night shifts, and other "fringes" has an effect on average hourly earnings particularly during the approach to and relapse from full employment. The introduction of welfare plans also adds to labor costs and purchasing power, and may be counted as a change in average hourly earnings.

2. The "job mix" is important. Shifts in employment from industry to industry, area to area, and plant to plant — given the variations which exist in wage levels among industries, areas, and plants — influence average hourly earnings,[24] as do changes in the general level of skill required.

3. The wage structure of the nation is flexible and changes in it have a distinguishable impact, as for example, the tendency of wages in low paid areas, industries, plants, and occupations to rise particularly rapidly under conditions of full employment and to fall more rapidly in depressions.[25]

4. The administration of the wage structure varies from time to time. Upgrading of workers in prosperity and downgrading in depression, by changing titles and thus pay without changing work assignments or wage structures, have an appreciable effect. Incentive plans, similarly, may be administered loosely or tightly.

5. General movements in the national wage schedule are particularly significant. This schedule moves up with increases in the related factors of prices, employment, and profits, and down when they go down, although more reluctantly. Unionism, particularly when it is young and aggressive and tormented by organizational and personal rivalries, may have some effect on the level of the whole schedule, for wage increases are both an offensive weapon of unions and a defensive weapon of employers in an organizational period (as in 1937). Rising productivity, in the long run at least, also pulls up the national schedule of rates; and short-run variations in productivity have an underlying effect, as will be noted below. The pattern of leadership and imitation, and the deportment of the leaders of the moment, are significant, as is governmental policy — *vide* the NRA period (particularly 1934), World War II, and the first postwar round of wage increases in 1945-46.

Average hourly earnings will vary with changes in each of these five items, but the last is normally the most important. The potential difference between

24. Variations in the "job mix" raise average hourly earnings more in prosperity and lower them more in depression than would otherwise be the case. "During the rapid downturn in business after 1929, there was a comparatively small decline in employment in the relatively low-paid industries, notably some of the consumption-goods industries, and this tended to lower the general average." Bowden, *op. cit.*, p. 525.

25. See, for example, Nedra Bartlett Belloc, *Wages in California* (Berkeley: Institute of Industrial Relations, University of California Press, 1948), Chapter 6; and John T. Dunlop, "Cyclical Variations in Wage Structure," *Review of Economic Statistics* (February 1939).

changes in average hourly earnings and in "wage rate schedules" (approximately item 5), however, was dramatically demonstrated in the report of the National War Labor Board which showed that, for the period January 1941 to October 1944, the former had gone up 50 percent and the latter only 20 percent.[26]

Short-Run Divergent Tendencies of Productivity and Wages

Impact of the Business Cycle — Reference to the factors affecting short-run variations in man-hour output[27] and average hourly earnings helps explain why the two have behaved as they have. The fluctuations of the business cycle have different, and sometimes opposite, impacts on them. In the early upswing of the cycle, as in 1933 to 1935, both will tend to rise, although at uneven rates. Higher levels of capacity allow fuller utilization of overhead workers, new equipment is installed, and skilled workers and managers and adequate raw materials are available. Increases in the cost of living, employment and profits, along with revived unionism, encourage or permit wages to rise.

Under conditions of full employment, as in World War II, wages will tend to rise more rapidly than productivity. Not only will the general upward movement of rates be strong, but the wage structure will tend to be compressed by the upward surge of low wages. The administration of wages will become more lax and more premiums will be paid. Man-hour output, at the same time, may be less amply encouraged. The supply of skilled workers is likely to be exhausted, more marginal workers are drawn into the employed labor force, discharge is less of a penalty, and turnover and absenteeism are increased. Managerial ranks are diluted by "green hands," and the pressure to watch costs is reduced. Raw materials are in less adequate supply, and firms of lesser efficiency are able to undertake or expand production. An enlarged volume of new equipment is an offsetting factor.

The early downturn dampens further rises in average hourly earnings, as in 1920-21 and 1930. Even if wage schedules rise slightly, stricter personnel administration and the cessation of premium pay, among other factors, have a

26. National War Labor Board, *Wage Report to the President on the Wartime Relationship of Wages to the Cost of Living* (Washington: 1945), p. 15. See also John T. Dunlop, *Wage Determination Under Trade Unions* (New York: Macmillan, 1944), pp. 19-27; and Temporary National Economic Committee, *Industrial Wage Rates, Labor Costs and Price Policies,* Monograph No. 5 (Washington: 1940) for discussions of the greater flexibility of average hourly earnings than of basic wage rates.

27. For an outline of a cyclical pattern for "technical change" (not as inclusive a concept as changes in man-hour output) similar to that set forth below for man-hour output, see Committee on Price Determination, Edward S. Mason, Chairman, *Cost Behavior and Price Policy* (New York: National Bureau of Economic Research, 1943), p. 166.

depressing influence. Man-hour output, however, may take a spurt. The least efficient workers and firms tend to be weeded out. Competitive pressures are again felt by workers and managers, and raw materials are in better supply. Capital investment may be directed more at improved efficiency through new equipment than at new construction for expansion. In the depths of a depression, as in 1932, average hourly earnings are under considerable downward pressure, and man-hour output also may sink, particularly because of low levels of operation even for the efficient firms.

Wage Setting Process — Aside from the differential effects of the business cycle, there is a second good reason why man-hour output and money wages may have divergent tendencies in the short run. This has to do with the operation of the wage setting process. Wages and productivity, in the short run, may be linked together primarily in three ways: 1) directly, 2) indirectly through profits, and 3) indirectly through prices. It will be suggested that the third of these is generally the most important and outweighs the others in the short run, and that this particular linkage has a tendency to force wages and productivity in opposite directions.

Direct Linkage of Productivity and Wages — Little direct connection exists between changes in man-hour output and average hourly earnings in the short run. Variations in productivity create few effective pressures focussed on the wage setting process. Statistics on productivity changes are not quickly and generally available, and are noted for their gross deficiencies. Man-hour output changes quite irregularly from plant to plant and industry to industry, and thus has no uniform effect on the determination of wage rates through the decisions of employers and unions, even when adequate knowledge about it exists. Divergent viewpoints on the distribution of productivity gains or losses reduce its acceptance as an equitable precept. Union members and unorganized workers alike do not press overly much for quick matching of wages to productivity when the latter is moving up, since this movement has little effect on their daily lives; and while employers may seek wage reductions when productivity goes down, these are resisted by the unions and workers, and employers are likely to have other channels for seeking or accepting adjustments. Thus changes in productivity lack four qualifications which make a wage influencing consideration significant: factual certainty, general applicability, equitable acceptability, and generation of strong pressures, on one or both parties, which have no other adequate outlet.

This does not mean that productivity changes have no direct effects on average hourly earnings. They may affect piece rate earnings. Also, if wage leaders nationally, regionally, or industrially base their wage decisions on a rise or fall in productivity, the influence of these decisions may be fanned out through the pattern-following process. Rises in productivity do help permit wage increases, and aggressive unions may take increasing advantage of this in the future. To the extent that they do, wages and productivity will be more closely related to each other.

Indirect Linkage Through Profits — An increase in productivity may work out its direct effects mostly on profits. This is apparently what happened, in large part, during the second half of the 1920s. Productivity went up substantially, while prices and wages held relatively stable, and profits rose considerably. It is possible to create a model of the economy in which the only immediate impact is on profits; wages and prices do not adjust until later, if at all. The chain of reactions then would go something like this: Productivity rises, profits rise, employment rises, and wages follow with a lag. Two links in this chain need examination. The increase in employment may be only a moderate one and take place after some substantial delay. Further, at levels of less than full employment, the supply curve of labor may be substantially horizontal, so that rising employment does not pull wages up very greatly. Under these conditions, which may not miss reality too widely, the effect of changes in productivity on wages is a delayed and dampened one.

Indirect Linkage Through Prices — Changes in productivity are much more effectively transmitted through the productivity → price → wage chain; but the effect may be the reverse. *Ceteris paribus*, rising productivity will tend to reduce prices; and if a substantial increase in man-hour output accompanies a downturn in economic activity the effect will be particularly noticeable. *Ceteris paribus*, falling productivity will tend to raise the cost of living; and if a decline in man-hour output comes at a time of full employment, the impact on prices will be especially great.

To the extent that changes in prices and man-hour output tend to have an inverse relationship to each other, so also will wages and man-hour output. For changes in wage rates, in the short run, conform much more positively to changes in the cost of living than to changes in productivity or profits. This is true for both organized and unorganized labor markets, and for both negotiation and arbitration in the latter case.

The explanations are easily discernible. Changes in prices generate much the greater pressures.[28] On the way up, changes in the cost of living have an almost instantaneous and conspicuous effect on the standard of living of the

28. For a discussion of the impact on wages of changes in the cost of living, see John T. Dunlop, "The Movement of Real and Money Wage Rates," *Economic Journal* (September 1938); and for a discussion of the impact on wages of changes in product prices see Dunlop, *Wage Determination Under Trade Unions, op. cit.*, Chapter 7.

workers. Wives, in particular, observe the increases, especially of food prices which are the most volatile. Many wage increases originate in changes in the cost of the market basket. With prices rising, the employers' ability to pay is likely to be increasing and the labor market tightening, so that employers may be both able and willing to raise rates. When product prices (and thus also the cost of living) are on the way down, employers rather than unions take the initiative in trying to change wages. Ability to pay tends to decrease and the labor market to loosen, so that employers are both less able and less willing to raise wages, despite any increase in productivity. The workers also press less for higher wages and are less averse to decreases in average hourly earnings, although they oppose reductions in scheduled wage rates.

The cost of living, also, is almost universally regarded as an equitable consideration in wage determination. Further, its impact on workers is relatively uniform throughout the economic system, and it thus serves as the most consistent wage influencing factor in setting "patterns" and in the imitation of those patterns. Finally, cost-of-living statistics are widely accepted and quickly and extensively publicized. Wage changes are closely geared to changes in the cost of living; and, thus, to the extent that changes in productivity impel prices in the opposite direction, wages, also, will tend to move in the opposite direction.

The direct linkage of productivity and wages and the linkage through profits tend to pull wages after productivity, while the linkage through prices tends to push them apart and normally overshadows the other two in its short-run effects. In an inflationary period, for example, with man-hour output retarded, wages would be expected to follow prices up rather than productivity down; and in the downturn of the cycle, with productivity rising and prices falling, wages would be expected to remain stable or fall, although rising productivity would have a cushioning effect.

Reference to past experience indicates that money wages are, in fact, more sensitive to the tug of prices than of physical productivity, directly or through the profit linkage; and, when the pulls are in contrary directions, prices will usually exercise the more attractive power.

The period 1926-29 is illustrative. Productivity rose substantially and profits were at a high level, but the cost of living held quite steady. Wages held steady also. Wage advances did not match the upward trend of productivity. The recent postwar period is another case in point. In 1946 and 1947, the cost of living rose substantially and so did average hourly earnings. Productivity, for a multiplicity of reasons, fell. To the extent the decline in output per man-hour encouraged the rise in prices, it propelled wage rates up also. In

1948, productivity, with reconversion problems largely overcome, started upward again, and the cost of living became somewhat more stabilized as did wage rates. Many more forces than these, of course, were at work.

By early 1949 the price level was turning down. At the same time, a substantial rise in man-hour output was in prospect, a consequence of a heavy volume of new investment and reinvigoration of the competitive spirit. If productivity were to catch up by the end of 1951 with the long-term average increase of about three percent a year, it would need to rise about 10 percent a year in 1949, 1950, and 1951. To the extent that such a development, or anything approaching it, would hold down prices, it would hold down money wages also. Again, as in the past, productivity and money wage rates would not be moving at the same rate, in the same direction. Should this prospect eventuate, the "eternal" problem of the day may appear to be not how to restrain wages so they may no more than keep pace with productivity, but rather how to spur their advance.

Judging by earlier experience, if they are to progress together it will be because of a forced marriage, not for love but for the convenience of others. Many proposals have been made for attaching them together, two of which will be discussed.

Industry by Industry Harnessing of Productivity and Wage Rates

In the long run, wages tend to rise somewhat more in those industries with rapidly increasing productivity than in those where productivity is constant, falling, or rising at a slow rate.[29] It has been suggested, however, that wage changes should be geared more closely to productivity changes, industry by industry. Peter Drucker, for example, while cognizant of serious limitations, has proposed that "the average efficiency of an entire industry be taken as the basis for the settlement of wage demands."[30] This is the "one yardstick which will give a satisfactory answer." Desirable as reference to this yardstick might be for a number of reasons which Drucker sets forth, it would introduce unqualified chaos into the wage structure.[31]

From 1939 to 1947, output per man-hour rose 100 percent in the rayon

29. Dunlop, "Productivity and the Wage Structure," *op. cit.* See also Jules Backman and M.R. Gainsbrugh, *Behavior of Wages*, Studies in Business Economics, No. 15 (New York: National Industrial Conference Board, 1948), pp. 52-60.

30. Peter Drucker, "Who Should Get a Raise, and When," *Harper's* (March 1946).

31. "Common laborers in technologically advancing industries would be receiving far more than skilled workers in other industries." Slichter, *Basic Criteria Used in Wage Negotiations, op. cit.*, p. 23. See also John T. Dunlop, "The Economics of Wage-Dispute Settlement," *Law and Contemporary Problems* (Spring, 1947).

industry and fell 10 percent in anthracite coal.[32] Any close reflection in wage setting of this divergent change would have impossibly distorted the wage structure. Moreover, such distortion would have been completely unacceptable to the anthracite miners even under other leadership than that currently available. Any arbitrator or union or employer negotiator who attempted to follow such a maxim would find his decisions lacking in compliance. Within my own arbitration experience, cases have been argued almost simultaneously involving industry-wide bargaining systems where application of this principle, using the same base period, would have doubled the wages of one group and cut those of the other in half. Neither such decision would have fallen within the outermost limits of expectation of either of the parties subject to it. Adoption of this principle for the determination of wages, plant by plant or occupation by occupation, would miss reality by an even greater margin.

Matching Wage Increases with Overall Gains in Productivity

Alvin Hansen has suggested, instead, that "wages in general should rise in accordance with average overall gains in productivity."[33] A progressive industry should raise wages "a little more than the average" and a stagnant industry "could scarcely be expected to raise wages as soon or even as far." Given our present system of wage determination, it is difficult to envisage how this principle would be applied to individual wage decisions. How can the employer or the union be expected to ignore the many other factors affecting wages, some of which are more persuasive, such as changes in the cost of living, the tightness or looseness of labor markets, expansion and contraction of employment, rival unionism and leadership,[34] prices for the products,[35] the degree and stage of union organization, and ability to pay (which is, of course, affected by productivity, product prices, etc., thus indirectly bringing them to bear on the wage setting process)? In the interest of general price stability would a union accept a three percent productivity increase, for example, when the cost of living had risen ten percent, or an employer yield such an increase, when the market for his products had collapsed? Would John L. Lewis find tolerable a two percent increase year after year if his industry was stagnant, while some other union leader in a progressive industry was winning four percent? Can any inflexible formula satisfy the

---

32. Bureau of Labor Statistics, *Output per Man-Hour Trends for 1947, op. cit.*
33. *New York Times Magazine, op. cit.*
34. For a discussion of political forces and considerations in wage setting see Arthur M. Ross, *Trade Union Wage Policy* (Berkeley: University of California Press, 1948).
35. The strong impact of product prices on wages is demonstrated by Dunlop, *Wage Determination Under Trade Unions, op. cit.*, Chapter 7.

requirements of the parties in collective bargaining for very long?[36] The unions, at least, would need to be rather more self-effacing than they have appeared to be in the past. Keynesian proposals may lead to the "euthanasia of the rentier,"[37] but the business agent cannot be expected to disappear so painlessly.

Even if scheduled wage rates could be tied to overall gains in productivity, average hourly earnings might still fluctuate substantially for the reasons set forth earlier, and upset the stability of per unit labor costs and purchasing power. The proposal neglects too much of the dynamics of wage determination.

Moreover, if changes in average hourly earnings could be linked to the average long-run gain in productivity of three percent per year, how could man-hour output be brought to leash? Between 1919 and 1948 it dropped as much as seven percent in one year and rose as much as fifteen percent in another. Since both average hourly earnings and man-hour output fluctuate considerably, it would seem almost equally desirable to influence the latter as the former. Per unit labor cost can hardly be stabilized if only one of the variables is controlled; and the blame for instability in the relationship cannot in good conscience be assessed only against wages when the historical record is viewed.

The national wage structure and changes in it do and must serve more purposes than cost and price stability, important as they are. They must gain consent. Some structures and some changes make more of a contribution to law and order than others. The demands of both power and distributive justice must be acknowledged to an acceptable degree. Labor market and product market forces need to find some expression outside the confines of a wage policy based on average long-run gains in productivity.

Realistic Prospects

An alternative to these two proposals is the encouragement of conditions under which productivity and wage rates will most nearly choose to advance together. Since full employment tends to fire up the latter more than the former, the proper degree of failure to achieve full employment might be one answer — just enough to retard undue wage advances and simultaneously encourage competitive efforts to increase efficiency at normal rates. To accomplish this, however, would be to sacrifice production to get productivity,

36. See the discussion by Arthur M. Ross of "The General Motors Wage Agreement of 1948," *Review of Economics and Statistics* (February 1949).
37. Keynes, *op. cit.*, p. 376.

and it is the overall level of production which makes the greater contribution to total welfare.

If we must have full employment to get maximum production, then it may be better to have it permanently than intermittently from the point of view of matching man-hour output and average hourly earnings. If full employment lasted long enough, some of the factors which have an adverse effect on productivity might be overcome — inexperienced workers and managers, inadequacy of equipment, and irregularity of flow of raw materials, for example. On the side of average hourly earnings, certain forces which raise them excessively tend to exert themselves only once — the compression of the wage structure by raising its lower end, the loosening of wage administration, and the introduction of overtime and night shift differentials. If full employment were to be accompanied by stable prices, achieved largely through devices other than wage policy, the likelihood of approximating the norm would be greatly increased.[38] Evenly balanced changes in man-hour output and average hourly earnings may be as much the result of stability as they are a cause.

A really close coupling, however, would require more centralized policy determination by government[39] or by industry and organized labor than now exists.[40]

In the absence of continued full employment, price stability and coordinated control, the principle that wages and productivity should proceed together lacks certain ingredients for successful application. In the long run, while it may be satisfied, as between 1919 and 1945, it is not fully meaningful, since important and upsetting divergences can and do occur in the short run. In the short run, it is impossible and perhaps also unwise to implement it with any great precision. It is perhaps of more avail to inquire what will happen when productivity and wages fail to accommodate each other and how to overcome any unfavorable effects. As a device for rallying public support around measures to alleviate such consequences, when wages depart or

38. A real dilemma presents itself. Prices can hardly be stabilized without stabilizing wages, and wages can hardly be stabilized without stabilizing prices. But it is at least as correct to say that wage stabilization depends on price stabilization, as the other, and more customary, way around.

39. The ultimate implication of the policy may well be such control, if it can effectively be exercised. See O.W. Phelps, "Collective Bargaining, Keynesian Model," *American Economic Review* (September 1948).

40. Unified labor and management policy holds no complete assurance, however, of fulfillment of the principle. See H.W. Singer, "Wages Policy in Full Employment," *Economic Journal* (December 1947).

threaten to depart too far from a reasonable relationship, the proposal has more merit than as the basis for specific wage bargains.

A small degree of satisfaction may possibly be derived from the short-run disharmonies. The apparent long-run harmony of the two variables is perplexing in the light of their short-term divergent behavior. How does it happen that over certain long periods they keep pace with each other, as shown by Hansen for the 75 years before and in this article for the 25 years after World War I, when over shorter periods they move so differently? No full explanation of this seeming contradiction will be attempted here. One possible answer is that it has just happened. Productivity has been rising secularly by a very substantial amount, and wages, for other reasons, have been rising also. The percentage increases over long periods of time, without benefit of any economic law, have turned out to be about the same.

A more comforting explanation might be that it is the short-run disharmonies, through a series of self-correcting movements, which cause the long-run harmony. Productivity runs ahead during the downswing and depression, and wages keep up or move out in front during the upswing and then jump ahead when the peak is reached. Over several turns of the wheel, they average about the same pace. If in the short run they cannot move together, but it is still desirable to have them do so in the long run, then the short run disharmonies may help achieve this end. A public wage policy, under these circumstances, which attacks wage changes in any single year as "out of line" with productivity changes, would need to be examined in the light of the long-term correspondence of wage and productivity changes.

Too great an emphasis on the evident long-run harmony, however, can be misleading. While productivity and wages did keep pace with each other 1840 to 1914, and also 1919 to 1945, they did not if certain other periods are taken, such as 1914 to 1945, 1919 to 1949, or 1933 to 1949. The price level was approximately the same in 1914 as in 1840, and in 1945 as in 1919; but it was not approximately the same in 1945 as in 1914, or in 1949 as in 1919, or in 1949 as in 1933. Real wages follow productivity; and when in the long run the price level does not change, money wages also follow it. The long-run harmony of productivity and money wages occurs when in the long run the price level is roughly stable.[41]

41. This statement, of course, can be reversed; and it can also be said that, in the long run, the price level will be roughly stable, if there is a long-run matching of increases in money wages and in productivity.

SUMMARY

1. Man-hour output and average hourly earnings in manufacturing moved quite divergently in three-fourths of the years, 1919 to 1948, and in every one of eight subperiods.

2. The proximate determinants of changes in man-hour output and average hourly earnings are quite different.

3. The business cycle affects these determinants in such a manner that man-hour output and average hourly earnings cannot be expected to move closely together in the short run.

4. The wage setting process, also, is such that the direct influence of productivity and the indirect influence, through effects on profits, in the short run, are overshadowed by other factors, particularly price changes, so that productivity does not pull wages directly after it.

5. Proposals to tie wage rates to changes in productivity, industry by industry or over the whole economy, ignore certain realities of collective bargaining and important functions of the wage setting process.

6. The creation of conditions under which wages and productivity will tend to move more closely together, and the acceptance of moderate deviations from the suggested norm of constant "efficiency wages," are suggested as a more realistic approach.

PART III. The Impact of Bureaucratic Control

Governmental Wage Restraints:
Their Limits and Uses
in a Mobilized Economy

W AGES ARE ALMOST never, in the strict sense of the word, stabilized. The situations in which they might be — a static, traditional economic system or one under absolute dictatorial control — lie outside our current interest. Even in a democratic state with a dynamic economy they are, however, almost always restrained. The employer, acting under the whip of economic forces, is the customary agent of restraint. The union, acting primarily under the impact of political pressures, is an important agent under certain restricted circumstances. The government, however, is frequently the chosen instrument of restraint in a mobilized economy.

The discussion which follows will be concerned, first, with a discussion of the parties to the wage restraint bargain in a mobilized economy; second, the upper and lower limits of a governmental policy of wage restraint; and third, the circumstances which will place the policy at one or the other of these limits or somewhere in between. At the end a few comments will be made on developments of the past year.

THE PARTIES

Wage restraints are exercised through people and institutions and a realistic appraisal of the possibilities requires an analysis of their likely behavior. If we are to assume reality, of what does this reality consist?

The Employers — Speaking broadly, the employers of the fifties differ from their counterparts of World War II in at least two major respects: they believe that industrial peace pays and they have a certain kind of faith in the government. Both of these observations, but particularly the latter, require

Reprinted from *Papers and Proceedings American Economic Review*, Volume XLII, No. 2, (May, 1952).

some explanation. Industrial warfare was costly; and it was found that concessions, particularly of wage increases, to the unions were not so burdensome as once thought. Even without industry-wide bargaining, wage increases spread quite uniformly throughout an industry; so that the first man to make a settlement is not for long, if at all, in an unfavorable competitive position. Nor will government allow industry as a whole to be severely caught between the nether millstone of higher labor costs and the upper millstone of a fixed volume of effective demand or rigidly set price ceilings. Here is where the faith comes in; and this faith is that neither fiscal and monetary policies will be so restrictive nor price ceiling so inflexible that the added costs cannot largely be offset by higher prices with unreduced volume. The faith goes beyond the current arrangements to the post-mobilization period, and it is widely believed that the government will support the higher cost structures when that time arrives. All this is based on the conviction that government must be more dedicated to maintenance of full employment than of the price level.

There is an exception to this, however. In a period of imminent disaster, which is defined a little later, the government would act quite differently. It might impose a strict pay-as-you-go program or expenditure rationing or remove "pass-through" pricing formulas, but this would be only for the duration of the crisis and simultaneously the wage policy would also be tightened. In the meantime, employers have no great incentive to exercise strong wage restraints and when the crisis comes others will take on this responsibility. Employers behave best as cost controllers when faced with a scarcity of effective demand either in fact or in prospect. Their vision of industrial peace at the cost of wage increases is not today daunted by the terrors of bankruptcy; and their faith in government is a faith that moves wage levels.

The Unions — The two crucial factors on the union side are that the unions are mature enough to be wage conscious and responsible enough to their members to want wage increases. Their maturity means that they will no longer forego wage increases for the sake of improved institutional security, as they did in World War II, although the union shop is still worth some money. Their contracts are already fairly well stocked with fringes, although pensions and health and welfare plans are still spreading. The wage and the wage alone is more nearly the sole center of interest. This means that the wage line can less readily be held by creating diversions elsewhere as did the War Labor Board.

Further, the unions are responsible — to their members; and their members

want wage increases from their unions. The general wage increase is particularly important if the mobilization effort starts, as it has this time, from a base
of full employment rather than mass unemployment as in World War II, for
maintenance or improvement of the standard of living must come more from it
than from raising hours to normal levels, moving from unemployment to
employment, or employing secondary workers in the family.

We have in the United States no fully developed union movement, in the
European pattern, with its labor party branch, and so the only people the
unions must and should be responsible to are their members. Only when the
unions develop a political party do they become widely responsible to the whole
economy, for then one of the "memberships" to which they appeal is the
electorate. Unions are particularly "responsible" when their party is the government. Then and only then are they likely to approach the economists'
definition of a "responsible" union: one which hesitates to ask for a wage
increase for fear of upsetting the economy. For then they must not only get
employers to agree to wage advances but a majority of the electorate must be
persuaded of their desirability, and the latter is the more difficult feat. Only
when unions are more concerned with broad political gains than narrow wage
advances will they be really responsible.

To be fully responsible in this sense, it is not enough, as is sometimes
suggested, that the unions be highly centralized and capable of making a
single national bargain, but they must also be in a position of appealing to a
wider constituency than their own members. Thus it is not alone the centralization of the union movement in Norway which makes it responsible but also
the fact that the labor party is in power; and in England, where the unions are
much less centralized, they also have acted comparatively responsibly when
the labor party constituted the government. The more political unions become, the better the economists like their actions, for they start bargaining
actively with the electorate as well as the employer and the former sets the
higher value on overall price stability.

American unions bargain with employers and represent the short-run sectional interests of their members as workers. (In discussing the likely "responsibility" of unions, three questions need to be raised: On whose behalf
are the unions bargaining — their own individual memberships, all organized
workers, or all workers? With whom are they bargaining — their own individual employers, all employers, or the electorate? Of what time span are they
thinking — the short run or the long run? As unions move from the first to the
last of each of these possibilities, they are likely to become more "responsible.") This self-interest does not mean that they have no concern for the

public welfare when public and sectional welfare diverge, but only that the self-serving interests of their constituents are uppermost. These private self-interests can be damaged by ill-advised actions which adversely affect elections or the passage of laws; and in a real national crisis the members subordinate their immediate individual interests to the more general requirements of national well-being.[1]

Until the recent postwar period, American unions had never had great power in an inflationary period. They discovered that sizable increases could be obtained for their members under such conditions and that union wages could be kept up with or ahead of the rising cost of living. However valid this experience may be for a mobilized economy, inflation is not now considered such a disaster as when it was assumed that wages must always lag behind rising prices.

The Public Members — At this point I should like to make three assumptions (the second of which will be temporarily relaxed a little later) which I believe to be realistic about the agency which will administer government wage restraints. First, it will be tripartite, although if it were not, there would probably be little change in basic policy except as caused by reduced skill in development and reduced acceptance in application. Second, it will be devoted solely to wage controls (including the handling of disputes), for if the same group of people were to administer wage and price controls, then their interests would be more mixed than if wages alone.[2] The labor members would want at one and the same time to be tough on prices and soft on wages; and the industry members the reverse. Third, the partisan (industry and labor) members of the board faithfully reflect the general sentiments of the group from which they are chosen. If they do not, they probably will not survive long as members, but while they do they may greatly affect policy development.

The public members essentially are mediators and they mediate primarily between the labor and industry members of their board who (according to the third assumption above) represent the general interests of unions and management respectively. (There are two other views of the public members:

1. For an illuminating discussion of political ceilings on wage demands, see Melvin W. Reder, "The General Level of Money Wages," *Proceedings of the Third Annual Meeting, Industrial Relations Research Association, 1950* (Madison: 1951), pp. 186-202.

2. For a discussion of the relationship between administrative arrangements and policy see Murray Edelman, "Hypotheses on the Relation between Governmental Organization and Labor Policy," paper presented before session of American Political Science Association, San Francisco (August 1951).

1) they directly represent the public interest in stabilization and are the guardians of the public interest against the special interests of industry and labor; and 2) they are the representatives of industry and labor against the consuming public and are useful to the parties by placing their "Good Housekeeping" seal on the actions of the parties. According to the latter view, it is essential that the public believe in the integrity of these keepers of this seal, but at the same time the seal should be available upon demand by the parties.)

Public members are chosen usually from among the experienced people in the field, and the experienced people are all, in part at least, mediators, else they could not have gained much experience. Even if mediating were not their inclination and often also their part-time occupation, the situation would require them to mediate. They like to get along as well as possible with the people they live with every day. They cannot fire the industry and labor members, but the industry and labor members can withdraw their approval of them. Moreover, the industry and labor members can withdraw from the board and stop its operations. Labor withdrew from the Defense Mediation Board early in World War II and it ceased functioning; three times the War Labor Board in the last war was threatened with disruption;[3] and the industry members withdrew very briefly and informally from the Wage Stabilization Board early in 1951 and the labor members for a longer time and more formally.

The first imperative for the public members is the survival of the board, and this requires that their actions be as acceptable as possible to the labor and industry members. In a specific dispute case, also, the dominant concern is to get the case settled, provided it can be settled in a manner which will not disrupt the board. Only under the most compelling circumstances, such as might arise out of relations in the coal or steel industries, will the public members endanger the cohesion of the board for the sake of settling a single case. It might be necessary, for example, as in the case of the National Defense Mediation Board, in order to avoid a national coal strike, for the public members to support a settlement which would disrupt the board. The public members must of necessity, if they are to hold the board together, be more concerned with what is acceptable to the labor and industry members than with what is acceptable to them as individual citizens, if this happens to be at variance. In acting in this fashion, they are serving the public interest in preventing or settling disputes, in avoiding challenges to the authority of

3. See William H. McPherson, "Tripartitism," in *Problems and Policies of Dispute Settlement and Wage Stabilization during World War II*, U.S. Bureau of Labor Statistics, Bulletin No. 1009 (Washington: 1951), p. 256.

government, and in preserving collective bargaining; but they may not be stabilizing the level of wages. If the unions want substantial wage increases and the employers are willing to grant them, then the policy of the board will be set to permit them; and if the unions are willing to forego substantial increases and employers fight them, then the policy will reflect these circumstances, too. If the acceptable compromise is not effective stabilization, stabilization is more likely to be ignored than the compromise.

There is one situation, however, where the acceptable compromise and effective stabilization will be very much the same thing. During a time of imminent disaster, an overall settlement of stabilization policy is likely to be negotiated formally or informally at the Presidential or Congressional level, and this will lower the level of union demands and employer concessions. Under these conditions, the public members can aid in the development and application of the overall settlement. Thus the public members are not wage stabilizers but stabilizers of relationships; and in the course of performing this latter function they may also restrain wage increases. The public is not an independent force at work on the public members except in a crisis and then through the person of the President or through Congress. I neglect here the Director of Economic Stabilization or his equivalent, for he cannot prevail over the wishes of a tripartite board except as he represents the wishes of the President.

The public members are given two assignments which normally are contradictory in their requirements: to mediate and to stabilize. As mediators they are supposed to help industry and labor reach a mutually acceptable bargain. As stabilizers they are expected to represent in the area of wages the anti-inflationary interests of the public. We have explored above the wage restraint interests of the employers and the unions. The public interest in wage restraint remains to be stated. The ideal wage restraint policy may be rather rigidly defined as one which maintains stable efficiency wages — wage rates rise only with rising productivity. Changed wage rates, under such a policy, would in and of themselves have no inflationary effects either by raising per unit costs or per unit effective demand.

We may speak of two wage policies: the union-management wage policy, which is that policy mutually most acceptable to these two parties, and the public policy as just set forth. Let us assume, as is very likely to be the case, given the interests of employers and unions as we have seen them above, that the union-management policy is substantially above the public policy. Then the public members have two alternatives. One is to insist on the public policy and then they will shortly cease to be public members; and the other is to help discover and then adopt the union-management policy. The latter is by all odds the more likely course, but it leaves the public members in the unenviable position of accepting a wage policy above the level of public policy. The only way out of this difficulty is to bring the level of the union-management policy down closer to the public policy, and there is very little the public members can do about this.

There are two general situations where the two policies are likely to be brought closer together: first, where the same tripartite board determines wage and price policy and thus where the unions may settle for lower wages in return for controlling the employers' prices; and second, where, in a crisis, the President or Congress brings about an overall stabilization settlement among the various parties at interest in our economy.

The clean-cut answer to the dilemma of the public members is to give them a single assignment — mediation of the union-management policy;[4] and to assign to the President and Congress responsibility, when the occasion demands, for creating a situation in which the union-management policy can be as close as possible to the public policy. The public members should be viewed as the neutral members of the board — neutral as between industry and labor — and not as the representatives of the public. They are not directly responsible to the public, but to industry and labor; and even if they were, they have not the tools at their command to discharge such responsibility effectively. Their central responsibility is to the joint desire of management and labor to accommodate their separate interests sufficiently to permit them to live together.

Reference throughout has been to the public members of the National Board. The public members of the regional boards (and case analysts at both the national and regional levels) have quite a different role to play. They are not to mediate between the parties before them but to enforce in individual cases the national wage restraint bargain made by the public members of the National Board. Their task is the faithful administrative application of this bargain. Their greatest virtue is the staunch defense of the integrity of this bargain; and their greatest crime is its violation.

THE LIMITS

Given the employers, the unions, and the public members as they are, what are the lowest and highest levels of wage policy which may realistically be

4. This is both an immensely difficult assignment, because of the great heterogeneity of interests on both the union and management sides, and an immensely useful function, because of the importance of preserving domestic tranquility.

expected? We are concerned here with policies and not with the specific wage increases which these policies will permit in actual situations.

The Lower Limit — In World War II the key wage stabilization policy was the Little Steel formula. Its purpose and to a lesser extent its consequence was to break the connection between rises in the cost of living and general increases in wages. The conditions which permitted the survival of the Little Steel formula cannot again be duplicated in the United States: the advent of a war in the midst of an unresolved gigantic conflict between large-scale industry and new and insecure unions, and in the wake of a great depression. Mass conflict and mass unemployment set the stage for the successful defense of the formula. Employers were predominantly antiunion and they fought wage increases as part of the battle against unionism; and they expected a postwar depression and did not want to get caught with high wage rates. The unions quite regularly took a union security item such as a maintenance-of-membership clause or some of the many new fringes, like vacations with pay, in lieu of greater wage increases. Union members, with a decade of depression behind them, settled for better jobs or even jobs at all and overtime pay and did not insist that general wage changes keep up with the cost of living. The recalcitrance of the employers, the insecurity of the unions, and the depressed condition of the workers made possible the Little Steel formula. With the union-management wage policy set at low levels, it did not substantially exceed the level of public policy and the public members could both mediate between labor and industry and serve the anti-inflationary interests of the public. Even then, however, tight wage policies, such as Executive Order 9328, had to be foisted on an unwilling Board and on the public members by the President or his representatives. Employers are no longer so recalcitrant, unions so insecure, and workers so docile and, as a consequence, tight governmental wage restraints are no longer so possible.

Since the conditions which permitted the Little Steel formula are not likely again to occur, in all likelihood the tightest formula which could survive more than very temporarily is one which ties changes in wages to the cost of living and beyond that allows little or nothing. A cost-of-living formula itself can be either tight or loose depending on the nature of the index, how the base date is manipulated, the tie-in between the index and wage rates, and the lags which occur. A tight application would include substantial lags in adjustments either through delayed adjustments on a time basis or by withholding them until the index had made substantial gains. What is necessary, however, is the assurance that wages will be adjusted in some fashion to offset rises in the cost of living.

There is one dominant reason for believing that stabilization policy will be tied to cost of living. The cost of living is the most universally accepted basis for wage adjustments in a period of rising prices. In all the democratic nations at war in World War II, including Britain and excepting the United States, a cost-of-living relationship of one kind or another was the keystone of the wage stabilization program. Since the war, in each of the democratic nations which has had a formal wage policy by agreement of the parties or by government action or a combination of both, adjustment of wages in some fashion to reflect the changes in the cost of living has been the basic principle. While this is the likely lower limit for policy, this does not mean that wage increases would be low in amount, since if prices went up substantially wages would also.

The Upper Limit — The upper limit can be stated almost as precisely: a policy which permits adjustments in line with what would happen normally in a full but not overly full employment economy. What would happen normally under these conditions? Wages would rise roughly in line with the rise in the cost of living, if any. Beyond that there would be a rise in the real value of the hourly rate. In the five countries which he studied for the period 1860 to 1939, Phelps Brown found that real wages rose persistently from year to year by about the same amount. For the United States the annual increase was a little over 1½ percent.[5] Further, certain adjustments take place in rates between jobs and between plants for the sake of greater "equity"; and fringe benefits are improved somewhat.

This suggests that the highest policy would be one which allowed wage offsets to the cost of living on some reasonable and not spurious basis; an additional adjustment, whether called an "improvement factor" or not, which would allow real hourly rates to rise the normal amount; corrections of bona fide intraplant and interplant "inequities"; and improvements at the customary pace in fringe benefits, which at the present time means some limited extensions of pensions and health and welfare plans. In addition, such a policy would include provision for normal day-to-day wage movements involving individual employees: promotions, merit raises and the like; and for the elimination of substandard rates of pay.

This policy is defined as the upper limit for a general wage policy primarily on the belief, which may be a mistaken one, that it is an acceptable maximum to the important unions in the nation (with perhaps a few notable exceptions). This assumes that the situation is such that the unions are willing to accept

5. E.H. Phelps Brown and Sheila V. Hopkins, "The Course of Wage Rates in Five Countries, 1860-1939," *Oxford Economic Papers* (June 1950).

some policy. They may, of course, be unwilling to accept any policy at all. This policy makes more than nominal gains consistently available; and allows the wage structure to continue its life largely undisturbed. At the same time, anything beyond these overall limits would appear unreasonable to much of industry and would certainly embarrass the government. There is no automatic mechanism, but only likely acceptance, which makes this the upper limit policy.

Is This Wage Restraint? — The first policy, while leading in some sectors, such as government, to more rapid rises if the cost of living is rising, would, on balance, most assuredly dampen wage increases, but is the second any wage restraint at all? It would probably not reduce significantly or at all the key bargains in our economy, for they would probably not exceed these limits; and in the periods when this policy is appropriate, they are not likely to be restrained very much in any event. What it would do would be to keep the non-key bargains in line with the normal pattern. Rather than control only the key bargains, as has sometimes been suggested, it would make more sense to control only the non-key bargains. For it is some of them which tend to get out of line in a period of overly full employment; a union is "on the make" or decides to take full advantage of its unusual bargaining position; or employers try to hold their labor in or recruit more labor to low wage plants or industries.

The nation's normal wage structure is generally a good one for the purpose of a mobilized economy. It provides substantial differentials for the construction and heavy industries over service trades and the light industries, and this aids recruitment into the essential lines. The problem is to hold down the rates in the less essential areas and thus to preserve the normal and useful differentials. Fortunately the people who can best be restrained — the unorganized employer and the small union — are the ones who most need to be restrained from breaking through the normal hierarchy of differentials. (While they can be restrained most easily at the formal level, they are, however, the ones most likely to evade the regulations and create an enforcement problem.) Not only does it have unfortunate results for manpower allocation if they do, but such actions would upset normal wage relationships and cause union and employer unrest.

One of the great contributions of the upper limit policy would be the restraint of the individual runaways. If this were done, wage adjustments for the sake of manpower allocation would be largely unnecessary, for the customary wage structure has already made them. There are important exceptions to this where a plant or industry or region has its character radically changed; for example, if an atomic bomb plant is introduced into a low-wage area. The central theme of this policy is to restrain those who both can be and need to be restrained. It would hold wage movements in an overly full employment economy to the pattern of a full employment economy.

THE PERIODS

We are dealing in a field where every case may be a special case, as was the situation in World War II. The factors to be considered are numerous, complex, and changeable. While realizing that no great precision is possible, there are three generalized periods in a mobilized economy which it seems most useful to posit in gaining an understanding of wage policy. To each of these periods a fitting wage policy is related. This will be an *ex post* view of what to the policy maker is always an *ex ante* situation.

The Pre-Crisis Period — This is the typical period of preparedness, of the garrison state, of the continuing "cold war." The percentage of the nation's capacity devoted to military ends is above the peacetime normal and there is likely to be mild inflationary pressure. But there is no war and no public sense of imminent threat. Relatively little overtime is being worked. The unions are not willing to give a no-strike pledge, nor the employers a no-lockout pledge, although it might be held that membership in a tripartite board is the equivalent of a limited no-strike and no-lockout pledge, in that labor and industry, so long as they remain represented on the board, are declaring their general acceptance of the program and thus disclaiming a general attack on it. Wage restraint can be only minimal, for the unions in the absence of a no-strike pledge are declaring their individual right to revolt against any restraints. The public and the government in the face of this will settle for industrial peace.

What is the proper wage stabilization policy in a period such as this when wages cannot be stabilized? The only likely policy is the upper-limit policy described above — a policy which tries to preserve the normal full employment pattern against the effects of individual runaways. Such a policy would provide a degree of equity in the treatment of wage earning groups, prevent unwise pirating of labor, and preserve customary differentials for the sake of manpower reallocation. It would be largely acceptable to the unions and thus serve as the basis for the settlement of wage disputes disrupting or threatening to disrupt essential industries; and at the same time it would not cause disputes either by leading too far in advance of what the employers would be willing to grant under the circumstances or by falling too far below what the unions could accept. For the sake of these purposes some uncertainty in the specific actual policies is probably desirable. A policy with some indefiniteness gives both the parties and the board more leeway to meet the needs of individual cases. It is a policy which the powerful unions would in all likelihood be willing to see applied against less powerful unions which tried to get out of line. The public, which likes to see something done, would think it saw something being done; and the existence of a wage policy makes price control politically possible. The suggested wage policy will make the unions less interested in pressing for effective price control, but strict price control under the conditions assumed here is somewhat unlikely anyway. None of these purposes can be served as well by the voluntary control through exhortation recommended by some, for its range of usefulness is so narrow as to be almost nonexistent.

It is the nature of this policy that it is not "tough," and in being loose, particularly if it is in large part self-administered, is not so subject to certain of the standard attacks of some economists against direct controls: the red tape, the faulty allocation of resources, and the temporary postponement of inflation and thus also of adequate fiscal and monetary measures. Particularly by not raising grave enforcement problems, it saves strong direct controls for emergency use later on, while providing the ready-made machinery for their application. Severe direct controls wear out relatively quickly and it is best to preserve their availability for a time when they may be greatly needed.

This policy would permit a mild inflation from wage sources if other factors were favorable, since it would allow the raising of both costs and purchasing power per unit of product, and without causing unemployment this could not be fully offset by fiscal and monetary measures. It would not, by itself, force a substantial inflation; and a mild inflation can make a contribution in drawing forth resources and satisfying the powerful groups in society, provided it does not get out of hand.

The full possibilities of this upper limit wage policy may not be continuously exploited. In advance of Congressional action on an important law, as in the case of the Defense Production Act of 1951 or the presidential elections in 1952, the unions have and will act circumspectly. Also, if there is a lull in economic activity (for example, as consumer and business inventories are reduced), the employers and the unions alike may proceed rather slowly.

The Crisis Period — The crisis period is one of imminent danger to the nation either because a major war has broken out or because one is thought so impending that a sudden and drastic jump in the percentage of national capacity devoted to military purposes is required, or because inflation is proceeding at so rapid a pace that the consumers have mobilized effective pressure against the government. This is the moment for the overall political settlement by the President or Congress. This settlement would no doubt include readjustments in price policy affecting farmers and businessmen and in fiscal and monetary measures. Part of the settlement would probably be a no-strike pledge which is the *sine qua non* for effective wage restraints. At this point, the wage policy could probably be moved precipitously from the upper limit to the lower limit; and administratively should be turned from self-administration to bureaucratic control. For bureaucratic control can delay wage movements for at least six months. Some consider the great contribution of the War Labor Board to have been the paper curtain it set up against wage increases.

Such a strict wage policy probably could not be held for very long, but while it was held, time would be gained for the market and for government controls to redistribute resources to meet the changed demand without violent wage movements and for fiscal and monetary controls to take effect. It is assumed that strict manpower and materials controls would be imposed during such a period.

The Continuing Crisis — Such a strict wage policy is best fitted for the original crisis period. It would soon wear out under the impact of union challenges, employer violations, and growing antagonism to controls. The memory of World War II at the present time gives rise to a certain cynicism about the effectiveness of enforcement. Unfortunately, a mobilized economy cannot always count on having a fresh and inexperienced generation with which to work. The "disequilibrium system" worked so well in World War II because it was so virginal.

Both because the line could not be held indefinitely and because other anti-inflation controls are more effective and desirable economically over the longer run, it would be likely that the wage policy would rise again, perhaps slowly at first, from the lower limit toward the upper limit. This would be the most difficult and perplexing period for the board.

The Three Periods — Viewed broadly, then, there appear to be three general situations — the pre-crisis, the crisis, and the continuing crisis periods — with a wage policy of the normal full employment pattern for the first, of a strict cost-of-living formula for the second, and a gradual movement from the latter toward the former for the third. Price stability is the key to wage stability in each of these periods and under each of these policies. Since prices are most likely to be stable in the crisis period, under the impact of the whole complex of policies appropriate to such a period, wages are likely to be most stable also.

A wage policy in a mobilized economy is supposed to perform several completely inconsistent functions: prevent inflation, allocate resources effectively, draw forth additional resources into the market, impose equality of sacrifice, settle disputes, preserve collective bargaining, and maintain unions and their leaders in unimpaired condition. One nice thing about these tests is that almost no conceivable action of a governmental wage board could fail to find support among them. Obviously the board will pick and choose. In the pre-crisis period it will look more toward industrial peace, in the crisis period to wage rate stability, and in the continuing crisis period from the one to the other. The only time, however, when it will look strongly toward wage stability is in a crisis period when wage stability and industrial peace are made compatible by an effective no-strike pledge.

Before turning to some comments on the current situation, I should like merely to note that while I have talked about three periods, certain fitting policies, and restricted basic factors, there are certainly other situations such as invasion and a post-crisis period, other policies such as the "iron ration," and other possible factors such as a revolutionary union movement.

WAGE RESTRAINTS IN THE CURRENT MOBILIZATION ECONOMY[6]

In relation to the developments of the past year, there are three central questions: What were the major policy alternatives before the Board? Has the Board been an independent force to raise wages? What are the proper tests of the Board's performance under current conditions?

The Major Alternatives — The Board never considered adopting a new Little Steel formula which would break the connection between wages and prices. At the outset the Board had before it two major alternatives: a modified Big Steel formula and the General Motors formula. The Big Steel formula was a 10 percent increase; the General Motors formula called for automatic cost-of-living escalation and an improvement factor. The Board adopted, as a first approximation, a modified Big Steel formula. As it turned out, this was not as approximate as we thought. It provided for a 10 percent wage ceiling at a time when the cost of living had risen by 8 percent, and for a review of this ceiling when new cost-of-living figures became available. When this turned out to be unacceptable, the General Motors formula became, in substance, the new ceiling. The Board has not yet located its own stabilization points but rather has accepted the points set by the steel, auto, and, to a lesser extent, coal bargains.

6. For general reviews of the work of the Wage Stabilization Board, written from contrasting points of view, see George W. Taylor, *A Report on Wage Stabilization*, U.S. Wage Stabilization Board, August 31, 1951; and Herbert R. Northrup, "Wage Stabilization: From Special Case to General Policy," *Management Record* (November 1951).

Has the Board Raised Wages? — The Board has been referred to as the "Wage Ratchet Board"[7] and the "Wage Stimulation Board."[8] Undoubtedly some bargains have been at higher levels because of the policies of the Board. Essentially what the Board has done is to take the top national bargains and turn them into governmental policy. In this form, these bargains have had more attractive power to all sorts of people than they otherwise would. If in the name of industrial peace the key bargains are accepted and if in the name of equity the same standards are set for others, then some wages will be drawn up closer to the levels of the key bargains than would otherwise happen. The alternative would be to discriminate by having one set of rules for the powerful and another for the weak. However stabilizing this might be, it would soon be the object of vehement protest.

While setting a higher target for some, the policy of the Board has restrained others. Cases have been modified or denied; and parties have settled for less than they otherwise would knowing that their cases would be modified or denied if they did not. On balance during the past six months, which have been marked by a lull in business activity, I am inclined to think that the elevating effect has been greater than the retarding effect. (The two effects together have helped preserve the customary differentials in the wage structure: government employees are receiving somewhat more and textile workers somewhat less than they otherwise would.) This is, however, a narrow view to take. The higher policy levels were essential to industrial peace and were required to afford to labor treatment equivalent to that accorded industry and agriculture under the Defense Production Acts of 1950 and 1951.

Tests of Performance — Wage restraints can have only a relatively minor effect on the total wage and salary bill of the nation. In World War II, changes in basic wage rates were responsible for only about one-third of the increase in weekly earnings in manufacturing;[9] and pay rolls were additionally increased by added employment. Because the work week has gone up so little as yet this time, changes in basic wage rates have been a more dominant factor, but about half the increased nonagricultural pay roll in 1951 over 1950 is due to increased employment alone.[10] The chief reliance in controlling effective

7. See reference in William S. Hopkins, "Wage Stabilization: Policy and Programs," *Proceedings of the Twenty-sixth Annual Conference of the Western Economic Association* (September 1951).

8. See reference in Richard A. Lester, "Wage Troubles," *The Yale Review* (September 1951).

9. See John T. Dunlop, "An Appraisal of Wage Stabilization Policies," in *Problems and Policies of Dispute Settlement . . . , op. cit.,* p. 174.

10. "National Product and Income in the First Three Quarters of 1951," *Survey of Current Business* (November 1951).

demand arising from wages and salary payments cannot be placed on wage restraints. They affect only rates. Earnings and pay rolls would rise even with steady rates; and rates cannot be held steady.

Appropriate tests in the current situation in judging the performance of the Board are these: How well has it preserved the normal full employment wage pattern? Has it contributed to industrial peace? Has it held its policies tentative so that they could easily be adapted to meet a crisis need without breaking commitments? Has it adequately rationalized its policies for the pacifying effects which such rationalization can have on the expectations of the populace? Aside from noting that the Board of late has been very adept at divining where the parties will be and getting there first with a permissive policy and has kept its policies tentative and explained them well to the interested public, I should like to comment briefly on the first question. The normal full employment wage pattern is a realistic upper limit for wage restraint in a period such as this, and the Board has kept generally within this pattern. It can, while staying within this pattern, round out its policy by permitting an extension, in some fashion, of the General Motors "improvement factor." It seems both likely and fitting, if somewhat unstabilizing, that it should do so.

A final word on the role of the economist as a policy maker in the area of wage restraints. The public members on a wage board should be above all else good mediators and the ideal mediator cares mostly about the fact of an acceptable settlement. The economist *qua* economist is apt to care too much about the content of the settlement, although acceptability is, and by the nature of the situation must be, the ultimate reference. The general public should look to the public members to mediate industrial peace and to the President and Congress, if anywhere, to stabilize the economy.

PART IV. "The California School"

Economic Analysis and
the Study of Industrial Relations

T HE DESCRIPTION and analysis of industrial relations have traditionally fallen within the jurisdiction of the economists. More recently,
sociologists, psychologists, and even anthropologists have entered the field
and made important contributions. It has become almost fashionable to say it
belongs to everybody except economists. Economics does not afford a complete explanation of industrial relations, nor does it so pretend. A more
serious charge is that economic analysis has not been adequate within its own
special area.

Traditional economic analysis has not been adequate in the area it has
sought to explain for at least three reasons: To begin with, it has paid too little
attention to its assumptions; and assumptions can be as important as internal
logic. Also, there has been too ready dismissal of the "imperfections"; and it
is often the imperfections that constitute the general case rather than the
exceptions. And, thirdly, the model of the trade union has been inadequate.
The first two limitations have been generally discussed and increasingly recognized. The third is a more recent realization.

The model of the trade union used by the more traditional economists has
assumed the following, among other things:

That an identity of interests exists between the union and its members.
The union is assumed to have the representation of its members as its sole
function.

That the union endeavors to maximize the wealth of its members, variously
defined. As a corollary, power is important as it leads to wealth.

That the union "sells" labor. It acts like other sellers and it is (or it should

Reprinted from *Proceedings*, Third Annual Conference on Research and Training in Industrial
Relations, University of Minnesota, 1947.

be) concerned with both volume and price. Thus is it said that unions either do act or should act like other economic institutions.

This model leaves a great many actions of trade unions unexplained, except by reference to irrationality and uneconomic behavior. A few examples will suffice. Why do unions strike when "strikes don't pay"? Or why do employers accept strikes when they also don't "pay" them? Traditional strike theories indicate that strikes should be rare. Strikes cost money to both sides, and it pays each side to settle to avoid this cost. Yet strikes are not so rare as these theories would suggest. Are "irrationality," "lack of acequate knowl-edge," and "burnishing the weapon" sufficient explanations? Why, for ex-ample, are strikes continued, or why do they occur at all, when the parties are separated by only one cent per hour?

Why do unions seem largely to ignore the employment effects of their actions? Presumably they should be interested in both price and volume. In fact, however, they are usually only concerned with price. This would seem to be uneconomic. It may cause unemployment and the loss of wealth to the total membership. Yet the admonitions of economists to be concerned with volume seem to fall on deaf ears.

Why do unions seem to prefer falling real wages (as in a period of inflation) to rising real wages (as in a period of depression)? It may somewhat exagger-ate the actual situation to suggest that unions look upon periods of falling real wages as "good times" and rising real wages as "bad times." This concentra-tion on the money, instead of the real wage, would seem to be uneconomic. Why, also, are unions more interested in changes in the level of wages than in the level itself? And why are they more interested in the relative than the absolute amount of wages, if maximization of wealth is their aim?

Why is the "pattern" of wage adjustments so significant? It cannot con-ceivably be based on labor market and product market considerations industry by industry or company by company. Yet in recent years it has been the strongest single force in wage determination. Attention to the "pattern" again would appear to be uneconomic.

Why do unions prefer industry-wide bargaining? Industry-wide bargaining often costs them the loss of strength which comes from self-denial of the "whipsaw" technique. The strength of the employers to resist is increased, and the ability of the union to prosecute a strike is decreased. The whole industry is shut down by a strike. No individual employer needs fear loss of business to his competitors. All members of the union are without work rather than only some. Public opinion is directed against the union. Yet unions almost universally seem to prefer industry-wide bargaining.

The traditional model is inadequate to explain many of the more important actions of unions. A more adequate model emerges if the traditional assumptions are reversed.

1. The union is different from its members. It has its own institutional requirements and its own survival needs. Not only may the desires of the union be different from the desires of the members, but they may in fact be in conflict. Thus there are "union demands" as compared with "membership demands." One clear case of divergence of interest is where the union seeks to prevent its membership from shifting to a rival union which the members think might serve them better.

2. The union is not solely interested in wealth but also in its own sovereignty and integrity. When the "chips are down" it is more concerned with the power of the institution than the wealth of its members. It will sacrifice the latter for the former both in the short run and the long run. It is particularly when the pursuit of wealth and the pursuit of power come into conflict that the traditional explanation breaks down. As long as these two pursuits are consistent with each other, the traditional model is adequate. The trade unions have no single end (wealth) and sometimes do not have the traditional goal of wealth at all. Thus the allocation of means is more difficult for the union leader than has often been assumed.

3. The union is not engaged in selling labor. It is more like a price-fixing institution. The labor is then "sold" by the individual worker. The union is a price-fixing institution only partially concerned with the employment effects of the price, even under the restricted circumstances when it is interested at all.

A realistic model of the trade union is that of an essentially political rather than economic institution. The union leader acts under pressures from many sources: its members, rival leaders in the union, rival unions, its own employer, other employers, the government, and perhaps even the consumers. The union leader tries to make adjustments, under pressures, to permit his survival and that of the institution. It is more fruitful to look toward politics, rather than the profit-making enterprise, for analogies.

It appears that the more insecure a union is, the more political and the less economic it will be. Thus the craft union, with its greater institutional security and its homogeneous membership, may be the less political and the more economic (aside from those instances where it becomes involved in jurisdictional disputes).

Economic analysis is useful in the study of industrial relations in seeking relationships between cause and effect, between decisions and consequences. It is, for example, essential for an analysis of the consequences of trade union wage policies on the industry or the nation. Its model of the firm is moderately good, and thus it can help offer explanations of why a firm acts as it does in collective bargaining. Economics is useful also in describing the surrounding environment and the basic economic forces at work.

Consequently, it is not suggested that economists abandon their former jurisdiction. It is suggested, however, that a combination of politics and economics will provide a more realistic understanding of industrial relations. Collective bargaining is carried on between largely economic institutions (the enterprise) and largely political institutions (the unions). In our increasingly highly organized economy, more diverse interests need political reconciliation. In large corporations and employers' associations, there may be no single goal of wealth even on the management side.

This change in the corpus of economic analysis to make it a combination of politics and economics should enable it better to tackle the major problems of industrial relations. It should help to illuminate the pursuit of wealth and power (and their interactions) by the economic interest groups of labor and capital; and this is a basic modern problem. It should help reduce the area of presumed irrationality and the conflict between "theory and practice." It should broaden the area subject to explanation and reduce the area outside the system of analysis. It should help make something systematic out of what theory has disregarded.

Further, this change may be helpful in the determination of policy. For example, our society has been largely concerned with an economic settlement of the industrial relations problem, when it may be in fact a political settlement which is required. Can industrial peace be bought with high wages or can it only be achieved by giving institutional security to unions and employers through a political settlement? Is industrial relations conflict not more political than economic warfare? As a further example, what is a responsible wage bargain? It is usually said that the union leader acts responsibly if he pays attention to the employment effects of a wage bargain on the industry and the nation. Under some circumstances, this might require, at least on the level of the individual firm or industry, a policy of lower and lower money wages. Yet any leader who followed such a policy would so upset his union as to prejudice peaceful industrial relations. Turnover in leadership, wildcat strikes, and rival unionism would be some of the results of acting in an "economic " way. By acting in a political manner and by adjusting to pressures, the trade union leader maintains stability. Rather than being antisocial, this may be socially desirable. The successful reconciliation of pressures may be as great a contribution to the body politic as acting in an economic way. Responsible union leaders need to be successful politicians at least as much as good economists.

Economics can continue to make a central contribution to the study of industrial relations if it pays more attention to its assumptions, if it is more concerned with the "imperfections," and if it develops a more adequate model of the trade union. Labor economics so developed can provide illumination so that Fred Harbison's famous drunk can go look in Central Park where he really lost his watch.[1] The economics of labor needs to become the economics and politics of industrial relations.

1. Frederick H. Harbison, "A Plan for Fundamental Research in Labor Relations," *American Economic Review* (May 1947).

Index

Hartley, Byron, 53n
Hayek, Friedrich A., 2, 3, 44
Hicks, J.R., 2, 3; labor market definition by, 38n2; on labor's income share, 93; "labor standard" concept by, 7, 131; on mobility and wage rates, 6, 34, 39; on union impact on inflation, 131; on wage setting, in labor market models, 39, 40, 43; on wage "system," 153n33
Hildebrand, George H., 130n1
Hiring hall, 50
Hirsch, Julius, 170n16
Holland. *See* Netherlands
Hollberg, Otto, 149n6
Hopkins, Sheila V., 195n5
Hopkins, William S., 201n7
Howe, Christopher, 11n14
Hoxie, Robert Franklin, 2
"Human Relations School," 2, 3

IAM. *See* International Association of Machinists
Improvement unionism, 97, 103-104
Income, private, 110, 114
Income, total, 110
Income redistribution: inflation makes inequitable, 129; unions' effectiveness at, 125, 165; U.S. and Great Britain compared, 112, 122, 126
Income shares: absolute vs. relative, 127-128; aggregate functional, 94-95; agricultural, 122-123; and business cycle, 102, 106-107, 111, 112, 115, 123, 125; class, 92-93, 104-105, 108, 125; and decision-making power, 125, 126-127; elasticity of substitution, 93, 99n; foreign trade affects, 122-123, 124; functional, 92, 94-95, 127; in Great Britain, 117-122, 127-128n67; in hard and soft markets, 100, 120-121, 124, 141; interest, 111, 127; international data on, 122-124; and "legislative enactment," 125; personal, 92-93, 94, 95, 128n67; in primary and secondary distribution, 108; and productivity, 94, 95, 99, 103; profits, 99-102; rents, 105, 107, 108, 111, 125, 127; social relations affect, 94; statistics lacking, 89; theories of, 90-95; transfer payments, 128; union impact on, 125, 165-166; in United States, 109-117, 126, 127-128
Income shares, labor's, 9, 10; in Australia, 122-123; in Canada, 123-124; constancy of, 89, 93, 127-128n67, 140; and decision-making power, 98-99, 105, 106, 125, 126-127; defined, 95, 127-128; in Great Britain, 117-122, 127-128n67; in marginal-productivity theory, 92, 93; in

natural-class theory, 90-91; in natural-individual theory, 93; in New Zealand, 122-123; in Russia, 108, 123, 124; in social-class theory, 91-92; in social-group theory, 94; taxation affects, 112, 121-122, 127; union impact on, 98-108, 112-117, 124-128; in United States, 109-117, 124-125, 127-128
Individual responses, in labor market, 25, 44, 45, 148-149, 166
Industrial markets: institutional rules in, 27-29; internal markets in, 30; movement within, 32, 33, 34; ports of entry, 30-31
Industrial relations, 1-3, 4, 205; California School, 13-17; recommendations for study, 207-209
Industrial system: external environments influence, 59; inflation-fighting recommendations for, 146; industry-wide bargaining, 55, 56, 206; industry-wide decision making, 55, 65-66; producer concern in, 51, 52; sovereignty in, 51-52; unemployment in, reaction to, 33; wage differentials in, 47-49
Industrial unions: conflict with craft unions, 34; control in, 50; and job evaluation plans, 78; movement in, 50-51; power of compared to craft unions, 163n61; seniority in, 33, 37; skill in, 157-158, 163n61; supply and demand in, 35-36; UAW as, 58-59. *See also* Unions
Industrialization: affects wage differentials, 10, 161; income distribution stages in, 165; inflation and, 13, 129
Industry. *See* Employers; Management
Industry-wide bargaining, 55, 56, 206
Industry-wide decision making, 55, 65-66
Industry-wide job evaluation, 78
Inflation: administered, 13, 135; capitalism and, 129, 144, 145; constant, sources of, 13, 129-130, 144-145; controlling, 13, 16, 145-146, 192, 198, 199; direct-controls unionism during, 108; economists' views of, 130-132; improvement unionism and, 103-104; industrialization and, 13, 129; New Deal unionism and, 107; productivity/wage divergence and, 178; types of, 131; unemployment and, 7, 13; union impact on, 10, 16, 134, 143, 144, 145; union power during, 190; United States, labor's income share and, 111-112, 113, 115; wage-policy unionism and, 105; wage restraint and, 13
Inman, J., 158n50
Institute of Industrial Relations, 4, 16, 41n9
Institutional behavior, of unions, 207
Institutional markets. *See* Labor markets, institutional

Lipset, Seymour M., 31n20, 34n24, 51
Little Steel formula, 194
Livernash, Edward Robert, 71n10
Lockheed Aircraft Corporation: joint job evaluation plan, 58; postwar job evaluation plan, 66; in SCAI plan, 56, 65; union activity at, 68
Logan, A.F., 53n
Los Angeles, California, 56, 150
Lumber industry, 57

Maclaurin, W. Rupert, 8, 28n11, 48n27
Malaya, 123
Malm, F. Theodore, 51
Malthus, Thomas Robert, 90
Management; conflict among, 8, 64-65; in job evaluation plans, 64-65, 73, 79, 80, 83, 85; as labor, 127; and productivity/wage rate harnessing, 182
Manager, bureaucratic, 36
Managerial unionism, 97, 106, 125
Manufacturing, productivity and wage rates in, 168-172
Marchal, Jean, 104n35
Marginal-productivity theory, 92, 93
Maritime trades, 26
Markets: hard, 100, 141; soft, 120-121, 124, 141. *See also* Labor markets; Product market
Marshall, Alfred, 3, 40, 93
Marx, Karl, 4-5; economic changes since, 127, 128; as social class theorist, 91, 92
Marxist economists, 2, 3, 4-5, 17-18
Mayo, Elton, 2, 3
McCaffree, Kenneth M., 162n58
McNett, Tom, 53n
McPherson, William H., 191n3
Meade, James Edward, 44, 45, 46, 52
Mediators: as parties to wage restraint, 190-193; requirements for, 191-192, 202
Mercer, S.R., 53n
Michels, Robert, 13
Middle East, 92
Mill, John Stuart, 94
Mining industry, 111, 163
Mobility, 31, 34, 37; inflation and, 130; job classification restricts, 73; in labor market definition, 39; movement distinguished from, 31n19; in New Haven, 31n20, 50-51; unionization as substitute for, 160; and union impact on wages, 136. *See also* Transfer.
Monopoly: in social-class theory, 91-92; in social-group theory, 94; by unions, 9, 15, 16, 44, 45, 48, 130, 144
Moore, Geoffrey H., 108n
Morale, 54, 57, 80, 173

Morse, Wayne, 58
Morton, Walter A., 107, 131
Motivation, and union power, 156-159, 165, 166
Movement, 23-34; barriers to, 23-24, 28-29; and business cycles, 41-42n10; costs of, 38; as definition, 38-39; in institutional market, 42, 43, 50; in managed market, 45; mobility distinguished from, 31n19; in natural market, 41; in neoclassical market, 40; in perfect market, 39, 45; reasons for, 48
Myers, Charles A., 8, 28n11, 29n14, 48n27
Myers, Frederic, 154n41
Myrdal, Gunnar, 6n6

Nashua, New Hampshire, 29n14
Nathan, Robert R. Associates, Inc., 169n8
National Defense Mediation Board, 191
National Union of United Welders of America, 58, 59
National War Labor Board (NWLB): controlled wage changes, 67, 85, 188, 199; disruption threatened, 191; economists on, 13; ordered job evaluation plan, 55, 57-58; "Re-Study Committee," 76; wage data by, 5, 40-41, 62, 174-175
Natural-class theorists, 90-91
Natural-individual theorists, 92-93
Neoclassical theorists, 2, 8, 9, 35, 93
Netherlands: postwar wage increases in, 142; social partner unionism in, 132; wage differentials in, 152, 158, 162; wage-policy unionism in, 103, 105
New Deal unionism, 97-98, 106-107, 125
Newell, Ralph, 53n
New Haven, Connecticut: labor mobility in, 31n20, 50-51; wage differentials in, 150
New Zealand, 122-123, 152
Nicholson, J.L., 49n27
Noland, E. William, 28n10
North American Aviation, Inc., 56
Northrup, Herbert R., 24n4, 30n16, 200n6
Northrup Aircraft, Inc., 56, 58, 65
Norway: centralized union movement in, 161, 189; direct-controls unionism in, 98; postwar wage increases in, 142; wage differentials in, 152, 158, 161
NWLB. *See* National War Labor Board

Oakland, California, 31n20, 41n9, 51
Ober, Harry, 151n14, 152n20
Occupations: in communal ownership systems, 26-27; in private property systems, 27-29; wage differentials among, 40, 152-153, 157-164 *passim*
Oil economies, 92
Oligarchy, 13, 16
Oxnam, D.W., 151, 152n22, 154, 163n62

97-98, 106-107, 125; quasi-revolutionary, 96; pure and simple, 97, 99-102, 124; sectional bargainer, 133, 135, 189; social partner, 132-133, 135; volatile, 96; wage-policy, 97, 102-106, 124-125
United Auto Workers (UAW): "improvement unionism" of, 97; as industrial union, 58-59; in SCAI plan, 56, 58-59, 68; wage setting by, 76, 101
United Kingdom. *See* Great Britain
United States: "American-type" unionism, 107; annual real wage increase, 195; direct-controls unionism in, 98; general level of wages in, union impact on, 138-143 *passim;* improvement unionism in, 103, 105; income redistribution compared to Great Britain, 112, 122, 126; inflation record, postwar, 145; labor market alternatives in, 45-46; labor's income share in, 89, 91, 94, 109-117, 121n60, 127-128; mediating wage policy in, 190-193; productivity/wage rate policy in, 168; sectional bargainer unions in, 133, 143, 189; standard wage rates in, 101; union responsibility in, 189-190; union types in, 98, 103, 105, 107, 133, 143, 189; wage differentials in, union impact on, 149-162 *passim;* wage stabilization in evaluated, 200-202
United States Bureau of Labor Statistics, 5, 58n4; productivity/wage rate data by, 168-172
United States Steel Company, 74
United Steelworkers of America, 74
United Welders of America, National Union of, 58, 59
University of California, Berkeley. *See* Institute of Industrial Relations

Wage controls, 11; as inflation solution, 146; and unions, 135, 139. *See also* Wage restraint; Wage stabilization
"Wage-cost inflation," 131
Wage differentials: "compensation," 152n19; "elastic," 149n6; industrialization affects, 10; institutional behavior and, 148-149; interarea, 10, 151-152, 155, 157, 160; interfirm, 10, 150-151, 155, 157, 159-160; interindustry, 10, 47-49, 153-155, 159, 163-164; interoccupational, 10, 152-164 *passim;* interpersonal, 10, 149-150, 155, 157, 159; in job evaluation plans, 149, 158; male/female, 149-150; manual/white collar, 162; for skill, 10, 152-153, 157-165 *passim;* types of, 148; union motivation and, 156-159; union power to change, 159-165
Wage drift, 141, 142, 143

Wage fixing, 14, 15, 52
Wage market: collusion in, 41, 45; defined, 38-39; disjointed from job market, 42-43, 69; equity in, 40, 41, 43, 45, 48; evaluated, 45, 46-52; institutional, 42, 43-44, 48, 52; managed, 44, 45, 46; natural, 40-41, 42; neoclassical, 40; as "orbit of coercive comparison," 43; perfect, 39
Wage-policy unionism, 97; effect on income shares, 103-106, 124-125; types of, 102-106
Wage rates, productivity and: comparative behavior, 168-172; compatibility of, 11, 167-168, 172-175; harnessing, proposals for, 179-183, 184; short-run divergent tendencies, 175-179, 183, 184
Wage restraint: administration of, 12, 199; circumstances for, 13, 197-200; efficiency wages in, 192; evaluated, 11-13, 143, 200-202; in Germany, 142; in Great Britain, 141; in Holland, 142; in Korean War, 12-13; limits to, 193-197; in mobilized economy, 199-202; parties to, 187-193; periods, 197-200; public interest in, 192-193; runaways, 12, 196, 197; wage drift follows, 141, 142, 143; in World War II, 12-13, 191. *See also* Wage controls; Wage stabilization
"Wage slide," 160
Wage stabilization: formulas for, 194-195, 199, 200; evaluated, 12; limits to, 193-197; possibility of, 187, 191-192, 194; price stabilization and, 182n38, 199; in World War II, 57, 191, 194, 195. *See also* Wage controls; Wage restraint
Wage Stabilization Board, reviewed, 191, 200-202
Wages: administered, 135, 138, 140, 145, 146; cost-of-living formula for, 194-195; in craft unions, 34, 68, 155, 157-158; determinants of average hourly earnings, 173-175, 180; efficiency, 94, 184, 192; environment affects, 53, 54, 59-63, 70-71; equity in, 40, 41, 43, 45, 48, 59-63, 66, 70-71, 81-84, 103, 195; "fair-share" policy, 103, 124-125; fringe benefits, 101, 152n19; "going rate," 5; guaranteed, 35; "improvement factor," 195, 202; institutional rules affect, 34-36, 37, 42, 43-44, 52; and job disutility, 8, 62, 72-73, 80-81, 162, 163; in job evaluation plans, 53, 54, 66, 69, 77-84 *passim;* and job responsibility, 74-75; "just wage" concept, 156; labor market tightness affects, 178, 180; labor scarcity affects, 56; manipulation techniques, 61-63; minimum, 151; and morale, 54, 80; policies, 192-200; prices and,

104n*33*, 139, 182n*38*, 199; productivity
and, 139, 140, 184; rate ranges, 63, 76-77,
80; real, 97, 167n*1*, 167n*2*, 195; rigidity of,
102, 124, 139n*16*, 162-163n*61*; in SCAI
plan, 57, 59-63, 69, 72-73, 85; and skill, 8,
62-63, 72-73, 74-75; standard rate,
100-101, 125, 154-155; structural mechanisms evaluated, 45, 46; supply and demand
affects, 39, 42, 43, 44, 48; unemployment
and, 140, 141, 144, 145; uniformity in, 41,
78, 150, 151, 156-165. *See also* Unions,
impact on wages
Wages, general level of: in institutional market, 49-50; in job evaluation plans, 54;
sources of increase in, 144-145; union impact on, 9-10, 82, 105, 134-145 *passim*
Walker, Francis A., 94
Walras, Léon, 93
War Labor Board. *See* National War Labor
Board
Warren, Earl, Governor of California, 16
WCAC. *See* West Coast Aircraft Committee
Wealth of Nations (Smith), 53-54
Webb, Beatrice and Sidney, 3; introduced
"standard rate," 100; on "legislative
enactment," 125; as social-group theorists,
94
Welfare provisions, 41
West Coast Aircraft Committee (WCAC), 58;
Boeing actions, 60, 72-73, 74, 75; chair-
man on job evaluation acceptance, 81; un-
ions represented on, 85; "Washington
Agreement," 75
West Coast airframe industry. *See* Boeing
Airplane Company; Southern California

Aircraft Industry plan; West Coast Aircraft
Committee
Western Europe: labor-party unionism in, 189;
union impact on wages in, 142-143; wage
differentials in, 152, 154
"Wisconsin School," 2, 3, 17
Witte, Edwin, 2
Wolman, Leo, 155n*42*
Wootton, Barbara, 103
Work group, 36
Work permits, 35n*27*
Work sharing, 35
Workers: as capitalists, 127; classification of,
62-63, 66, 67, 73; in institutional markets,
22-25; job evaluation complaints by, 67;
job market participation by, 41-42; job re-
evaluation to attract, 62; in managed markets, 45; manual/white collar, wage differentials, 137, 162; morale of, 54, 57, 80,
173; motivating to organize, 68, 147, 157;
in natural market, 41-42; in natural-class
theory, 90-91; in natural-individual theory,
92-93; in neoclassical market, 40; in perfect
market, 39; preferences of, 21-22, 25;
postwar demand for, 61; security of, 27, 28,
32, 33, 37, 70, 73, 208; in social-class
theory, 91-92; in social-group theory, 94,
128; in structureless markets, 24; wage
equity views, 81. *See also* Unions
World War I, 112, 117, 168, 169
World War II: labor's income share in, 111-
112, 117, 120, 123, 124; productivity/wage
rates in, 175; wage data from, 40-41, 49;
wage restraint in, 12-13
Woytinsky, W.S. and Associates, 154

The Autobiography of Alice B Toklas

By

Gertrude Stein

© 2011 Oxford City Press, Oxford.